Power Politics

Power Politics

ENVIRONMENTAL ACTIVISM IN SOUTH LOS ANGELES

KAREN BRODKIN

RUTGERS UNIVERSITY PRESS

New Brunswick, New Jersey, and London

Library of Congress Cataloging-in-Publication Data
Brodkin, Karen.
    Power politics : environmental activism in south Los Angeles /
Karen Brodkin.
        p.   cm.
    Includes bibliographical references and index.
    ISBN 978-0-8135-4607-0 (hardcover : alk. paper)
    ISBN 978-0-8135-4608-7 (pbk. : alk. paper)
    1. Environmental justice—California—South Gate.   2. Student
movements—California—South Gate.   3. Hispanic American high
school students—California—South Gate—Political activity.   4. Sunlaw
Energy Partners (Firm)   5. South Gate (Calif.)—Environmental
conditions.   I.   Title.
    GE235.C25B76 2009
    363.7'05250979494—dc22
                                                        2008051479

A British Cataloging-in-Publication record for this book is available
from the British Library.

Visit our Web site: http://rutgerspress.rutgers.edu

Manufactured in the United States of America
Typesetting: Jack Donner, BookType

CONTENTS

PREFACE AND ACKNOWLEDGMENTS

THIS BOOK TELLS THE STORY of a successful grassroots campaign against building an electric power plant in a part of Los Angeles County already burdened with polluted air. Its heart is the story of how the environmental justice organization Communities for a Better Environment (CBE) and its youth group, Youth for Environmental Justice (Youth-EJ), went about defeating a power plant during 2000 and 2001, when California seemed to be in the midst of its worst electricity shortage ever. These activists saw themselves as environmental Davids against the Goliath of Big Power. Marianne Brown, Erin O'Brien, and Bryce Lowery at UCLA's Labor and Occupational Safety and Health first connected me with these activists, for which I'm grateful. My biggest thanks go to CBE staff, and to the high school students who did the outreach and education that mobilized South Gate residents to become involved. They opened their files and shared their ideas and expertise, their notes, artwork, and photos with me. I also thank their teachers at South Gate High School, who are also important players in this narrative.

As I pursued this story, it got more complicated. The good guys and bad guys were not always who I expected them to be. The big power Goliath saw itself as David too. I began to feel like I was solving a mystery, and as with reading a mystery novel, I found myself entering unfamiliar territory.

The issue was deeply entangled in local and statewide politics that sometimes had little or nothing to do with electricity, and sometimes had much to do with its technology and political economy. Activists may try to shape the policies and practices of legislative and regulatory bodies, but they usually do it from the outside, because that is where grassroots organizing is especially effective. Like those I study, I am seldom privy to the metaphorical smoke-filled back rooms of politics, where the landscape of activism is sculpted.

The study of grassroots activism and the issues connected to it are areas of research I know something about, but I am no expert on energy, deregulation, emission control technology, or the politics surrounding any of them. When I discovered that it was going to be impossible to tell the story of grassroots activism without telling these stories too, I sought help.

South Gate city councilors and city clerk, another set of key players in the book, gave me a tutorial on the back rooms of city politics, and a good education on their differing perspectives about the power plant and the campaign against it. I thank city clerk Carmen Avalos for guiding me through an enormous amount of city data and Erick DeLeon of her office for finding and photocopying documents. *Los Angeles Times* reporters Richard Marosi and Hugo Martin offered invaluable background information on South Los Angeles politics. I was also fortunate to get a crash course on South Los Angeles history and politics from George Cole, Bell city councilor and longtime labor activist in South Los Angeles. I also owe debts of thanks to Dave Sickler and Goetz Wolf of the Los Angeles County AFL-CIO and to Vince Avila of the South Gate Police Officers Association.

It is hard to write about a power plant controversy without some understanding of energy production, emission control, and deregulation policies, as well as state energy and air-quality politics. I've had some expert tutors. Robert Danziger, Sunlaw's founder, explained the company's technology and what it was up against, and suggested where I should look for evidence. Anupom Ganguli of the South Coast Air Quality Management District tutored me on emission control systems, testing, and AQMD's protocols. Mark Abramowitz and V. John White, environmentalists who work on improving California's air quality, helped me to understand statewide energy politics and emission control systems, and guided me through the legislative and regulatory landscape.

There's always the risk that a little learning is a dangerous thing. I hope I got it right, but the mistakes are mine.

Excellent volunteers assisted me in conducting interviews at South Gate. Jennifer Tucker conducted a number of them and joined me in several others. Youth-EJ member Victoria Gutierrez also helped interview. South Gate alum Sylvia Zamora, who was conducting research on the power plant for a Smith College undergraduate project, and I shared our interviews, and Zamora shared her survey of South Gate residents with me.

Rocio Barraza, Oscar Gutierrez, and Blanca Martinez, three South Gate High alums, conducted their own research as part of an undergraduate anthropology project at UCLA. I owe them all deep thanks for their important contributions.

I have presented some of the analysis in this book at meetings of the American Anthropological Association, the Canadian Anthropological Society, and the Society for North American Anthropology and benefited greatly from participants' feedback.

For reading and insightful commentary on early chapters, I thank Sherry Ortner and Tritia Toyota, colleagues at UCLA, and Alvaro Huerta. Bob Gottlieb, Hilary Cunningham, and Jeff Maskovsky read the full manuscript, and their thoughtful readings and incisive critiques helped strengthen it greatly.

Finally, I thank Sandi Morgen for the title, Yuki Kidokoro for the cover photograph, and Carollee Howes for listening to me wrestle with this project for so long.

Power Politics

Introduction

ON TUESDAY JANUARY 23, 2001, a school night, in the middle of statewide crisis-level energy shortage, some three hundred high school students and their parents marched from South Gate High School in southeast Los Angeles County to a meeting of the city council to tell their elected representatives that they did not want a power plant built in their city. They were referring to Sunlaw Energy Partners' plans to build the 550-megawatt Nueva Azalea power plant in their predominantly Latina/o working-class city. The major television networks dispatched helicopters and ground crews to cover the events, which were broadcast on the evening news. That fact alone made me sit up and take notice because this part of Los Angeles—South Gate, a low-income Latina/o community of largely new immigrants—gets almost no press or television coverage.

For most of the students, this action was their first foray into political activism. They had planned carefully, going door to door with leaflets they'd made, building giant papier-mâché puppets and noisemakers, and carrying bright signs with a red and yellow skull on them. Many of them had written and practiced speeches that they hoped to deliver to the city council. Their message was clear. This plant would add pollutants to the area's already toxic air. It wasn't good for the community, and it wasn't fair. Airborne toxins were already causing high rates of asthma and respiratory disease in South Gate. Corporations deliberately dumped and sited toxic industries in these low-income communities of color because they believed the residents couldn't fight back.

"When we got there," said Jackie Amparo, one of the student organizers who arrived at the high school early, "it was not that many people. . . . But then people kept coming and kept coming, and a lot of people went." Television news helicopters circled overhead, and the camera crews homed in on the giant puppet heads bobbing above the growing crowd and the dramatic skull posters, the signature image of the campaign. Some of their teachers were out there too, lending support. One of them, Veronica Sanchez, said it "felt wonderful, when we were marching to have my students tell me to stay on the sidewalk! It was good that they were the leaders and I was following their directions."

The regular Tuesday night city council meeting was already in session when the marchers got to city hall, where they had to run something of a gauntlet before they got into the council chambers. Some thirty union plumbers had turned out to support building the plant because it would create good jobs for them. "These guys wanted this job badly," said marcher Martha Andrade, "and they were not happy to see all of us protesters there, a whole bunch of high school kids." Jairus Ramos, a student organizer, described "this really big football player–type guy who was very intimidating when we were having this little press conference before we went into the city council. He was there heckling the students."

Once they got inside, students managed to get the power plant onto the council's agenda for discussion and to get the council to take a nonbinding vote on whether it supported the power plant. "Especially when we went to interrupt the meeting," Jackie recalled, "it was really—you could feel you have power. It felt, it's hard to describe it. Thinking, even though they are city council, they are representing us and basically we have power also, and we go in there and state our issue and they have to listen to us."

But the students were shocked at the behavior of their elected representatives and their elders in the audience. They heard adults on both sides of the issue behaving disrespectfully—shouting one another down and engaging in personal mudslinging. It felt like a three-ring circus.

The students were watching a slow motion, local political explosion, and the power plant issue had lit the fuse. The mudslinging the students testified to was not really about Sunlaw's proposed Nueva Azalea power plant; rather, the plant was a magnet for South Gate's local political factions, a battlefield on which they acted out other political differences. At the time, students were aware of none of this. And Sunlaw's officers were equally unaware of South Gate politics when they applied to build their plant in South Gate.

As the meeting dragged on late into the night, students hung in there for the public comment period so they could deliver their speeches, which they did, one after another. The television cameras kept rolling and broadcast them live on the ten and eleven o'clock news. In the end, the city council voted three to two to oppose building the power plant. Even though the council's decision had no authority, it was a statement. Some six weeks later, on March 6, South Gate voters defeated by two to one a referendum supporting the power plant. Although not legally binding on the ultimate decision by the California Energy Commission, the vote effectively stopped the project.

DEREGULATION AND CALIFORNIA'S ENERGY CRISIS

Part of what made this protest so unusual is that it occurred in the midst of an enormous statewide power shortage.[1] Professional and public opinion agreed that California desperately needed more power plants to produce the electricity required by its growing population and economy. In this context, environmentalists and advocates of clean and green sources of power were pretty well shut out amid the public clamor for more power more quickly. Even mainstream environmentalists had no visibility in this climate.

We now know that the shortage was a product of the state's 1996 deregulation of the production and sale of electric power, and of energy companies gaming the market (a topic to which I return at the end of the book). But that was not widely known in 2000 and early 2001, when South Gate students were protesting plans to build this particular plant. At that point, the energy crisis that deregulation created definitely influenced California and local public opinion about the plant.

Deregulation affects this story most directly because it made it economically possible for Sunlaw Energy Partners to find a market for the electric power it might produce and encouraged the company to build its own plant. Sunlaw's main business, however, was not producing electricity but producing what promised to be a less-polluting emission control system for gas-fueled power plants. The large plant that Sunlaw hoped to build was to be an end run around California's big energy producers and a way to showcase Sunlaw's new technology. To set the stage, we need to take a brief look at California's deregulation of electricity.

Deregulation was directed at the private sector, mainly "the big three" power producers and retailers: San Diego Gas and Electric

(SDG&E), Southern California Edison (Edison), and Pacific Gas and Electric (PG&E). Before deregulation, these three companies were state-regulated, private monopolies that produced and sold most of the electricity in California.[2] These companies lobbied strongly—to the tune of $4.3 million plus another million in campaign contributions—in support of deregulation. The 1996 legislation (which passed with little opposition) took several steps to deregulate the wholesale price of energy—what the big three and other private companies responsible for selling electricity to consumers paid—by creating a partially open market for buying and selling electric power one day at a time. To do this, it created the California Power Exchange as a nonprofit agency responsible for buying and selling power for the whole state at auction and setting wholesale electricity rates based on free market prices among wholesale sellers. The big three power companies gave over control of their electric transmission lines to another new independent agency, the Independent System Operator (ISO), to allow electricity to be more freely bought and sold on what became "the grid."

The free market argument behind this move was that encouraging many independent energy producers to participate in California's power market would increase competition among power producers, increase the supply of energy offered, and hence lower prices. The big three retained their responsibility for providing power to consumers and were to become in essence middlemen between wholesale power producers and retail consumers. Deregulation was attractive to them because it allowed them to sell off "stranded assets" in the form of old and inefficient power plants. The legislation was premised on the expectation that were the big three to sell off their old and expensive power production plants and instead purchase electricity on the open market, where newer companies with newer plants dominated, they would cut their wholesale costs and increase their retail profits.

Legislation early in 1998 opened the door to deregulating retail energy prices, which is when problems became visible. This legislation encouraged these private providers of electricity to consumers to sell off their power plants. It did so by putting a ceiling on the rates they could charge consumers until they sold off their capacity to produce electricity. Then they would be able to raise rates if necessary. The big three power companies, now competing with an increased number of large out-of-state wholesale electricity producers and suppliers, including the soon to be infamous Enron, began the process of selling their productive assets so that they could lift the cap on their retail price (the cost of power to consumers). In all, they sold off about 40 percent of their productive capacity. According to Thornberg (2002), neither the power companies nor the officials involved in deregulation ever considered the possibility that the wholesale cost of energy might rise rather than fall. However, if that were so, the ability to raise rates was an incentive that would be hard to justify to the public.

By mid-1999, far ahead of expectations, SDG&E completed divestment of its power plants, and thus began the first test of a deregulated market for selling retail power. Instead of wholesale prices decreasing, however, they skyrocketed statewide by 2000, and the price of electricity to consumers in the San Diego area increased by 300 percent. The free market was working just the opposite of what its advocates had predicted.

Edison and PG&E still owned their power plants and thus could not raise their rates. Their position was even worse than that of SDG&E because the wholesale cost of energy had risen to a price that was greater than the retail price at which they were allowed to sell, and they could not pass the increase along to consumers. As a result, they had to borrow heavily to fulfill their contracts. This situation ultimately led them to file for Chapter 11 protection from bankruptcy (from which they have since recovered fully).

Several factors were blamed for the high wholesale costs. On the demand side, 2000 was a year with a very hot summer. On the supply side, a severe drought in the Northwest decreased supplies (and increased the price) of hydroelectric power from an area upon which California relies heavily. Also on the supply side was a dramatic nationwide rise in the price of natural gas. Most power plants in California are natural gas plants.

The energy crisis became very serious and very public in the summer of 2000—just as Sunlaw Energy Partners was preparing its application to build the 550-megawatt Nueva Azalea power plant in South Gate. In May, California had a stage-two power alert as its reserve supply fell to 5 percent of need. The following month, PG&E instituted a number of planned rolling blackouts to avoid larger and unplanned statewide blackouts.

Supplies were dangerously low in part because many out-of-state power companies had decided to close down plants for extended maintenance during a period of California's peak demand (Berthelsen 2002). At the time, however, the brownouts, shortages, and rate hikes were attributed to rapidly rising demand and inadequate supplies. So, in the summer of 2000, when Sunlaw Energy Partners prepared to move forward with its plant, the energy climate in California was one in which both expert and popular opinion perceived that demand for electricity was increasing and more power plants were desperately needed.

By August, when Sunlaw's application was complete and filed, the shortages, brownouts, rolling blackouts, and price hikes were only getting worse. By December 2000, when student environmentalists were holding their first big community event to oppose the building of the plant, California was paying $1,400 per megawatt hour for wholesale electricity. In comparison, in 1999 the average wholesale cost was $45 per megawatt hour. President Clinton's Federal Energy Regulatory Commission was stepping in to impose a cap of $150 per megawatt hour on wholesale energy prices, and in early January, California's Public Utility Commission instituted a consumer rate hike. As Sunlaw's public relations campaign in South Gate was explaining that the Nueva Azalea plant could offer South Gate relief from blackouts and skyrocketing electricity prices, Governor Gray Davis declared a state of emergency on January 17, 2001, which was to last until November 2003. Relief from this threat would be nice indeed.

Although the first murmurs of price fixing were beginning to emanate from public officials as early as August 2000, they did not have much traction. Even when Democratic governor Gray Davis, who inherited deregulation from his Republican predecessor, charged in August 2000 that the system was being manipulated, no one seemed to hear him. And on February 1, 2001, the state legislature was willing to approve spending up to $10 billion of public funds to buy electricity (on top of a previous allocation of $400 million). Common sense of the times held that Californians had to control their energy appetite, and, more important, something drastic had to be done to increase the supply of energy. Sunlaw seemed to be making the right proposal in the right political climate.

YOUTH ACTIVISM AND THE POWER PLANT

I became interested in this struggle because I couldn't believe that high school students would be able to stop a power plant, much less do it while California seemed to be facing its most massive shortage of electrical power ever. Less than a year before high school students made the power plant major news in South Los Angeles, the world had been given a glimpse of a global upsurge of youthful social movements that created a new politics against globalization and free trade at the protests against the closed-door meetings of the World Trade Organization (WTO) in Seattle. CNN heralded the week of huge demonstrations of 50,000 to 100,000 as a wave of "'60s style activism." It attributed the passion of the demonstrators to the fact that "young people—Generation X" finally had an issue to care about (CNN 1999). As is often the case, however, what the media thought was brand new had been building for at least a decade. The youthful demonstrators in Seattle, like the high school students in South Gate, were the crest of a much larger wave of national and global youth activism that had been gathering force over the course of the 1990s.

In the summer of 2000, the youthful energy that first appeared in Seattle continued in Los Angeles, when thousands of protesters, most of them young, converged on the Democratic National Convention. The theme of the protests was "Human Need, Not Corporate Greed." Before the convention, youth activists held weeklong training sessions during which organizers led a huge variety of workshops, from direct democracy and globalization-style free trade, and civil disobedience, to puppet and visual art making, music, street theater, and the "Billionaires for Bush, or Gore." The convention venue was surrounded by a twelve-foot fence, and the city was occupied by an enormous number of heavily armed police from across the state. Police provided their own theater of mass force, and some 10,000 mainly young demonstrators—ranging from the bicyclists of Critical Mass, to black-clad anarchists, antiprison activists, immigrant rights workers, and antiglobalization and environmental groups—countered it with their own forms of non-violent theater. Not least of these was a concert by Rage Against the Machine, which was a big draw for high school youth. Many of the protest organizers were veterans of Los Angeles' vibrant labor upsurge in the 1990s, and attendees included a few high school students from South Gate who knew things "weren't right" and were searching for ways to change them.

The Los Angeles movement was propelled by immigrant workers' activism and was deeply intertwined with largely college and high school student–led opposition to a series of anti-immigrant and anti–affirmative action voter initiatives. The synergy of these movements galvanized high school and college students and transformed many of them into full-time activists. Some became environmental justice organizers because they saw it as "environmentalism with an edge"—environmentalism with a strong social justice orientation. The organizers of Communities for a Better Environment, the environmental group that led the campaign against the power plant, were young and had cut their teeth in this mix of labor issues, immigrant rights, and antiracist activism. A variety of Los Angeles community groups also had their own political education academies and curricula for high school students, and activist high school students across the city enjoyed solid networks with one another. As a result, during the 1990s, young Los Angeles activists created a new political cohort with its own signature politics (Brodkin 2007). Their movement linked economic and environmental justice and participated in larger national networks of social justice and antiglobalization movements.

SOUTH GATE AND THE POWER PLANT

To understand why South Gate high school students were the catalyst for blocking construction of a power plant in the midst of a statewide energy crisis, it helps to know something about the history and the people of South Gate and Southeast Los Angeles County more generally.

The population of South Gate, like that of the surrounding area of Southeast Los Angeles County, is mainly Latina/o, with both Chicana/o and new immigrants from Mexico and Central America. Southeast Los Angeles County has long been the industrial heart of the West Coast. Home to the ports of Los Angeles as well as oil refining, aircraft, steel, and other heavy industry since the 1920s, it remains a core industrial area centered around garment, metal, and furniture manufacture as well as trucking and rail transport. It is also a hot spot for airborne toxics, from the ports at San Pedro and Long Beach, from the railroads, freeways, and diesel trucks that crisscross the area, as well as from industrial dumping. Residents of Southeast Los Angeles County have long been low income and economically working class. Before the 1970s, South Gate was virtually all white; by 1990, it was mainly Latina/o.

Environmental justice arguments made sense to the working-class Latina/o majority of South Gate residents. They had plenty of experience with California's racism and anti-immigrant sentiment in their daily interactions and with a series of recent statewide voter initiatives that denied public services to the undocumented, prohibited bilingual public education, and ended affirmative action. And they had plenty of experience with respiratory ills and toxic spills.

The high school students who became the public face of the campaign against the power plant were environmental justice activists. They learned their environmentalism from the California environmental justice organization Communities for a Better Environment (CBE). The environmental justice concept and a national environmental justice movement emerged from a growing awareness in the 1980s and 1990s that this nation is sharply divided around access to a healthy environment. Those who enjoy easy access to the cornucopia of things available in our consumer society seldom live or work near the toxic dumps, pesticide-laden fields, or polluted air and water that are part of their production process. This phenomenon is not accidental. Environmental justice activists and researchers have shown that low-income communities of color have been the destination of choice among toxic industries across the country. Throughout the nation, a shockingly high percentage of people of color live in close proximity to hazardous dumps and industries. In the Los Angeles area, 91 percent of the 1.2 million people who live within two miles of toxic waste sites are people of color (Wilson 2007). The South Gate activists' campaign was a classic example of what Robert Gottlieb (2005) calls a "risk discrimination" battle against yet another form of racial discrimination. The concept of risk discrimination gained legal and policy standing under the Clinton administration, largely as a result of the grassroots strength of the environmental justice movement, as we shall see in chapter 2.

Acknowledging that the odds were against them, environmental justice activists portrayed themselves as David battling a corporate Goliath. But most grassroots environmental campaigns are like that, and most environmental Davids lose to corporate Goliaths. Not this time, however, and I wanted to know how they did it.

Indeed, that was my first research question, and it led me to analyze this struggle as a classic environmental justice battle that pitted working-class people of color against an array of big corporations and their political supporters—here, a big power producer wanting to try out a new emission control technology in an area already overburdened by toxics. Such behavior was part of a long history of using working-class communities of color as guinea pigs or dumping grounds.

From this perspective, I came to agree with the activists that much of their success resulted from the fact that their message resonated with South Gate residents, that they ran a participatory grassroots campaign and built leadership in the community, and that they had a well-thought-out campaign strategy and used the mass media effectively. Still, many environmental justice campaigns do these things well, but most do not win or win so quickly and decisively. It soon became clear that this kind of grassroots campaign may well be necessary, but it is not sufficient. So I began to look at the particulars of this struggle, what organizers think of as the local and political conditions under which they act. When I did this, I heard two other explanatory stories of what happened and why.

In the first of these, Sunlaw Energy Partners and its founder, Robert Danziger, saw themselves as environmentally conscious businessmen and also environmental Davids, in this case battling the Goliath of much bigger energy corporations. They had developed what seemed to be a safer and cleaner system of emission controls for power plants. But, they argued, big power had a great investment in the old technology and was determined to keep Sunlaw's better product off the market and away from regulatory control. Highly regarded local legislators with good environmental track records supported building the power plant because of its potential long-term benefit to California's air quality. So too did the city workers' union (SEIU), the pipe fitters' (plumbers) union, and the Los Angeles County Federation of Labor (AFL-CIO). For unions, support of the project presented an opportunity for them to work with environmentalists, especially an environmentalist who promised to hire union labor. Both labor and legislators actively campaigned for the power plant. Sunlaw's technology held out the long-run promise of cleaner California skies, and the company promised that all construction and maintenance work would be union labor. Both unionists and political officials who supported the plant did not talk about racism or xenophobia or address the arguments of environmental justice activists about racial discrimination in siting environmental hazards. Instead, they emphasized the shared working-class interests of residents, namely, that the plant would bring union jobs and much-needed revenue for city services.

The array of forces in South Gate was somewhat unusual. The WTO demonstrations in Seattle in 1999 gave a prominent public profile to labor support for environmentalism in the much-publicized images of teamsters and turtles marching together. That image represented a double surfacing of new forces. Its telegenic puppetry and pageantry highlighted the emergence of a new, international and youthful movement for social justice encompassing both environmentalism and economic justice (more on this in chap. 2).It also heralded a kind of public emergence of labor union environmentalism. In California, labor and environmental justice activists were often allies in struggles against toxics. Their usual opponents were big corporations. Sunlaw and its supporters portrayed themselves as leading a working-class environmental struggle, with labor and progressive environmentalists united behind a joint agenda of good jobs and clean air. In this struggle, however, a kind of teamsters-and-turtles coalition was arrayed against environmental justice activists.

This story gave me a different perspective on the power plant struggle. If both constellations of activists saw themselves as representing low-wage constituents, what might I learn by looking at both environmental justice and this teamsters-and-turtles coalition as different models of working-class environmentalism?

By working-class environmentalism I mean simply a range of environmental politics that speaks to interests that its proponents believe are important to low-income and blue-collar wage workers. Good jobs, safe working conditions, and nontoxic neighborhoods are all important interests, but they are in short and precarious supply among America's working class. Gottlieb argues that labor unions have historically prioritized jobs and embraced safety and health at work and neighborhood only conditionally and ambivalently (Gottlieb 2005, 347–388). But the kinds of environmentalism that have traction and vitality in working-class communities (most notably, environmental justice and antitoxics) show that safety and health at home and work are important issues as well.

Thinking about movements and organizations that address any of these three issues (including and in addition to unions) as working-class environmentalism raises important questions for the future of environmentalism. What can comparing their campaigns—the strategies, discourses, and goals or visions—tell us about what a successful working-class environmental movement needs to look like? What are working-class priorities? How do they address the intra-class differences created by institutional xenophobia, racism, and sexism? More to the point here, will expanding the question about why environmental justice activists prevailed, to include Sunlaw's supporters among possible models for working-class environmental directions, give us a clearer picture about what works and what doesn't for a working-class environmental movement?

Local supporters of the power plant in South Gate had still a third explanatory story. For them, the controversy wasn't at all about whether or not to build a power plant. The real fight was about getting rid of Albert Robles, South Gate's crooked city treasurer, a Latino politician who built an electoral base among new immigrants—and who happened to be against the power plant because, so people believed, Sunlaw had refused his request for a bribe. Anti-Robles forces regarded his opposition to the plant as merely a smokescreen behind which he hid his corruption. A number of elected South Gate city officials, the police department, as well as a slice of older white and Latina/o South Gate residents explained things this way.

The supporters of the Nueva Azalea plant were a disparate coalition held together largely by opposition to political corruption. Labor and state legislators were at the core of bringing the power plant and anticorruption issues and their potential constituencies together, so that opposition to Robles became a good reason to support the plant. Among adherents of the merged story, environmental justice activists figured in only as Robles' goons or dupes. The anticorruption movement ultimately became a grassroots movement that crossed ethnic lines, although that happened after the power plant was no longer a live issue (Quinones 2007). Despite the fact that all officials avoided race talk and spoke about South Gate only in class terms, it was hard to ignore anti-immigrant sentiment inside the coalition. Support for the plant was mainly about taking any opportunity to move against Albert Robles, but many who hated Robles also opposed the power plant. In addition, an indeterminate but visible part of the energy among some whites in the coalition looked like a coded way of expressing resentment that Latina/os had taken over what these whites saw as their city. Latina/os in this coalition shared their white neighbors' anger at corruption, even if they did not share their anti-immigrant sentiments, or perhaps their support for the power plant.

The anticorruption story shows that issues that seemed to have nothing to do with the power plant in fact had an important impact.

When the anti-Robles movement became linked to the power plant, it made xenophobia and public silence in South Gate about things racial visible. When xenophobic sentiments surfaced in the context of the power plant campaign, they raised new questions about what ethnicity and anti-immigrant sentiments had to do with people's views on the power plant. Environmental justice activists explained their position as simultaneously supporting environmentalism and opposing racial discrimination. Their opponents did not address these arguments, nor did they say anything publicly about racial or anti-immigrant sentiment. What was the impact of anti-immigrant sentiment and immigrants' knowledge that it was alive and well even if officials did not talk about it? What was the impact of environmental justice talk about disparities in pollution among white and Latina/o neighborhoods? And most important, was working-class environmentalism that appealed solely to shared class interests viable?

My interest in this struggle soon expanded to looking at the racial elephant in the living room: how racism, xenophobia, and widespread refusal to talk about them affected this environmental struggle, and what lessons it might have for progressive social movements more generally. South Gate was not unusual. Many progressive groups—labor unions, for example, seem actively to avoid talking about race even when there is cross-racial cooperation (or maybe especially then). So in addition to telling the fuller—and intrinsically dramatic—story of how environmental justice activists managed to stop the power plant, this book explores the consequences of race talk and race avoidance, and their lessons for working-class environmentalism.

Two important studies of the state of environmentalism, Mark Dowie's *Losing Ground* (1995) and Robert Gottlieb's *Forcing the Spring* (2005; see also Szasz 1994), offer insightful analyses of the ways that race and ethnicity (as well as class and gender) map onto other fault lines that exist within the wider environmental movement. One fracture onto which issues of race maps is about the ways environmental organizations are structured. Gottlieb shows how a wide variety of locally based environmental groups—antitoxics, antinuclear, and environmental justice groups—built a strong movement in the 1990s, predominantly in working-class communities, especially among people of color. These groups shared a belief that building a democratic and participatory movement was the most effective way to create real change. All were grassroots movements, and to many in the 1990s they were the only movement-like part of the environmental movement. Not only did this strand of environmentalism energize those who bore the brunt of industrial toxics, but it energized others by connecting visions of a greener planet to visions of social justice. The core constituencies of the locally based organizations tended to be working class and nonwhite, and to have women prominent in their leadership (Bullard 1994, 2005; Checker 2005; Cole and Foster 2001). Environmental justice activists took the lead in pushing both the mainstream and white grassroots antitoxic activists to take on dumping and siting toxic industries in communities of color as an issue for all environmentalists.

The more established wing of the environmental movement has not been constituency based but rather staff based. It relies on salaried professionals in organizations staffed by legal and scientific experts. Its actors were upper-middle class, almost all white, and male. By the 1990s, Dowie was one of many who thought that the environmental movement had lost its vision and become routinized as a professional-driven legal and lobbying effort concentrated in a few large nonprofit organizations. The largest mainstream environmental organizations remain principally organizations of boards of directors, paid professional staff, and fundraisers, operating without real memberships or popular participation. Gottlieb analyzed the path by which a few of the largest environmental organizations, the "big ten," came to be the only voices of environmentalism with which corporations and policymakers were willing to negotiate. These organizations became a kind of special interest group (expert advocates for "the environment") arrayed comfortably alongside business and government, and engaged with them in high-level, largely closed-door policy negotiations. Their actions antagonized grassroots environmentalists and, as we will see, the environmental justice activists in South Gate.

The mainstream organizations had little concern with the environmental issues that people of color and poor whites were struggling with, and they were uneasy with the organizing and popular mobilizing strategies that the mainly women-led antitoxics movements were using to good effect. In addition, there existed a visible streak of xenophobic population control and anti-immigrant sentiment within the environmental mainstream (Gottlieb 2005, 327–336). By the nineties, to many potential young activists, environmentalism looked like a movement run by and for middle-class white American citizens.

By the end of the 1990s, when the power plant struggle was beginning, largely as a result of challenges from grassroots environmentalists, mainstream organizations began to broaden their agendas to include toxic dumping, hired a few women and people of color, and became somewhat less cozy with large corporations. The 1999 antiglobalization demonstrations at the Seattle meeting of the World Trade Organization brought together a wider spectrum of environmental groups and issues. The demonstration's focus on the human and environmental devastation wrought by global corporations sounded a theme that has since become more popular in the mainstream. In addition, as Gottlieb shows, antipesticide activism and food safety have taken root as issues in working-class communities in the form of urban farming, farmers' markets, and school cafeteria activism, expanding the vision of grassroots environmentalists. Although the divide between mainstream and what were in the nineties termed "alternative" environmental groups has gotten less sharp in the last decade, still there are significant differences in their visions of what a movement should be. Gottlieb suggests that the ways mainstream and grassroots environmentalist organizations worked to attempt to defeat Bush in 2004 showed these differences clearly. Mainstream organizations targeted battleground states and focused on "upper middle-class suburban voters, the constituency they considered most interested in environmental questions." But locally based environmental organizations added an electoral focus to their "existing organizing and constituency work in their own regions and neighborhoods." The latter, Gottlieb suggests, shows the "potential for providing a different and broader environmental message, one that could begin to break the movement out of its confinement as a white middle class–based interest group concerned with preserving environmental amenities and instead reinvent itself as part of a movement for social and environmental change" (2005, 406–407).

By 2009 there is even more widespread concern about the state of the environment than there was in 2000. Global warming probably has the highest media profile, followed closely by public awareness about the health hazards caused by the dumping of industrial and nuclear toxics, the unsafe nature of our food supply, and the loss of public green spaces and species diversity. Today there are many vibrant and locally based environmental movements that are also grassroots movements. Grassroots movements have a good track record of reshaping the ways people think—the common sense of the times. By doing this, they expand the politics of the possible.

THIS BOOK IS A CLOSE-UP look at how one group of environmental justice activists managed to defy the odds and stop a power plant in South Gate. It is also a comparison of the relative strengths of two forms of working-class environmentalism—one grassroots and racially inflected, the other centered in progressive institutions and officials and race avoidant—as models for future directions. More specifically, I tease out the ways that the race consciousness of environmental justice offers a more robust practice and vision of a working-class social justice agenda and multiracial collaboration. In this book I make clear that understanding how race and ethnicity, racism, and xenophobia shape the daily life of grassroots movements is a key part of the repertoire of insights needed to build that broad, participatory, and multiracial environmental movement.

People's willing involvement is the very foundation of grassroots social movements. Activists' search for mass appeal is just the surface of a deeper inquiry in which they try to figure out how to link what drives them to what might drive large numbers of potential participants to embrace the goals and strategies of a movement as their own. I've argued elsewhere that one key task activists perform is to facilitate bringing their own visions and social identities and those of potential constituents into a harmony that explains willing political activism as the right and obvious thing to do. In so doing they create a movement's collective political actor, a political identity that is more than a demographic. It is an identity infused with a cultural and political perspective that embodies the movement's social values, its vision as well as its energy (Brodkin 2007).[3] Political identities are inherently unstable precisely because they are always objects of ideological struggle. In those struggles, each side tries to create a political culture of potential constituents that embeds the obvious rightness of its actions and beliefs.

We know that race and ethnicity are social identities that have a strong influence on the way people interpret the social world. They are not the only ones, but they are important. At the same time, race and ethnicity need to be part of the portrait and hence part of the explanation about why the movement's particular course of action and vision are the right and obvious ones for its desired political constituency. This is especially so for social movements seeking multiracial constituencies, including the spectrum of grassroots environmental movements. We are just beginning to think about how race and ethnicity play out in the daily life of these movements.

In South Gate, it became clear that ethnic identities, especially those of whites and Mexican and Central American immigrants, were at the root of very different versions of working-class environmental politics. Environmental justice activists created a widely resonant political identity of what an environmentalist looked like and fought for, and the face of that identity was working class, Latina/o, and immigrant. The identity was both strength and weakness. As we shall see, South Gate's population of Mexican and Central American ancestry included many families that had been in California for as long as their white counterparts, and families that were solidly middle class. Their opponents sought to create a race- and ethnicity-neutral working-class environmentalism and environmentalist. Their results were also mixed, and ultimately ethnic avoidance proved a more serious weakness than ethnic identification.

The debate about the power plant created a perfect storm as each constellation of local actors and the allies who supported them collided in dramatic ways. Each explanatory story mobilized supporters and opponents (many of whom had no history of local activism) because they tapped into important local issues and social identities that the formal political process did not address. The overlap of environmental concerns with a web of racial subtexts helped to make the power plant issue deeply important to a wide swath of the city's residents for a range of different reasons.

Because the campaign around the power plant came to be part of the disparate agendas of different interests in the city, it became an issue that was widely owned and deeply invested in. People paid attention to the flyers and mailers from both sides. Fairly early in the controversy this situation generated a great deal of buzz. I was attracted by the television and print news reporting of environmental justice discourse and high school students' activism. The *Los Angeles Times* and the local newspapers generated their own buzz about South Gate's flamboyant and corrupt city treasurer, who subsequently received a ten-year federal prison sentence for stealing some $20 million from the city treasury of South Gate (Marosi 2002c; Silverstein 2007).[4] The

CEO of Sunlaw Energy sent mass mailings to every South Gate resident telling the story of his small environmentally conscious company fighting big energy and the benefits the plant would bring to the city. Unionists talked and sent out mailers about the power plant as a creator of jobs and a union-friendly and environment-friendly business. Many parents worried about the dangers to the health and safety of their children. All of this discussion generated a widespread sense that the power plant issue was important in an immediate way to many people's strongly felt concerns and daily lives. This kind of buzz invited people to own the issue both personally and as part of an investment they shared in their everyday social groups, whether school, civic or church.

Race and ethnicity were important organizers of pro- and anti-plant sides, but their role was seldom obvious or straightforward. Neither side was organized on ethnic lines: the largely white Downey board of realtors opposed the plant, whereas the South Gate chamber of commerce supported it. South Gate's Latina/o elected officials were almost equally divided in their allegiance. The historically white South Gate police force had Latino as well as white police officers supporting the plant. The environmental justice activists included white residents of South Gate and neighboring cities as well as Latina/os.

The different lived histories of white and Latina/o working-class residents acted both for and against the environmental justice campaign. Environmental justice messages resonated strongly with Latinos, and especially with their children, but environmental justice activists also spoke publicly about and brought racial differences into the arena of public discourse. Some whites who opposed the plant resisted confronting race or class discrimination as they affected quality of environment.

PLAN OF THE BOOK

By the time of the referendum in March 2001, I knew I wanted to write the story of how students stopped a power plant, but I also wanted to write it from the perspectives of actors on different sides of the issue. After the referendum, I began to interview many of the high school activists, CBE staff, high school teachers, city councilors, the city clerk, union officials, and adult community members who had been actively involved. I also interviewed a number of private and public environmental experts, political analysts, and journalists familiar with politics in Southeast Los Angeles. All uncited quotations in this book come from my interviews with the speakers or from interviews conducted by the two research assistants. In addition, South Gate High alums have also done research on community responses to the power plant, which they have shared with me. Because there were lingering fears that plans to build the plant might still be alive, some activists continued working on the issue through the fall of 2001. I participated and observed during this phase and attended several community and city council meetings.

With a few exceptions (noted in the text), I have used people's real names in this book, with their permission, because this is their story, their perspectives, and they are key analysts. Some interviewees are public figures; others are not. Social science scholars normally do not use real names, largely to protect those with whom they work. I've tried to balance giving credit where it is due and doing no harm to those I've interviewed. I've come closer to historians' protocols of using real names yet bestowing anonymity on sources where appropriate. Statements that interviewees did not wanted attributed to them are reported as unattributed, or the sources are noted as anonymous interviews. Things people told me but did not want passed on are not in the book.

The first four chapters set out the historical background and the origins of the three struggles that became intertwined as the citywide battle around the power plant. Southeast Los Angeles County's history as a center of heavy industry and working-class residential life that has undergone major economic and demographic changes and accompanying ethnic tensions provides the backdrop to the plant controversy. The ways that people understood their city in terms of industry, class, and race influenced how they interpreted the controversy over the plant, and the complex way that ethnicity and race factored into the power plant controversy.

Chapter 1 discusses the racial dynamics of South Gate's history and introduces the local political players, and the ways that race and immigration shaped their fortunes and their conflicts. Chapters 2 and 3 are about environmental justice activism. Chapter 2 sketches the history of the environmental justice movement and its beginnings in Southeast Los Angeles County. Chapter 3 tells the story of how Communities for a Better Environment and their high school activist group, Youth for Environmental Justice, came to organize a campaign against the power plant. Chapter 4 tells Sunlaw's story: how Robert Danziger and his associates came to develop a less polluting emission control system for conventional power plants. It traces their struggles with big power providers to market their technology, and with state political agencies that helped and hindered their efforts as part of the process that led them to want to build a big plant in Southeast Los Angeles.

Chapters 5–8 describe the unfolding and playing out of the power plant struggle from 1999 to its resolution in March 2001. These chapters are about political drama, the "who-shot-john" and the day-to-day strategies and dilemmas of local players on both sides. To explain why environmental justice activists prevailed, I show how each side's messages played with different constituencies in South Gate, and why the constituencies heard them as they did. I also highlight what xenophobia and race avoidance looked like in those events, and how they animated people on both sides of the issue. Chapter 5 focuses on the makings of a perfect storm from its beginnings in 1999, when Sunlaw first presented its proposal to build a power plant to the city council, and when its city treasurer, Albert Robles, began to flex his political muscles. It chronicles the development of pro- and anti-Robles factions in South Gate, Sunlaw's contact with South Gate's contentious government, CBE's introduction to Sunlaw and South Gate, and the creation of a local movement against Robles and in support of the power plant. Chapter 6 is about the embrace of environmental justice ideas by South Gate High School students and teachers. Chapter 7 focuses on the high school students as they became the public face of the anti-plant campaign. Chapter 8 analyzes the activities and strategies of both the pro- and anti-plant forces in what turned out to be a very short, intense, and often ugly struggle. It focuses on what helped the environmental justice campaign succeed and queries what success looks like for a grassroots movement.

The conclusion looks to the future. It examines the campaign and its lessons for working-class environmentalism, including the role of race and race avoidance in shaping the outcome of this struggle. It looks as well at the evolution of environmental justice politics in Los Angeles and some of the vibrant coalitions and campaigns they have begun to generate.

CHAPTER 1

South Gate Transitions

I'm a labor guy; I have been a UAW international representative. I worked at General Motors from '55 and [in 1982] I became the first Latino [city councilor] in the City of South Gate. And I served as the mayor twice.

[The City Council] didn't want public housing because they didn't want blacks. And I said wait a minute. They are lying to you. We are taking block grant funds to put it into the infrastructure to clean up the streets and the potholes. The city is deteriorating. We have fourteen percent unemployment, General Motors is closing down, Firestone, Weiser Lock. And I said the only way to build it is to create jobs, so you to do it through taking block grant funds and getting an aggressive redevelopment program in here. So we embarked on that. And in '83 to '88 we probably had the most vigorous redevelopment in the history of the city. We turned the city from fourteen percent unemployment, and I did it based on jobs.

—Henry Gonzalez, South Gate city councilor

When we first moved here, General Motors was still here. My dad works for Toyota. A lot of people work in factories, living in Southeast LA, I guess after the civil rights movement, because before that it was a segregated area from what I understand. When I first moved out here I remember derogatory comments from these older whites. They felt they had a right to say offensive things like "you stupid Mexican" to me in the late '70s early '80s. So for a long time I think that whoever held the power in the city, maintained it for a long time. I think that is changing.

—Leticia Ortiz, South Gate High teacher

SOUTHEAST LOS ANGELES COUNTY is the industrial heart of Southern California. It includes parts of the city of Los Angeles, the ports of San Pedro and Long Beach, and a multiplicity of small towns, one of which is the city of South Gate. Beginning with oilfields in the 1920s, and exploding during World War II with heavy manufacturing industries, Southeast Los Angeles remains today the industrial core of Los Angeles County, and the county remains the major West Coast manufacturing center of the nation. In the last thirty years, big changes in demography and economics have left their mark on the area's politics. South Gate, like its neighbors, went from being a white working-class city whose workers held well-paid, unionized industrial jobs to a Latina/o and new immigrant working-class city whose workers hold low-paid and nonunion jobs.

Throughout the transition, South Gate has remained a city of relatively high homeownership, a good place for working-class families to live, and a city with a working-class sensibility. South Gate is also a place where publicly unspoken racial divisions and pro-union sensibility coexist and shape people's outlooks. All of these characteristics played important roles in the ways that different sectors of the community interpreted the power plant and the message of its opponents.

DEMOGRAPHIC AND ECONOMIC CHANGES IN SOUTH GATE

Like other small towns in Los Angeles County's industrial belt, South Gate was built by migrants from small midwestern and southern towns, who arrived in a steady stream, attracted by cheap land and jobs in the sun. Across Southern California, starting in the early decades of the twentieth century, local real estate entrepreneurs bought land, platted it, and advertised build-it-yourself home sites as a chance to own a slice of the Southern California paradise. Becky Nicolaides' *My Blue Heaven* (2002), a superb history of South Gate during 1920–1965, chronicles its growth as a white working-class suburb of homeowners and shows how the mix of industrial work and suburban homeownership shaped the residents' politics about class and race. South Gate's attraction for working-class migrants was the chance to buy land at an affordable price and to slowly build a home, grow food, and raise a few head of livestock on one of the three tracts that ultimately became the city of South Gate. Their numbers swelled greatly in the 1930s, with the arrival of refugees from the Oklahoma, Arkansas, and Texas Dust

Bowl, who came to work in Southern California's booming oilfields and nascent industries.

Although the city was relatively poor prior to World War II, the postwar industrial boom brought prosperity and even affluence to the area. This good life rested heavily on employment at the large, unionized factories that sprang up in the area, most notably GM, Firestone Tire, and Weiser Lock, as well as on jobs at the smaller manufacturing and trucking firms that employed so many of the area's residents. The large union firms set the wage levels for blue-collar work throughout the area, and as a result, the smaller firms also paid relatively well.

Rhonda Nitschky described growing up in Southeast Los Angeles toward the end of this prosperous period:

> I am forty years old. I grew up in Maywood on 52 Street, which is as close to Vernon as you can get. My dad worked in a factory that made cardboard boxes and my mom was a teller at B of A [Bank of America], and they built a house in Maywood really close to the third industrial belt around the Southern Pacific Railroad yard. So I have grown up living around factories and truck depots.

The city of Huntington Park, which borders South Gate, was a commercial center for the area. Nitschky continued,

> When I was young, Pacific Boulevard in Huntington Park was the chic shopping place to go in the LA area, not like Rodeo Drive, but they had big movie premieres. And it changed just that much in forty years. When I was a kid, the area was mostly white and it was mostly blue collar. A lot of people—a lot of those people were immigrants from other states like from Oklahoma and Texas and Arkansas during the dust bowl, and those were the kinds of people that came out here and worked in the factories and built a lot of the factories and the industries. The more prosperous ones went off to the aerospace jobs and were over on this side of the 710 freeway, and that started changing even when I was a kid.

Nicolaides shows South Gate as a self-consciously white-only city from the beginning, and also almost equally as a working-class-conscious city. Both sentiments grew even more powerful in the aftermath of World War II, as the civil rights movement and postwar prosperity grew more or less side by side in the fifties and early sixties. Nationally and in Los Angeles, unions were at their peak strength and delivered good wages and benefits to their members. In return, workers were loyal to their unions, and white workers were willing to support union demands that employers hire black and Mexican workers into those good union jobs. Beginning with some albeit reluctant government pressure to hire nonwhite workers in defense industry plants during World War II, the nascent civil rights movement in Los Angeles was able to open up jobs for black and Mexican workers in Southeast Los Angeles' heavy industry. The unions that South Gate's working-class residents supported, especially the United Auto Workers, were also committed to desegregation, and South Gate's union members supported desegregation at work as well.

When it came to integrating schools and neighborhoods, however, South Gate's white working class was adamantly and unabashedly segregationist. They developed a version of white working-class political sensibility that rested on seeing themselves as "the hardworking, taxpaying, homeowner." In their homeowner's hat, they resolved to keep South Gate white as a way of marking their rightful place in respectable middle-class society. During the postwar decades, for the first time in American history, the suburbs that exploded across the country allowed blue-collar workers to enjoy the nation's most important marker of middle-class status, a one-family home. All these suburbs were white only; builders simply refused to sell to black families, and usually most other nonwhite ones. Postwar suburban politics became deeply invested in keeping neighborhoods and schools segregated. As Nicolaides put it, "To maintain their place in the postwar suburban world, South Gate residents felt the need to assert their whiteness all the more stridently. The pursuit of the American Dream had become a zero-sum game. And the victories, ultimately, bittersweet" (2002, 274, 327).

The idea that their shot at the American Dream was imperiled by school and residential integration may well have animated blue-collar segregationism among these homeowners. The transformation of zero-sum thinking about dismantling segregation into reigning policy and popular understandings of affirmative action came from much higher circles, however. In her superb book *Freedom Is Not Enough*, Nancy MacLean (2006) shows how, by the early seventies, neoconservative intellectuals, largely Jewish, and policymakers were transforming popular understandings of positive steps to eliminating racial barriers into quotas for hiring and college admission. "Ironically, it was the Irish Catholic Daniel Patrick Moynihan who sounded the alarm most powerfully for a new conservative Jewish identity politics that marched under the banner of color-blindness. 'If ethnic quotas are to be imposed on American universities,' Moynihan warned in a widely noted 1968 speech, the Jews will be almost driven out'" (MacLean 2006, 198). Other neoconservatives spread this interpretation of affirmative action. "Alleging 'the reinstitution of discriminatory measures against the Jews,' [Norman] Podhoretz in 1971called [affirmative action] a symptom of a fearsome new anti-Semitism by which Jews must inevitably be harmed. The zero-sum groupthink perspective which the neoconservatives urged on affirmative action was nowhere more bluntly stated than in Podhoretz's 1972 goad: 'Is It Good for the Jews?'" (198).

MacLean argues that the zero-sum interpretation of affirmative action gained a moral legitimacy that old-style conservatives and opponents of integration had lost because it came from an ethnic group that was a long-standing advocate of civil rights for African Americans and whose members had themselves been victims of discrimination.

Zero-sum thinking redefined the meaning of fairness and antidiscrimination. The core criterion for fairness became merit, which was the plaintiffs' argument in the *Bakke* and *Defunis* cases before the U.S. Supreme Court. The plaintiffs—both white, Jewish men rejected for admission to medical and law school—argued that admission of more minorities meant that fewer and probably more qualified whites would be admitted to professional schools.

This shifting discourse about fairness had two important concomitants. First, it left no way to talk about or deal with ongoing patterns of racial unfairness without the argument being construed as entitlement to violate the rights of another group, and hence divisive. The discourse of meritocracy makes it difficult to address the persistence of racism—without a real danger of being misunderstood as divisive. The second concomitant has to do with feelings about the state of American society. Affirmative action promotes and rests on a kind of "rising tide raises all boats" optimism, whereas zero-sum views rest on and generate pessimistic fears of "limited goods." In retrospect, the shift in the way that many Americans, including South Gate residents, came to understand affirmative action is not fully surprising. By the midseventies, the national and local economic picture was no longer rosy, and things continued to worsen with the beginnings of de-industrialization in the late seventies.

In the South Gate of the mid- to late sixties, these views led to a major shift as working-class residents, disaffected and alienated from labor and New Deal Democrats, made the city a Republican political stronghold.[1] Nicolaides attributes some of this shift to growing business unionism—a focus on wages and benefits for members and a retreat from organizing the unorganized. The powerful unions that commanded South Gate workers' allegiance abandoned a wider vision of improving life for America's blue-collar workers. By confining themselves to wages and working conditions of the already unionized, they left the field of public policies and civic culture to more conservative forces and offered no organized alternative to segregationism in local politics (Nicolaides 2002, 251).

The 1965 Watts Riot only hardened South Gate's burgeoning segregationist views. Watts is an African American neighborhood in the city of Los Angeles that borders South Gate to the west. The prospect of school busing—with students from the western part of South Gate being bused to school in Watts—was an inflammatory political issue in the early sixties. During the Watts Riot in 1965, "the South Gate police hauled shotguns and tear gas out to blockades they'd set up at streets passing from Watts into South Gate. And residents stood guard over their homes, some on rooftops, others on porches, some brandishing weapons, many fearing that the riot would spill over into their own domestic space" (Nicolaides 2002, 1).

What happened in South Gate was part of a much wider white backlash to integration in Southern California and the nation. White working-class Southeast Los Angeles feared school integration and, worse, Mexican and black families moving into the neighborhood. When Rhonda Nitschky began school in the late sixties, her mother sent her "to a private school through the sixth grade, which was all white, not so much a prep school, but just my mom didn't want me in public school. Even though she was a bank teller, she came up with sixty dollars a month to send me to a private school."

Resistance to integration did not take place in an economic vacuum. Between 1965 and 1983, Weiser Lock, Firestone Tire, and GM, the three biggest plants in South Gate, had all shut down, laying off more than 11,000 workers. The picture was repeated across the region as unionized corporations, such as Alcoa and Bethlehem Steel in neighboring Vernon, closed down and left town. The collapse of big industries continued into the nineties, when big aerospace companies such as McDonnell Douglas and TRW imploded. As Southeast Los Angeles hemorrhaged jobs, the brunt of the economic collapse was borne by black and Latina/o workers, who, being the last hired, were the first laid off. The timing couldn't have been worse. Massive layoffs occurred right after African Americans and Latinos had finally managed to break segregationist hiring barriers, gain union jobs, and enter local union leadership. Because black and Mexican workers were also younger than their white counterparts, they were not eligible for retirement and were never able to access the union's good retirement benefits. And because residential segregation prevented nonwhite workers from "follow[ing] their jobs to the suburban periphery, nonwhites were stranded in an economy that was suddenly minus 40,000 high-wage manufacturing and trucking jobs" (Mike Davis, as quoted in Nicolaides 2002, 329).

For working-class whites in Southeast Los Angeles County, that periphery lay to the east and south—away from Los Angeles and toward Orange County. In those years, Downey, home of Karen and Richard Carpenter, was a kind of border city, part Orange County, part working class. According to Rhonda Nitschky,

> Downey is a weird place. Downey is the kind of place where they used to have really, really racist cops. When I lived in Bell, I can remember people telling me about Latinos that wouldn't even drive through Downey because they knew they would get pulled over. Downey was totally white bread, and I can remember after I moved there things started to change because a lot of Koreans were moving and almost all the churches in Downey were taken over by Koreans because the population was aging, moving away, dying off, and the churches weren't getting younger members.

Nitschky added freeway building to the list of things that caused deterioration in Southeast Los Angeles. The controversy-filled Century Freeway, or the 105 freeway, runs east–west through the belt of Los Angeles County's working-class cities. Over much protest and many legal challenges, the state of California used eminent domain to seize and demolish a large number of houses along the route, but the actual building did not start for years. The years of living with blasting and

smashing on top of the demoralization that had developed among residents who were unable to stop the project were only heightened by
years of living with the wreckage before construction began. Nitschky
remembered those years: "They used eminent domain to cut down a
block of houses that belonged to Downey and South Gate, and it sat
vacant for more than a decade, and then they built the 105 freeway. And
it's really caused—between the losing [of] the aerospace jobs and then
having that whole swath of town come down and the whole recession
in the late eighties and first couple of years in the nineties, and then
the whole influx of the Latinos into the area—there's been a lot of
changes."

Industrial collapse, white flight, and damaged neighborhoods set
the stage for the major ethnic transformation that took place in South
Gate and neighboring cities between 1965 and 1980. Third- and
fourth-generation Mexican Americans and newer Mexican and Central
American immigrants were able to move from poorer neighborhoods
to Southeast Los Angeles cities that formerly had been determined
to keep them out. Between 1960 and 1980, South Gate's Latina/o
population went from 4 percent to 46 percent and then rose to 83
percent by 1990 (Nicolaides 2002, 328). Despite all the changes, there
are still fair numbers of white residents like Nitschky, who stayed, and
longtime Latina/o residents like South Gate city counselor Henry
Gonzalez, who moved in during the early years.

Younger residents have vivid childhood memories of these times.
Leticia Ortiz, who teaches at South Gate High School and also grew
up in Southeast Los Angeles in the late seventies and eighties, described
the anti-Mexican racism she experienced in South Gate, as quoted in an
epigraph to this chapter.

A few years older, and white, Rhonda Nitschky graduated from Bell
High School in 1978.

> I would say at that time, it was about 50/50 white and Latino.
> And the white flight was starting even then. I went to Nimitz
> Junior High School in Huntington Park [which had] a lot of racial
> tension, a lot of violence, drug use, and it was like a really scary
> experience for me coming out of this private school where all the
> kids were well behaved and there was never any kind of trouble. I
> had been really sheltered, and all of a sudden I'm in there with kids
> that have drugs and knives and guns in their lockers. There were

kids that got killed when I was there in gang fights. There was this whole like surfers versus cholos thing going on.

And it was the same when I went to Bell High School. They had racially motivated melees on campus on several occasions. And I had kind of been victimized in a kind of a girl joining a gang victim incident, initiation-type thing where they basically had to attack a white person in order to get into the gang or something. I was just walking through the hallway minding my own business at school, and all of a sudden I was walking by a group of Latino girls and I got punched in the face, without anybody saying a word, so hard that it knocked me down and almost knocked me out. And by the time I got up off the floor, they were gone. One of my friends was walking out of school, and she got slammed across the head with a wine bottle. And there were like weird incidents. And at the same time I am dating a Latino.

That experience may have helped Nitschky look at the racial dynamics in Southeast Los Angeles from two very different points of view.

When I was twenty-one, I was with this guy, and he had gone to Princeton. He was home on vacation, and he's wearing shorts and a shirt that had the Princeton logo on it, but he was driving his brother's big old bomb of a car. We were driving through Huntington Park, and it was my twenty-first birthday, and I had gotten snockered. I didn't drink until I was twenty-one, and that was it. And he was being the good designated driver, and I was sick laying down in the back seat of the car, and so he is driving real slow through Huntington Park at one in the morning. And all of sudden we get pulled over by the police. They come up to the car. This is 1981. They come to the car. They don't even ask for his ID. They tell him to get out of the car, slam him up against the side of the car, and he is going "What did I do?" And they are telling him to shut up, slamming his face against the side of the car. They are telling him he's weaving, and they have never looked in the back seat of the car. They didn't see me. And I just exploded out of the back seat of the car and started demanding names and badge numbers. And the police looked at each other, they didn't say a word. And then all of a sudden they run to the squad car and jump in and just burned rubber peeling out. They looked like Batman and Robin jumping into the Batmobile. It was so weird. I had thought civil rights issues were a thing of the past, and everything is all hunky-dory.

And that was my first exposure to racist cops and what people of color were experiencing in Los Angeles. And this was way before the Rodney King thing. I had no idea. So my first reaction is how stupid they are, how could they be so stupid. And I'm laughing because they looked so funny running away from me. And I turn around and I look at my boyfriend and he is just sitting there shaking with shame and with rage, and he couldn't even speak to me about it. It's like we were living together in the same city a few blocks apart and we were experiencing totally different lives.

I don't know where the anger and hostility of the Chicanos that I went to junior high and high school toward whites was coming from. It's like I had never done anything to them. I wasn't somebody who used racial epithets, had always considered everybody to be equal, and yet I found myself victimized from time to time. But it's hard for me to walk in their shoes and know what they experience on a daily basis.

I have seen too many things and I know some of the things that they have experienced. For instance, I stopped at a gas station and gone into the little fast food mart, and like walked through this door, gone in and had a black woman walking right behind me, and when she got to the door, the door was locked—that kind of thing in that area. So I can only try to imagine how that makes somebody feel. So I try to be sensitive, but sometimes I'm insensitive and don't understand things.

SOUTH GATE AND
SOUTHEAST LOS ANGELES TODAY

Today Southeast Los Angeles is still California's manufacturing center, but the manufacturing jobs are no longer union jobs, and the factories are small, unstable, and often outright sweatshops. The largest employers are relatively small apparel, metal, plastic, rubber, and furniture manufacturing shops, followed by small retail trade establishments and a fewer number of wholesale businesses (see table 1.1).

South Gate residents are still predominantly working class, but in 2000 they were 92 percent Latina/o, divided between Mexican and

TABLE 1.1

Businesses in South Gate, 1997

Major industry	Industry subgroup	No. of establishments	No. of employees
Manufacturing		200	7,603
	Apparel	23	1,614
	Plastic and rubber	13	642
	Metals	74	2,563
	Furniture	12	740
Wholesale trade durables		86	417
Wholesale trade nondurables		32	618
Retail trade		154	1,738
Totals		472	10,376

SOURCE: South Gate 2002.

Central American ancestry. Some families had been in California for two to four generations, and some had moved to South Gate from East Los Angeles, Watts, and neighboring cities; new immigrants were mainly from Mexico but also El Salvador, Guatemala, and other Central American countries, plus a few people of many other backgrounds. The city's population has almost doubled from 53,831 in 1960 to 96,375 in 2000, and is projected to come close to 104,000 in 2010 (South Gate n.d.). The population has gotten younger, falling from a median age of thirty-three in 1970 to twenty-six in 2000 (Institute for Homelessness and Poverty n.d.).

In 2000, South Gate household median income for its 22,194 households was $27,279, significantly lower than $41,000, the approximate median income for Los Angeles County in 2000 (Institute for Homelessness and Poverty n.d.). In respect to income, South Gate is a solidly working-class city, although it is not class homogeneous. Some 3,000 of its 22,000 households report incomes of between $50,000 and $75,000, and another 1,000 households report incomes above $75,000, putting about 18 percent of households solidly within middle-class income brackets. Although the data do not link income and ethnicity, we will see that most of the middle-income residents, like most city residents, and most South Gate leaders and professionals, are more likely to be of Mexican and Central American ancestry than white.

A little more than half of South Gate's 7.5 square miles are zoned for residential occupancy, with most of the area containing low-density, single-family housing. Another 39.7 percent is zoned as industrial, commercial, or mixed use, but mainly industrial, and 8.6 percent of the land is public, including a large, beautiful park in the eastern part of town (South Gate n.d.).

South Gate has its own internal east–west gradient (see table 1.2), based in part on its history of late incorporation of a number of disparate working-class tracts (Nicolaides 2002). South Gate shares its western border with the historically African American neighborhood of Watts. The physical border is the Alameda Corridor, a wide street of heavy industries, an old railway freight line, and in recent decades a long-term construction project, with its attendant dust and traffic jams, to build a high-speed below-grade railway to carry containerized freight from the Port of Los Angeles to downtown warehouses. The west side too is where industrial and mixed zoning is located, as well as where apartment housing is concentrated. It is the less desirable and poorer side of town. The eastern border is with historically white and more middle-class Downey. The 710 freeway also cuts through the east side of South Gate. This side of town contains mainly single-family housing and the city park. It is also where South Gate's remaining whites tend to live. In addition to the race, class, and industrial gradients, there is also an educational gradient. Children from the west side of town are bused to Jordan High School, a poorly performing school in Watts. Those from the east side of town attend South Gate High School,

TABLE 1.2

Ethnic and economic geography of South Gate

	East side census tract	West side census tract	South Gate
Ethnically Latino (%)	61	95.2	92
Owner-occupied housing (%)	83.1	52.2	46.9
Householders older than 65 (%)	12.7	3.5	4.8
Renter unit average size (persons)	2.79	4.36	3.9
Owner unit average size (persons)	2.8	4.84	4.33

SOURCE: U.S. Bureau of the Census 2000.

which has an excellent graduation rate and record of sending students to top colleges.

South Gate city councilman Hector De La Torre summed up South Gate's ethnic and generational demographics this way:

> I would say you could divide the city into four groups. One is the white residents, who tend to be older and to be working-class people. There is your second-, third-, fourth-generation Latinos, who in most instances tend to see things kind of like the white folks. They have lived in the city longer. They have deep roots in the community. And the third group is the immigrants. New voters who moved to South Gate from wherever they came from. In most instances they came from neighboring cities like Huntington Park, Lynwood, Bell. The fourth group is the children of immigrants.
>
> South Gate is perceived to be a better place than the cities immediately adjacent to us. Our home ownership rate, although by LA standards is not great, in our area is very good, nearing 50 percent owner occupied. We get a lot [of people who move] from South Central as well. My family moved into South Gate from South Central when I was three or four years old, so it's kind a normal migratory pattern into South Gate, and then, if people are successful in South Gate, they move east, Downey, La Mirada. It's kind of a stepping-stone community. For a lot of people, the first house they buy is in South Gate. They may have rented wherever they lived before and buy a house in South Gate. Schools are incredibly overcrowded and are perceived to be better than the schools of where they came from.

South Gate High School teacher Leticia Ortiz would agree with that analysis: "A lot of [our students] are immigrants or their parents are immigrants or they moved here from a place that was worse. So a lot of our kids, they have a lawn and backyard, and it's better than wherever they came from. It's better than South Central or better than Compton; it is better than Mexico."

Ortiz, however, sees upward mobility as shaping residents' political perceptions. "So I think a lot of our kids have a hard time thinking of themselves as oppressed because they compare it to something worse. We used to live in South Central. When we moved here from Compton in the '70s, moved to South Gate, it was like, wow we had a front lawn and a backyard—it looked like a little suburbia compared to where we used to live, and I think that's what a lot of our students—it's more like a first generation becoming more a second."

City clerk Carmen Avalos analyzed the politics of demographic differences across the east–west gradient.

> The west side of our city happens to be the less desirable area I think in the city [because] there is excessive overcrowding, parking problems as a result of that being more of your apartment district. You have a lot of newcomers who are immigrants in that area who have just become naturalized citizens. And therefore they are very limited in their understanding of the democratic process in this country and could be easily persuaded by anyone utilizing their ignorance about the process. I think it is kind of easier to take advantage of these individuals and I know because I lived in that area. That's where I grew up.

Sylvia Zamora, then a Smith College student from South Gate, conducted a survey of residents in the western half of the city in 2002 as part of a research project on the power plant. Her findings overlap with Avalos' description in that the majority of those she interviewed seemed to speak Spanish as their first language. They have lived in South Gate for well over a decade, however, and were also registered voters (Sylvia Zamora, pers. comm.).

Many undocumented immigrants had applied for amnesty under a 1986 law that allowed them to apply for citizenship after a seven-year wait. In the wake of California's passage in 1994 of a voter initiative (Proposition 187) that denied public services to the undocumented, many became citizens and registered to vote. As a result of that proposition and the organized effort to register new Latina/o voters, a fair number of relatively recent immigrants are registered voters and citizens in South Gate as well as elsewhere in California.

Downey is often the first stop for the upwardly mobile, who then move to more prosperous areas like Fullerton and Orange County. Rhonda Nitschky sees Downey, where she now lives, as being in the midst of an ethnic transition not unlike South Gate's.

> The population in this city [Downey] right now, I think is kind of barbell shaped. There's a lot of elderly white people, and

there's a lot of young Latino families that have only been here a couple of years, and a lot of them have young children. There has really been explosive growth of school children at the local schools. I could show you the schools right over by where the power plant was going to be—where there was one school, there are now two schools. They literally had to take out the playground and build an elementary school because they had so many school children. At first they couldn't believe that the population here in an established community was growing that much. They were hiring detectives to spy on school kids to make sure they weren't coming over the line from South Gate and Bell Gardens.

Smooth Transition or Unspoken Friction?

Given the rapid ethnic transformation throughout Southeast Los Angeles County, it is surprising that there is so little public talk about ethnicity or race in the city. It is particularly surprising because anti-immigrant sentiment was a big part of the California landscape during the decades of transition. It crystallized in 1994, with the passage of Proposition 187, a voter initiative (later declared unconstitutional) that denied undocumented immigrants access to health care and education. I suspect that the public silence about racism and xenophobia in South Gate, especially among progressive officials, is largely a response to the power of zero-sum thinking and a wish not to fan divisiveness. As we'll see, the prevailing public discourse is about South Gate as a working-class city. It alludes to ethnic diversity and inclusiveness but without triggering white sensitivities about race and immigration.

Many Latino residents who have lived in South Gate since the late seventies have experienced insulting remarks and other forms of interpersonal and institutional discrimination, and these currents of resentment and racism continue to run beneath the surface of city life. Privately, Latino residents, officials, and students speak often and matter-of-factly of that history—and its persistence.

Henry Gonzalez has been around labor and politics in South Gate for a long time. His South Gate roots go back to the days when South Gate was a white and white-run city. Politically, as Gonzalez states in the an epigraph to this chapter, he is a Democrat, president of the

Labor Council for Latin American Advancement of the AFL–CIO, and until he retired, an international representative of the United Auto Workers.

As a South Gate resident since 1961, he was among the first Latinos to move to the city. According to Mayor Raul Morial, Henry Gonzalez, who, in 1982 was the first Latino to be elected to the city council, "remembers a time when he worked here as a commissioner but wasn't welcome to live here." Morial also said that, privately, Gonzalez had told him lots of stories about his experiences with racism. Gonzalez himself doesn't speak much about racism, whether directed against him or more generally. As the lone Latino on a white, Republican-leaning council in the eighties, that avoidance was understandable. In one of this chapter's epigraphs, Gonzalez describes a situation in 1982 when his white colleagues refused to apply for federal funds: "They were saying too many strings tied, and you will have public housing," which he saw as saying in code that they believed taking federal funds would force South Gate to allow African Americans to live there. In urging the council to apply for federal funding, Gonzalez was careful *not* to address their wish to keep African Americans out of South Gate. He consistently stressed that in politics one has to get along with one's colleagues, to be political. And in this context, where he was new and the only nonwhite councilor, it made political sense.

As South Gate changed demographically, however, old adaptations might not serve so well. As a result of the 1965 changes in U.S. immigration law, ethnic changes occurred all across Southern California, from Chinese immigration to the San Gabriel Valley east of downtown Los Angeles, to Mexican and Central American immigration into South and Southeast Los Angeles.

Early forms of white backlash included "English-only" laws. Many cities discussed passing them, and a few did so (Horton and Calderon 1995). A proposal for such a law was among the few instances of public race talk I was able to find in South Gate's more recent political and civic life. It was a 1985 effort, when South Gate's population had become about 60 percent Latino, to change city zoning regulations to require that all business names be in English. Mayor Raul Morial, who has lived in South Gate since about 1970, remembered it as "an English-only initiative on the city ballot" and that many white residents supported it. It was not a voter initiative, however, but came from the city's planning commission. Morial was probably right about the anti-immigrant sentiment that prompted the commission. They recommended that the city council pass an ordinance requiring business signs to be in English and—referring to Asian businesses—in Roman letters, for public safety, so that police and firefighters could read them. The commission's recommendation came from the planning department, which claimed that there had been "a proliferation of business trade name signs written in languages other than English." Louis Bremer, the commission's chair, was quoted in the press as saying, "there are a lot of businesses coming out that are strictly in Spanish." A planning aide, speaking to the amendment requiring Roman lettering, even though there were no signs with Asian characters in the city, said that it was "just in case." A *Los Angeles Times* survey found few businesses with Spanish-only signs and mixed responses to the idea by businesses with them (Alfonso 1985a, 1985b, 1985c).

There was little support for the change, however. The predominantly white police department, then Mayor Bill DeWitt, who is white, and the predominantly white city council opposed the ordinance, while, ironically, Henry Gonzalez supported it (Rodriguez 1985). It was quietly dropped.

As South Gate's Latina/o population increased, so too did its participation in the city's civic and political life. An important milestone in 1990 was the decision of the South Gate Junior High School PTA to conduct its meetings in Spanish, with English translation. Although both PTA officers and school officials were worried—after the flap over the English-only signage proposal—there was no complaint, "just a positive response," according to the school's principal. More important, it resulted in an extraordinary growth in membership and vitality of the PTA in South Gate. By 1990, there were only 55 white and 40 black students out of 3,700 students in the school; the rest were Latina/o. With the switch to Spanish, and the election of a Spanish-speaking president, PTA membership more than tripled—from 466 to 1,455— and attendance at meetings rose steeply. So too did active involvement of parents with the school, in buying band and gym uniforms, and of the PTA and school in assisting families new to the country and area with health care information and with food assistance to the needy (Louie 1990).

All of this suggests a fairly smooth transition for South Gate, and indeed there is much to buttress this view. By 1996, four of the five city councilors were Latina/o and the face of elected governance was no

longer white. Several local political analysts believe that the transition of
power from whites to Latina/os in South Gate has proceeded amicably,
and that its historically white police force has also changed.

Others see it differently, however. One observer thought that South
Gate police "were the worst and most racist in Southeast LA" and
that it was the last to integrate Latinos into their command structure.[2]
Several others suggested instead that South Gate had experienced more
a semblance of change in the sense of a Latina/o city council, but not a
change in the locus of real power. They argue that South Gate's white
population has been able to hold onto civic power because they are the
core of the 24,000–25,000 registered voters in the city. As recently as
the early nineties, one claimed, whites could say publicly that they didn't
want Latinos in South Gate Park, and the city council supported that
request. One analyst pointed to the experience of the Oldtimers' Foundation, a civic group that has served meals and provided other services
for seniors since the late seventies. They used to use the Senior Center
in the park, a building that is a private facility on public property. Now
that the foundation is serving a predominantly Latina/o constituency,
they have not been allowed to serve lunch there, reportedly because
many of South Gate's older whites still do not want Latina/os there.
Several noted that South Gate is no different from other cities of Southeast Los Angeles with Latino city councils.

What I found surprising was that South Gate's progressive Democratic politicians and union officials, among those most likely to be
committed to building inter-ethnic harmony and ending discrimination, studiously avoided talking about these issues. Nor was it only the
older generation, those who entered politics in the days when South
Gate was adamantly white, who avoided race talk. Henry Gonzalez's
younger colleague on the South Gate city council in 2000, Hector De
La Torre, grew up in South Gate and describes himself as a progressive,
pro-union Democrat. He too stressed the class continuity of South
Gate's transition instead of the racial transformation: "I tell people all
the time that South Gate has not changed. They always talk about
how much South Gate has changed in the last thirty years, but I tell
people it hasn't changed. It was working class thirty years ago; it's a
working-class community today." And Julie Butcher, manager of the
Service Employees International Union (SEIU) local of South Gate
city workers, also stressed class or union continuities, suggesting that a
shared union tradition was responsible for a harmonious racial transfer

of power: "The transition from old white to Latino has been okay, a model for change. The city had a strong union tradition."

I think of this civic discourse as "union-speak," because, like labor union discourse, it talks about South Gate's working-class populace as if its members all had the same interests, and that those are working-class interests, which transcend or trump any other kind of interest. At its best, class talk is a hopeful, wishful discourse about cross-ethnic community solidarity. But it is also part of a larger pattern of avoidance that responds to zero-sum thinking about racial discrimination such that calling attention to race makes one vulnerable to charges of being divisive or antiwhite.

The absence of public discourse about such friction in a working-class city does not mean there is no ethnic friction or discrimination. Instead, the absence makes it hard to deal with the problem if you can't talk about it in governmental or official contexts. Without public discourse, discrimination and ethnic favoritism can continue as business as usual, because there is no socially acceptable way of calling attention to it. Persons on the receiving end of discrimination already know discrimination exists and usually appreciate its being acknowledged and addressed by civic leaders. The leaders' silence leaves a political vacuum for someone to say what everyone knows—that discrimination and friction exist.

Enter Albert Robles. Robles saw that political vacuum and used it to become South Gate's most powerful and, to many, its most dangerous politician. From the time he was elected to the South Gate City Council in 1992, until he was voted out of office in 2003, Robles could be found in the middle of virtually all of South Gate's political controversies. One cannot understand the controversy surrounding Sunlaw's proposed Nueva Azalea power plant without knowing something about Albert Robles.

Part of my problem of getting a handle on Albert Robles is that, although I was able to talk with those who became his political enemies, he did not respond to my requests for an interview. He has also said little publicly about his background except that he is a Mormon, was abused by his father, was a foster child, and lived in garages (Quinones 2001). During the period I was conducting my research, reports on Robles' behavior and alleged corruption were something of a cottage industry among members of the Los Angeles press.[3] I could find no record of Robles-initiated proposals or programs that appeared to advocate for or support the needs of new immigrants, or the needs of South Gate. And Albert Robles left no written record of his contributions. What looms large in written records and the recollections of those I spoke with are Robles' efforts to support himself with political posts and to exercise power. So, the Albert Robles who appears here is pieced together from these sources.

In an interview with *Los Angeles Times* writer Sam Quinones, Robles explained that he moved to South Gate in 1991, soon after graduating from UCLA with a major in political science, "because nature abhors a vacuum. Albert came to fill a need for leadership within the community." Robles described South Gate politics to Quinones as a struggle between an old guard and new politicians like himself who wanted to represent the voices of new immigrants (2001, 22). In the statewide political climate of the 1990s that was marked by xenophobic discourse and a stream of anti-immigrant voter initiatives, Albert Robles was able to build a political base among South Gate's newer immigrant citizens by addressing their perceptions of being treated as second-class citizens. Silence on the part of progressive officials about racism and anti-immigrant politics helped Robles achieve his goal. The only endeavors that Robles undertook on behalf of new immigrants, that I was able to find, were largely symbolic.

His most visible gesture was his effort to change the city's annual festival. South Gate is known as the Azalea City. The azalea is the city's flower, and the city's big civic celebration, or carnivale, is the Azalea Festival. At that point the festival had been held every March for the last thirty years. It is also an event that honors women over sixty, and the Azalea Queen was chosen each year from among this age group.

In 1994, soon after being selected by his fellow councilors as mayor, at the age of twenty-six, Robles seems to have been behind the push to change South Gate's annual civic celebration from the March date of the Azalea Festival to May 5, in effect replacing the Azalea Festival with Cinco de Mayo. According to press reports, the rest of the city council was surprised and not at all pleased. Residents as well as councilors complained. Some accused Robles of "petty politics and cultural favoritism." South Gate High School teacher Victorio Gutierrez spoke out against imposing a Mexican holiday on an ethnically diverse city that included many other Central Americans as well as Anglos. Mildred Ward, at the time the Azalea queen, noted, "We have no problem celebrating Cinco de Mayo, we just want the Azalea Festival to remain a tradition in South Gate" (Romero 1994). Ultimately it did, and a Cinco de Mayo celebration was added to the city calendar.

It is likely that a move to add city support to a Cinco de Mayo celebration would have provoked little in the way of opposition in 1994, when the city was overwhelmingly Latina/o, and when Cinco de Mayo had become as much a Southern California–wide celebration as a Mexican one. Although Robles did not say so, trying to do away with the Azalea Festival looks like a way of declaring that South Gate no longer belonged to whites but to Latina/os. The move clearly was provocative not only of the white old guard but also of residents and councilors with visions of multiethnic civic ownership. It was a message, a symbolic gesture to new immigrants, who were overwhelmingly from Mexico and potentially his political constituency.

Albert Robles owes his start to Henry Gonzalez, which is ironic in that they quickly became enemies. After college, Robles worked for the state assemblywoman who represented the district that included South Gate. Henry Gonzalez's wife worked in Southeast Los Angeles politics and met Robles, who impressed her, as he did many others, as smart and personable. She introduced him to her husband, who shared her opinion.

Henry Gonzalez, as the first Latino city councilor, encouraged promising young Latina/os to enter politics, but he rues the day he helped Albert Robles do so. Gonzalez recalled,

> I met with Albert, and he says to me, what do you think. I said, well, Albert, you are going to have to move into the community. They are going to rib you on the basis that you are a carpetbagger and they will criticize you on your youth, but I think you combat that with your education. You got a B.A. at UCLA, you're educated, you're articulate. I was not on the council then, [but] I supported him, opened the doors for him, introduced him to people and got people to support him, and got people to donate money to his campaign and he got elected.

Albert Robles was elected to the city council in 1992, and when Gonzalez was reelected to the council in 1994, he continued trying to mentor and help Robles. He also supported Robles' appointment as mayor.[4]

So then he was always griping about this and that. I said, look, Albert, you got to learn how to work with people. You get a majority and then you can do your program. I made a big mistake. From then on, everything he kept doing was using the city funds [for personal things]. I said you can't be doing crap like this. We slapped his wrist; the attorney slapped his wrist saying he couldn't be doing that, so then he just got power hungry.

Some who knew Robles were more forgiving, saying that Robles did take on issues of racism and xenophobia, but they also thought that he did so in ways that were sometimes racially divisive and other times simply self-serving or corrupt.

Still, back in 1996, long before he made the papers, Albert Robles was beginning to make enemies of his colleagues in South Gate government. Although Gonzalez quickly lost his enthusiasm for Robles, the two did not seem to have become overt political enemies until 1996, when Robles ran for a position on the Southern California Water Replenishment District (WRD) while he was also serving on the city council. The WRD is a little-known but important agency in charge of preserving and making constructive use of Southern California's groundwater. The position carried an annual salary of $23,400 (Quinones 2001, 22). While on the WRD, Robles managed to claim over $15,000 in reimbursed expenses for things such as acting and flying lessons (Martin 2004).

When Robles won that election, Gonzalez recalled, "I said, here's our chance to get rid of him. I didn't say anything and then later on when he got elected I laughed and I said, well, it's nice having you on the city council. He said what are you talking about. I said, you can't serve on the city council and the water board. It's a conflict. Well, you're crazy. So then they rechecked and it was right, he couldn't run for re-election. So then he ran for treasurer."

One thing everyone agrees on is that Albert Robles is a very skilled politician, and that he built a constituency of largely new immigrant voters, who helped him, and the candidates he supported, to win elections. Robles was elected to the post of city treasurer—a job that paid $69,000 a year—on his first try. Most of his long list of enemies argue that Robles built his political base among Mexican immigrants largely by playing on their naiveté about U.S. politics and by behaving like a Mexican political boss and adopting the practices of Mexico's long-ruling PRI political party—giveaways in exchange for votes. In Robles' case these ranged from hot dogs and sodas, plants and toys, to, at the end, a house (Marosi 2003a, 2003b). In Mexico, the argument goes, corruption and politics were synonymous, and however distasteful, Robles' behavior was in sync with new immigrants' understandings of U.S. politics. Combined with "playing the race card," Robles, by his symbolic gestures toward new immigrants, successfully portrayed himself for a long time as the champion of South Gate's new citizens.

He also managed to withstand a challenge to collecting his WRD salary (for the duration of a four-year term, 1996–2000) while serving as South Gate's treasurer. Bill DeWitt served on the city council during 1980–1990 and had been active in South Gate civic affairs since the late seventies. He is a businessman, owner of General Veneer, an established South Gate plywood company, and a member of Rotary and the chamber of commerce. He and Henry Gonzalez worked well together on a number of issues between 1982 and 1990, even though they came down on opposite sides of the English-sign proposal. DeWitt was not on the city council in 1997, but he was no happier than Gonzalez about Robles holding two well-paid public positions. So he contacted the California Attorney General's Office to request an opinion about whether there was a conflict of interest in Robles' holding of both offices. And, if so, whether he, DeWitt, had the right to sue as a private citizen and resident. The answer from the Attorney General's Office was that there was indeed a conflict of interest and that a lawsuit was appropriate (Lungren and DaVigo 1997, 97–206). DeWitt did not go forward with that lawsuit for reasons that are not clear—and Robles remained on the WRD. Later in 1997, however, DeWitt did sue the city for hiring an economic development consultant without posting the position or seeking applicants. It is unclear whether Robles or someone else made the hire, but DeWitt dropped his suit when the city agreed to fire the consultant and reimburse DeWitt for his legal expenses (Douglas 2000).

By this time, Gonzalez and Robles were becoming overtly antagonistic toward each other. When Robles became city treasurer, according to Gonzalez, "he starts talking about [getting a] majority [on the city council] and then he wants to get a job with the city as the city manager. So then they [the city council] put a referendum on the ballot that no elected official for two years after he leaves office could become [an appointed city official], and it passed, and so he is all upset and he blames me for it."

The friction that was beginning to develop between Gonzalez and Robles, and between DeWitt and Robles, was also developing between South Gate's municipal workers' union and Robles. City workers in South Gate are unionized. They are represented by SEIU Local 347, which also represents workers in the municipal governments of a number of cities. That local became involved in South Gate politics at about the time Albert Robles was elected city treasurer. Actually, Albert Robles was the reason for their involvement. According to Julie Butcher, Local 347's manager, Robles, as the city's new treasurer, went around asking which city staff had to pay child support, and he wanted the cell phone records of undercover South Gate police. The city council refused these requests, and Robles stopped signing city checks, including the checks for Local 347 members. City workers came quickly to fear Robles. In short, by 1997, Albert Robles was ruffling feathers among South Gate's older political establishment and civil service workers.

Small city politics in Southeast Los Angeles County were unusually turbulent during the years of political transition that followed the region's shift from white to Latina/o working-class residents. South Gate was no exception. Turbulence related to demographic changes interacted with generational shifts and aspirations of some of the younger political generation. Both Henry Gonzalez and Bill DeWitt are deeply rooted in South Gate. They are older men who have made their mark locally. Gonzalez's roots are in the UAW, and in the youth football league—a volunteer effort he started during the years he was not a city councilor. DeWitt's background is business, and his civic participation is in business groups as well as on the city council and planning commission. For neither is South Gate politics a full-time job or a stepping-stone to a political career or higher office, and neither supports himself with his political position.

Indeed, the city council in South Gate, like those in other California cities in its size range, considers membership on its council to be a part-time position. Given that the post paid about $7,200 a year in the 1990s, it is not a job to live on. Yet serving on the council offers public visibility, and it can also be a stepping-stone to a full-time political career, as it later became for Hector De La Torre, who now serves as representative to the state assembly for the district that includes South Gate.

By all accounts, the job was a stepping-stone for Albert Robles as well. In 1998, as a political unknown beyond South Gate, Robles entered the statewide Democratic primary and came in second for the post of state treasurer, a major accomplishment for a politically unconnected novice. He also managed to score a television appearance on *Cristina*, the Spanish-language equivalent of *Oprah* (Quinones 2001).

Robles' critics believe he was so good at winning elections because he took advantage of new voters' unfamiliarity with U.S. politics. It also seems that Robles presented himself as a champion of a large portion of the population who had no voice or explicit representation in city government, even if he did so only by taking pot shots and raising symbolic issues such as the Cinco de Mayo celebration. These two explanations are not incompatible by themselves, but they have different implications. The first suggests that new immigrants are not very competent politically; the second highlights the silence among South Gate's progressive politicians and labor leaders about ethnic friction and xenophobia. Given the disastrously corrupt state of politics in the United States in general, Robles' corruption and support look positively all-American. A public discourse about South Gate's working-class continuities and shared interests ignores deeply held divisions within South Gate's working class. At best, a class-transcendent discourse can be read as hoping that xenophobia and the damage it does will go away if no one talks about it. When Albert Robles said there was a political vacuum he intended to fill, it turned out to be the vacuum created by this silence, and those who were waiting for someone to address their feelings of exclusion and to validate their perceptions that xenophobia was alive and well in America became his constituents.

In the nineties, Albert Robles was beginning to offer one way of addressing exclusion, even if for motives that his colleagues in city hall were less than happy about. At the same time, in neighboring Huntington Park, a fledgling group with the innocuous name of Communities for a Better Environment was beginning to develop a very different way of dealing with some of the same injustices.

CHAPTER 2

Environmental Justice
and Communities
for a Better Environment

CARLOS PORRAS GREW UP IN TEXAS in the fifties and early sixties, and learned about politics in the Chicano movement of the late sixties and seventies. Porras knew racism firsthand, not only from whites toward Chicanos but from also fellow Chicanos toward African Americans.

> I have to say that I wouldn't be the person I am with the political beliefs that I have had it not been for the fact that my parents divorced and my mother remarried in 1956, and this was in Texas. She married a black man. I was seven years old. I remember the first time I saw him I kind of did a double take because his skin was dark. But the color thing was momentary, and then he was just another person to me. And he was a good person. But by the time I was seventeen, my god, I had learned so much about what [being black] meant to society. I went through betrayals because people who were my friends before they knew of my stepfather would turn their back on me and get hostile with me once they learned about my stepfather. I'm like, wait a minute, I'm the same kid I was yesterday before you knew.

Later in life, Porras became an environmental justice activist as a result of his job in the public works department of the city of Santa Fe Springs, in Southeast Los Angeles County. Working near an oil refinery made him aware of environmental health as a workers' issue, and later as a civil rights issue.

Unbeknownst to me the administration people in management of the city of Santa Fe Springs are bigots against Mexicans. Santa Fe Springs' population is 77 percent Mexican. These white people in this city management talking shit about Mexicans. I defended myself and they wanted to fire me. My co-workers [said] keep your mouth shut. I ain't keeping my mouth shut. So when they tried to fire me I organized. The superintendent was asked to retire, and the city engineer and director of public works were asked to retire because I went to politics. I went directly to the councilman who was a Mexican and told him what was going on. My co-workers saw that and they were like damn, we can't believe you did that, and can we elect you to represent us. I said, fine, go for it. I served for fifteen years alternately as president and vice president of that union.

Which segues into the environment. [Our local] represents all city employees, but I work in public works. Our public works yard is across the street from Powerine Oil Refinery. The oil refinery was documented in the [*Los Angeles*] *Times* back then as being the dirtiest refinery in the state of California with the most violations. But I'm not really all that worried about that stuff. I don't know about environmental health. I'm clueless like most of the public out there. I'm dealing with labor stuff. I want wages and hours and benefits.

This substance would come down all around the refinery for a mile in circumference, and it would get shot out with a flare and spewed all over the surrounding area wherever the wind took it. People noticed it because it was gummy stuff. If you didn't wash it off your car right away, it would start to eat the paint. So everyone is [saying] this refinery, look what it's doing to my car and look what it's doing to the paint.

The refinery has to do a PR thing [to] appease everybody, so they go to all the local car washes and get contracts, and they say, when it happens to take your car to the car cash wash and they will wash it free and we will pay for it. And so everybody starts doing that. Some people start abusing it. Then there's others who are saying that's not enough; why should I have to take the time out of my day to go to the car wash just because your refinery spewed this stuff on my car? So the refinery responds by hiring individuals to set up canopies in the parking lots of business parks, industrial parks around the refinery, including the public works yard. So here's this guy being paid eight, ten hours a day to do nothing more than wash and wax and detail cars. That goes on for about a year, everybody loving it.

In that same period of time, six of our public works guys retired. And in that year four out of the six died of cancer. And because we were a small public works unit, we knew each other's families. So naturally, I'm attending funerals this whole time. At the fourth funeral I'm sitting in a pew looking at the family grieving and another employee comes up and sits down besides me and says you know what, I just came from the car wash, and I think we need to have somebody. If that stuff is eating the paint off our cars, what is it doing to us? And is that why, when we retire, we are dead within a year? And I had never thought about it. I'm like, you might have something there. It turned into a political football that ultimately got me fired because city council, who had saved my job in the past, eighteen years before, was in bed with the refinery—campaign contributions, little parties, trips to Hawaii. We fought the refinery.

The city did not want us to take this up as a labor issue. And I said we are talking about our livelihoods here and we need some health and safety agreement, and they said, no, not now. We had already tried asking the air district. [They] said they were too busy. We tried asking the health department and they said, if there was anything wrong, they would have told you. And the city said we don't want you to deal with that, don't even ask.

I had an advisor that I had hired on the labor stuff and he said, I know these people at UCLA, why don't you go over there and ask them if they can give you any information. So I went to UCLA. Basically was asked to do a presentation for some graduate students who were looking for a project for their master's thesis in urban planning. They took it up.

The students' research, Porras explained, showed that the Powerine Refinery had a long history of "accidents" and that their emissions problems were far from unknown. When the findings were publicized, Powerine declared bankruptcy and shut down, and Carlos Porras had a new mission, to create a movement for environmental justice in Southeast Los Angeles County.

The idea of environmental justice and the movement itself grew out of scattered battles like the one that transformed Porras. The first salvo was fired in 1962 by Rachel Carson's best-selling *Silent Spring*, but credit for acting on that lesson belongs to the residents of Love Canal, a white working-class suburb near Niagara Falls, whose houses were built on top of a site that Hooker Chemicals had used in the 1940s and 1950s to dump toxics—a fact not disclosed to buyers. When oozing gunk began to show up in basements and around the neighborhood, and there seemed to be too much cancer to be an accident, women of the community took the lead in demanding answers. By the midseventies they had created a mass movement that, by 1978, had gotten the government to seal off the whole area and, in 1981, got the families relocated to new housing elsewhere (Gibbs 1998; Kaplan 1997; Rosenberg 1995). The movement charged that government and business were covering up widespread dumping and its dangers. In those years, the government and the public at large did not know much about the serious and long-term health dangers of toxic dumping. To a generation brought up with the idea of "better living through chemistry," the discovery that those chemicals could kill them was relatively new. These early battles exposed the prevalence and the dangers of industrial pollutants, as well as collusion between polluting corporations and the government agencies that were supposed to regulate them.

Environmental justice as a concept and a social movement built on these efforts. Its birth is usually traced back to 1982, when African Americans in rural Warren County, North Carolina, began a sustained protest against that state's decision to create a landfill in their community for PCB-contaminated soil from fourteen counties. The source of the PCBs was two companies, Ward Transfer Company of Raleigh, North Carolina, which sold PCB-soaked oil to a New York waste hauler, who had intended to resell it and turn a quick profit. But the Environmental Protection Agency (EPA) banned such re-sales in 1979, so the hauler cut his losses by illegally spraying all 30,000 gallons of the PCB-soaked oil along North Carolina's roads. It was the largest documented PCB spill in the country, and it was deliberate. The owners of both companies were ultimately convicted and jailed, but North Carolina taxpayers were stuck with the cost of undoing their mess (Bullard 1990).

In the northeastern part of the state, very poor Warren County was among the few North Carolina counties spared the illegal spraying. There, however, is where the state decided to build a massive landfill to accommodate the contaminated soil from the entire state. The landfill was built just outside the small town of Afton, home to mainly African Americans, as was the rest of Warren County. Federal regulations already on the books prohibited dumping PCBs in landfills, but the state managed to have them waived.

County residents, with women prominent among the local leadership, tried to stop the landfill—first by meeting with state officials to argue their case and then by bringing a lawsuit. When these tactics failed, they took direct action to block the 7,200 truckloads of the toxic waste brought to the landfill. Robert Bullard's pioneering *Dumping in Dixie* (1999) tells the story of their group, Warren County Citizens Concerned about PCBs. For years, they held large daily protests, marches to the dump, civil disobedience with massive arrests, and church meetings. They drew national publicity and support from civil rights, labor, and environmental leaders. Charles Cobb, head of the United Church of Christ's Commission for Racial Justice, played a leadership role in the protests. So too did Washington, D.C., congressional delegate Walter Fauntroy.

Even the head of EPA's hazardous waste implementation branch encouraged the protest. He told them, "Landfilling is cheap. It is cheaper than the alternative. The people who like to use landfills such as chemical industries are very powerful. No amount of science, truth, knowledge or facts goes into making this decision. It is a purely political decision. What they listen to is pressure" (Bullard 1990, 44). Eventually Warren County activists succeeded in forcing the governor to cap the dump and promise to detoxify the site when it became technologically feasible. It took until 2003, and more sustained protest and persistence, to get the state to fulfill its promise and to finally clean up the landfill (Bullard 1990; WARN 2003).

The Warren County movement was the first to argue that government and business deliberately concentrated their toxic dumping in communities of color. That charge was first made by the local NAACP chapter in requesting a preliminary injunction to block the dumping in Warren County.[1]

In June 1983, the U.S. Government Accounting Office (1983) published a study of the race and income demographics of hazardous waste landfills relative to the general population in eight southern states. The findings were telling. Three of every four hazardous waste landfills were located in or near communities of color; three of five African

Americans and Latinos lived in communities that had hazardous waste landfills. This study was the first of many that have since ascertained a clear and persistent national pattern of dumping toxics disproportionately in communities of color (Bullard 1994; Morello-Frosch et al. 2002; Wilson 2007).

The Warren County movement ultimately established a legal precedent for civil rights suits alleging racially disparate patterns of distributing environmental hazards. Environmental justice activists argue that polluters deliberately choose to dump toxics in poor communities of color because they believe that these communities lack the will and resources to stop them. Corporate opponents argue that poor people of color moved to areas that were already polluted because the drop in property values made housing affordable. On the face of it, Southeast Los Angeles looks like a poster child in support of the corporate case. Even when the area was white, it was an industrial center and had more than its share of airborne and chemical toxics.

Researchers studied this chicken-and-egg question by examining who moved into Southeast Los Angeles and when they moved in. They looked at all the polluting industries, landfills, and hazardous waste sites that were built or moved into Los Angeles County in the 1970s and 1980s. They found that these sites were concentrated in neighborhoods that "were two-thirds more minority than those neighborhoods [where they] were not. These newly toxic neighborhoods did indeed become more minority in demographics, but the gain in percent minority population was no faster than in the rest of the county" (Pastor et al. 2001, 2005). In other words, polluters targeted the working-class neighborhoods that were already most heavily minority, but minorities did not move into those neighborhoods any faster when they became toxic dumping grounds, as the lower-housing-price argument predicted.

In the wake of Warren County, local antidumping campaigns spread across the country, including Southern California. The communities where they sprang up looked a lot like South Gate. They were working-class communities of color and of new immigrants. African American residents who formed Concerned Citizens of South Central Los Angeles were among the first in the city to wage an environmental justice campaign when they mobilized against the city of Los Angeles' plan to build a huge incinerator in their neighborhood (Hamilton 1994). In nearby East Los Angeles, the historic center of the city's Latino population, a group called the Mothers of East Los Angeles formed in 1984 to successfully block the state of California's plan to build a prison in their backyard. When county agencies and a private company sought to build a large waste incinerator near the organization's East Los Angeles neighborhood, the Mothers mobilized again (Pardo 1998) and came to be a major environmental justice force in the city. These were well-fought campaigns that challenged the unfair practice of siting health hazards in communities of color. They garnered a great deal of popular support and helped put the concept (if not yet the term) of environmental justice on the Los Angeles map.

Environmental justice went public in 1991 as a national movement with the First National People of Color Environmental Leadership Summit in Washington, D.C. Organized by the United Church of Christ's Commission on Racial Justice, it brought together over a thousand activists and created a comprehensive document, "Principles of Environmental Justice." From its birth, environmental justice was as much about economic fairness as it was about racial fairness (Second National People of Color Environmental Leadership Summit 2002). The idea of economic justice had its roots in Martin Luther King's Poor People's campaigns of the sixties, which demanded equal access to decent jobs, wages, health care, and education for people of color and working-class whites (Environmental Justice Resource Center 2002). In April 1990, formation of the Southwest Network for Economic and Environmental Justice brought together a variety of local groups, with a heavy representation from youth, from California, Arizona, New Mexico, and Texas, around environmental and economic issues (Cooney 1999).[2]

The growth of this movement and its synergy with a wide spectrum of economic justice movements resulted in environmental justice becoming a legitimate, recognizable issue for the public, for federal and state governmental agencies, and, as a result, for business. According to many analysts, it also became the most vibrant and grassroots part of the environmental movement (Dowie 1995; Gottlieb 2005; Szasz 1994). Although none of the organizing, research, or litigation implied that environmental justice concerns would have a high governmental priority in relation to other considerations, they at least offered significant legal and political levers and ways of talking about environmental justice as a legitimate issue. In Southern California in 1990, the South

Coast Air Quality Management District (AQMD) established an Ethnic Community Advisory Board to advise them about air quality in minority communities.

In 1993, Carlos Porras joined Communities for a Better Environment (CBE). Until then, CBE's activities had been concentrated in the Bay Area of Northern California. It focused on combining scientific research and legal expertise to expose and fight industrial pollution and toxics in low-income communities of color. When CBE's Southern California office opened in the city of Huntington Park, in Southeast Los Angeles County, and Porras became its executive director, CBE added community organizing to its interests, becoming a hybrid environmental justice organization that combined professional expertise with grassroots organizing.

Although environmental justice was not a household word in Southeast Los Angeles, residents were all too familiar with the toxic hazards of industrial pollution. In 1986, a chlorine cloud from a burst pipeline at the Purex plant next door to an elementary school in South Gate sent twenty-seven children to the hospital. Neighbors discovered that the school was surrounded by industries that emitted toxic chemicals, including hexavalent chromium, the carcinogen later made famous by the movie *Erin Brockovich*. Parent protests resulted in shutting the school and moving it to a new site. Then in 1988, despite increased local knowledge about hexavalent chromium's dangers, teacher and parent protests were unable to shut down two schools in Bell Gardens located near chromium plants that had already been declared EPA Superfund sites. The following year, teachers and parents at still another elementary school, this one built right on top of a toxic dump, protested the sickening sludge and forced the evacuation of the school until the dump was effectively capped and monitored (Communities for a Better Environment [CBE] 1998).

Soon after CBE set up its Southern California office, it was recruited to participate in its first grassroots campaign by residents of Huntington Park (which adjoins South Gate), who were trying to get rid of an enormous mountain of concrete. Dubbed La Montaña, the concrete had fallen from a section of Interstate 10 when it collapsed during the 1994 Northridge earthquake. A local entrepreneur had found a site to store the debris, hoping to pulverize and sell it as building material to the Alameda Corridor project for its high-speed below-street-level rail freight line.

The problem was that the storage site for the rubble was across the street—a small street—from a residential neighborhood. Residents had been coming together and trying to persuade the city to take action against the dust and breathing problems it caused. CBE joined with them, helped them to pack city council meetings, take around petitions, and demand that the city study the dangers. At the city's request, and with some foot-dragging, the AQMD produced a study, which CBE and the neighbors challenged as inadequate.

The residents' goal was to persuade the city to declare La Montaña a public nuisance. Between a united and persistent neighborhood and CBE's technical resources, said Leilani Hickman, one of the local leaders, "we outlasted them. People learned how the system functioned." By winning widespread support among Huntington Park residents, as the CBE report put it, "neighbors made support for la montaña the political kiss of death in Huntington Park." In 1996 the city declared the mountain a public nuisance and forced the owner to get rid of it. This was CBE's first experience with collective action, and it drew attention from the press as well as from young activists wanting to engage with environmental justice issues (CBE 1998, 9).

Yuki Kidokoro was one of those activists. She first became interested in environmental justice as a UCLA undergraduate. Until the first Gulf War in 1991, she described herself as apolitical. It was a war she did not understand, and she went to a demonstration to learn something about what was going on. From there, she helped plan a day of education about the war on campus. This activity was a turning point for her in what she described as a shift from contributing to society by being a doctor or lawyer to thinking about social activism as an equally valid form of being socially useful. Kidokoro then made her way to UCLA's activist networks and got a crash course in what people in Los Angeles were doing to improve their lives. She became involved with the campus Environmental Coalition and through that was introduced to the concept of environmental justice and its connections to human rights. As a member of the coalition, she served on the board of Youth United for Community Action, a group that organized among people of color around environmental racism. She learned about popular education by working with Gilda Haas, head of Strategic Action for a Just Economy (SAJE) on a community scholars program at UCLA, with workers who had been laid off by Price Pfister, a faucet manufacturing company in Pacoima.

Kidokoro heard about CBE in 1994, when she came to Huntington Park to work on an environmental justice video about La Montaña for the Environmental Coalition at UCLA. There she met the CBE staff, including Carlos Porras, and returned in 1996 to work as a summer intern with CBE as part of her Urban Planning graduate program. When she graduated in 1997, CBE offered her a job as its first youth organizer, actually its first full-time staff organizer of any kind.

Kidokoro was part of the cohort of young Angelenos who came into political activism in the 1990s. Making it up as they went along was hardly unique in the organizations they joined and those they formed. Even more established groups were following that path as they tried to find new ways to reinvigorate democratic organizing across a wide spectrum of social issues, and especially to reach out to high school students. CBE was one of a number of community-based groups inventing some form of political and activist academies and workshops for high school students. Kidokoro's assignment was to develop a curriculum and offer training to youth. Although she had some background in popular education, working with youth was unfamiliar territory. As a person well into her twenties who was trying to organize teens in age-conscious Los Angeles, she worried, "Was I cool enough? What's cool?" CBE had no experience with youth work either, so Kidokoro was on her own. Within three weeks she'd designed a plan and begun making presentations to classes in Huntington Park High School. She was hoping to find students who would want to come to a series of after-school environmental trainings.

The concept of environmental justice resonated strongly with these students, most of whom were children of new immigrants, largely because it seemed to explain the impersonal or institutional aspects of the racism and anti-immigrant experiences they had had but for which they had no name, and which no one was talking about. Jairus Ramos, a Filipino immigrant in a largely Latina/o city, "knew things were wrong" and was already in search of ways to do something constructive about them. At school his first stop had been the environmental club, "but it was basically fund-raising and not doing anything active." He spent time in the library, "and listening to music that was political I guess, like punk rock or like old folk songs from the 60's." In his junior year, he was among the first students to come to Kidokoro's training. The concept of environmental justice put names and faces on the "something" he knew was wrong.

Part of Kidokoro's training included a Toxic Tour, something CBE had already developed as a form of education and organizing. It involves, first, research to learn about the chemicals used in production, waste, and emissions of various industries in the neighborhood, their potential health hazards, and the violations and fines that have been imposed on specific companies. The tour takes people past the industrial facilities in various areas of Southeast Los Angeles and explains their record and the hazards in the environment one is likely to encounter in the course of living or working near these facilities.

In the summer of 1997, fifteen students, including Alicia Gonzalez (a pseudonym) and Jairus Ramos, consistently attended Kidokoro's five-week training on toxins, health and public regulations, environmental justice, and community organizing. "As soon as the sessions were over," Jairus Ramos recalled, Kidokoro "asked if we wanted to keep meeting. And that's how we formed the Youth Action. It was in the summer of 1997, my junior year. Back then it was called EJTEA, and it stood for Environmental Justice Through Education and Action." When Alicia Gonzalez became involved with EJTEA, she brought her younger brother along with her. By the time he got to high school, he was a regular on his own.

Kidokoro's goal was to connect education to action. She hoped that the students would want to go from learning to getting involved. As she put it, "the message in the curriculum was that to make change you have to work as a group; can't do it alone." During the summer of 1997 and through 1998, EJTEA focused on political issues that students brought to the group. It felt to Kidokoro a little like flying by the seat of one's pants. The group had speakers from the United Farm Workers' strawberry worker organizing campaign tell them about the pesticide hazards that they lived with on the job and how they were trying to form a union to protect their health, as well as for economic benefits. They learned about antisweatshop organizing and listened to a speaker tell them about environmental justice issues in Burma, East Timor, and Chiapas—that it was a worldwide issue. "We went to lots of demonstrations to see what people were doing," Kidokoro said. "Then they began to initiate their own local actions."

Everything seemed important, and all issues seemed to be related. Deciding to focus on one thing wasn't easy. This part was hard, Kidokoro recalled, "not as exciting as attending demonstrations." First they had to go through a process of figuring out what they were concerned about. After much discussion, they decided that the three most important issues to the group were sexual harassment, overcrowded schools, and pesticides.

This process was hard for Kidokoro too. Being committed to building a group through democratic process meant that the issues should be those the group chose. But Kidokoro was organizing a group that would be affiliated with CBE, whose mission is environmental justice, not educational justice or sexual harassment. "It is a challenge," she said. "CBE is a bit schizophrenic. It's a bottom-up organization for designing campaigns, but it is also about environmental justice in a focused way." She desperately hoped that the issues the fledgling group wanted to take on would be issues CBE could see as part of its environmental justice focus. Her own interpretation of environmental justice was fairly broad, but she really hoped she wasn't going to have to interpret sexual harassment and police brutality as environmental justice issues. Fortunately the student group went with pesticides.

Their actions ranged from publishing a newsletter, to organizing toxic tours themselves, to demonstrating against the Niklor Chemical Company, which was manufacturing pesticides near a residential neighborhood in Carson. They also learned how to build air-sampling buckets to measure air pollution levels and to conduct their own research. In this last effort, students were part of a wider collaboration between CBE and academic researchers to examine air quality in communities of color (Morello-Frosch et al. 2002).

The EJTEA group also connected with other groups of activist high school students and participated in a citywide youth campaign in support of allocating public funds to repair schools in working-class communities of color, and in support of the Healthy Schools Campaign, a statewide bill to ban pesticides in California schools. On the latter issue, EJTEA held a rally at Huntington Park High School and participated in statewide events in support of the bill's passage. Although the bill passed the California legislature, the governor vetoed it.

Students also worked on CBE's 1997 push—a lawsuit and community campaign to pressure AQMD to strengthen environmental regulations in Southeast Los Angeles. Its focus was an AQMD regulation that set the maximum level of airborne carcinogens permitted at any facility. That level, set in the early nineties, allowed a plant to emit a level of cancer-causing toxics likely to produce a hundred additional cancers per million persons exposed, and for noncarcinogenic toxins it allowed an increase of up to five times the level that health experts considered safe (Environmental Justice Collaborative 2004, 11). The regulation did not take into account that low-income people of color were exposed to higher levels of toxics from many different plants and that their actual risk was much greater than the risk for white and middle-class people who lived and worked in a much less toxic soup. Students went door-to-door in their neighborhoods, leafleted at swap meets, and made presentations at their high school and other civic organizations. They estimated that they collected perhaps a thousand signed postcards in support and presented them to each AQMD board member. They also made a formal presentation to the board. These efforts were part of a larger, regionwide collaborative campaign that joined CBE, academic researchers, and community funder Liberty Hill Foundation. By 1997 that campaign, in connection with a CBE lawsuit, led to an AQMD promise to rethink the regulation, and in 2000 the South Coast AQMD lowered by 75 percent the allowable level of carcinogens (Environmental Justice Collaborative 2004, 11; see also Pastor et al. 2005).

The group also began to grow and changed its name to Youth for Environmental Justice, or Youth-EJ (pronounced Youth Edge). Perhaps most significant for its growth is that the Huntington Park group took the initiative in creating an ongoing coalition of youth groups in Los Angeles. In November 1998 this coalition held its first "For Youth by Youth" Conference, where citywide high school activists were able to share their experiences, and discuss issues and their perspectives on them. Youth-EJ held a second training and youth conference the following summer, in 1999. By that time Youth-EJ had a core group of activists with a solid background of knowledge about pollution in Southeast Los Angeles, an environmental justice perspective on its causes and consequences, a lot of experience in talking about these issues with students and adults, and some experience with making formal presentations. By the fall of 1999, when they were beginning to plan their third five-week training for the summer of 2000, the first rumors about plans to build a power plant in South Gate were just beginning to surface in the community (Kidokoro 1999).

CHAPTER 3

Creating an Environmental
Justice Campaign

JAIRUS RAMOS, ALICIA GONZALEZ, AND GEYMAN
HERNANDEZ were among some ten to fifteen environmental activists in Huntington Park High School's environmental club. Jairus and Alicia were graduating, and they felt a particular desire to recruit more members and to find ways of keeping up with people who left. They were also deeply involved in the planning discussions for the second Youth in Action six-week training camp an annual organizing effort to involve more high school students in environmental justice activism, scheduled for the summer of 2000.

The organizers' first priority was to find students who wanted to participate in the summer training. Most new individuals showed up because they were friends of one of the activists, or because they were looking for this sort of activity. Jackie Amparo came to the training because of her friendship with one of the activists. "I was just expecting to come to the training and it's over with. But to be exposed to all these different things, that was—I'd seen it on TV, people protesting, but I never thought of me doing that. It was a very new experience. I liked the training and that's how I stayed." Milton Hernandez (no relation to Geyman) became interested first in the Huntington Park High group and attended the summer training as a result of Geyman's invitation. "After the trainings, I wanted to do something about what I learned, so I got active." In 2000 the six-week-long training workshop, run by Youth-EJ during July and August, had some ten to thirteen student participants.

Because the plan was to combine education and hands-on activism, part of the leaders' planning process was to keep their eyes out for a good environmental justice issue with which students taking the workshop could get involved. At the last workshop session, CBE staff asked whether Youth-EJ and the new workshop attendees wanted to choose a campaign in which they'd take the lead. Ramos explained that this meant that the campaign "was going to be youth driven and youth led, and a lot of the decision making was going to be done by youth."

Deciding to take on an activist project was easy, but choosing one of the several possible issues was harder. Sunlaw's publicity campaign had already begun, and the Nueva Azalea plant seemed to be in the air from several different quarters. One student from South Gate who was at the workshop brought a Sunlaw flier to the group because she was concerned about it. Jairus remembered hearing talk around CBE back in midautumn of 1999 about the possibility of a power plant being built in the area. Sunlaw, however, was not the only possible project discussed. Another was preventing the CENCO Oil Refinery (formerly the Powerine Refinery that Carlos Porras had taken on years ago) in Santa Fe Springs from reopening.[1]

Jairus remembered that "the meeting where we decided it was pretty intense because people wanted to take on everything." There was a strong consensus that it should be the Nueva Azalea plant because power plants give off a lot of pollution, South Gate was very close, and, Milton recalled, "it hasn't been built so it's much easier to not let something pass than to shut down something." Newcomer Jackie Amparo was excited about the magnitude of what they were about to take on; she was encouraged after having learned of other environmental justice victories in the workshop, "and I thought, maybe we could succeed in this; it's worth a try. But what made me stay is that I really started to believe that it was not right, and I actually liked what they were doing and I was for it."

CBE shared the organizational philosophy, mission, and priorities of its youth group, but as a statewide organization with research and legal expertise, its position depended on doing its own evaluation of the project. The organization therefore requested intervenor status with the California Energy Commission (CEC). By so doing, they were entitled to receive all materials that Sunlaw submitted and to offer responses, challenges, and testimony, all of which became part of the evidence CEC was obliged to consider. CBE then assigned its staff scientist and its attorney to study Sunlaw's data as its application materials began to be submitted.

It was also the case, however, that CBE had already made a de facto decision, in light of its success in helping residents remove Huntington

Park's mountain of concrete rubble, to focus its energies on developing a democratic grassroots organizing approach to environmental justice. It had solidified that commitment when it hired Yuki Kidokoro to be its first youth organizer.

By late August 2000, all these factors created another dilemma in an organization that already had something of a dual personality. The youth group Kidokoro had initiated was busily working on a campaign to block the plant, while CBE—the sponsoring organization and her employer— was trying to figure out if it should oppose the plant at all. Kidokoro was promoted to CBE lead organizer and given the unenviable job of putting together staff who were studying the issue and youth who had already made up their minds to oppose the plant into what came to be called the Green Team. The team included student representatives Jairus Ramos and Milton Hernandez, CBE's attorneys Anne Simon and Will Rostoff, and its staff scientist, Bahram Fazeli, as well as Kidokoro.

Kidokoro was also part of a wider and multiracial cohort of Los Angeles activists who came of political age in the nineties. That cohort's politics includes a deep commitment to figuring out how to build leadership and knowledge, democratic groups, and campaigns among those with whom they work (Brodkin 2007). It is almost fair to say about them, or at least about their ideals, that making democracy work was as important as winning any particular campaign.

Kidokoro felt that democratic process was critical. She also believed that it was the only fair way to deal with the ever-present contradiction between CBE's commitment to community leadership and environmental justice: "What input do you get from community members and what decisions do you make as an organization based on our core values and our mission? Because we have a dual identity of wanting things be decided democratically, in a way where people could take ownership over a position, over a campaign. That was a struggle. The challenge was how to do it in a meaningful way."

As lead organizer, Kidokoro saw herself as responsible for creating an environment and process in which those decisions could be made. And she wanted the Green Team to be the place for figuring out how to proceed in a democratic way. There was a logic behind the formation of this team. CBE's commitment to democratic community-based environmental justice activism meant that it needed to give weight to Youth-EJ's position because youth were as much members of the community as adults were. Indeed, at this point, youth were the only local "community." But CBE staff members of the Green Team—organizers, a scientist, and lawyers—were older and had a lot more experience and technical knowledge than high school students. It was a difficult structure for developing a working consensus. Kidokoro worried especially about the power to silence others that specialized knowledge gives to those who have it. "At first my understanding of organizing was, having experts, lawyers, science, while they can be helpful, they can also be hindering in making people feel like, we don't know so we cannot move forward."

Her fear was that the high school students and any adults who might join the campaign would feel they had to follow technical experts instead of thinking about the issue from perspectives that came from living in an area full of airborne toxics. She felt that the Green Team needed to take a broad view of expertise to include that knowledge. Without it, there could be no democratic community-based organizing.

Kidokoro also wanted to clarify the specific contribution of scientific expertise to a democratic campaign. "Scientists can help us sharpen our arguments and add more information to our arguments. But ultimately, as people who organize know, information can be manipulated in many different ways; you can find studies that say no there isn't a problem here, or ones that says there is."

At first it sounded to me as though Kidokoro was saying that scientific expertise can't be independent of bias, and that each side chooses what it likes, which would have been strange for an organization that has focused most of its efforts on solid science (and sophisticated legal strategies). It turned out that her worry was quite different. It was that scientific expertise and social context were two parts of a whole analysis. A narrow focus on one part, for example, how much of a particular pollutant was being emitted, without attention to the other part, the physical and social environment in which that pollutant is being released, was only half an analysis. She insisted that pollution data had to be evaluated in ways that were specific to their social context. Were this plant to be located in a community that had little ambient pollution, the scientific analysis of the social and health impact of that particular quantity of pollutant would be very different than it would be in Southeast Los Angeles.

And finally, Kidokoro insisted that science should rest on the moral imperative of environmental justice and fairness: "bringing it back to values and rights rather than getting stuck on numbers is something that is a challenge, but I think it's a good one. It was an interesting challenge of how you bring in [science] in a way that helps, and I think we did. I think my role in lead organizing was trying to balance out hearing everyone's arguments, and really try to hold organizing up."

Bahram Fazeli, CBE's staff scientist, doesn't much talk or dress like the kind of expert who would intimidate high school students. He doesn't hang out in a lab—CBE's office doesn't have a lab. His cubicle looks pretty much like the tiny overcrowded cubicles of all the other organizers: lots of cartoons, leaflets, photos, Post-its on the walls, and piles of reports and unidentifiable papers stacked on bookshelves and desk and scattered across the floor. As a scientist with an activist sensibility, he seemed comfortable thinking like a scientist and an organizer at the same time. He shared Kidokoro's perspective that one had to think about pollution and pollution control in its social context: Who would benefit from Sunlaw's new technology, and who would bear the burden of the pollutants it added to the local air? Was this fair?

Early in the campaign, Fazeli was CBE's point person at the California Energy Commission's public meetings. The CEC is the state regulatory body with sole authority to review, grant, and refuse the licenses needed to build any power plant over fifty megawatts anywhere in California. In the spring and early summer of 2000, the CEC notified the city of South Gate and CBE of Sunlaw's application to build.[2] The agency's procedures required that it notify and request input from potentially affected public institutions and individuals. The CEC was to hold a variety of public hearings about the plant and its impact, and hear testimony by interested parties about their views on the plant's impact on communities and their environment. Institutions, municipalities, voluntary organizations, and individuals could become intervenors.

From early September 2000 until January 2001, the CEC held a number of workshops in South Gate and Downey for the general public and for interested city councils as the public outreach part of its process. All these meetings followed a similar format. CEC staff first spoke about the process of licensing, and Sunlaw spoke about their plans. At the end there was a question-and-answer period during which community members could speak and ask questions. Youth-EJ members attended a number of these meetings to ask questions and to make their views known to CEC members. Describing the first session, in South Gate, Fazeli estimated that about fifty local residents turned out, in addition to some twenty people from Sunlaw Energy Corporation, CEC staff, and staffers from the state senator's and assemblyman's offices, as well as a representative from the neighboring city of Downey. Sunlaw also provided English-Spanish translation and dinner for all the attendees, which Fazeli remembered as "a lot of good food! You can't really be critical of that aspect because the criticism has always been the public has been discouraged from attending public meetings, so it was like, look, we are just encouraging people to attend. Of course another aspect of it is that Sunlaw is trying to be a good salesperson, so there are two sides to that. I can't say it was a bad idea. I think they had an agreement with CEC to pay for the translator."

Reflecting the uncertainty that then existed within CBE, Fazeli wore two hats at early meetings. With one hat, he attended the meetings as a scientist to study Sunlaw's application for certification and to request additional information because of CBE's status as intervenor. Wearing another hat, he was also doing a little organizing—looking for people from the community who attended these meetings, who were concerned about the impact of the plant, and whom CBE might recruit should it decide to oppose the project. "Because there were no organizers in the beginning, I did a little bit of organizing too. People who went to the microphone and asked questions from Sunlaw, who were concerned. When somebody would finish talking I would get the person's name and phone number, and potentially that, if it becomes a campaign, then we have this [contact]. So in the beginning I did a little bit of everything."

Given CBE's commitment to grassroots community organizing, it was pretty likely, even by September, that the organization would end up opposing the plant. It became more likely in October, when two additional organizers, Alvaro Huerta and Angelo Logan, joined the team. On one track, CBE was studying the data. On the other, *if* CBE was going to get involved, the organization wanted its involvement to be at the grassroots level, *and* it brought two organizers on board before it made an organizational decision.

How Do You Build
a Grassroots Campaign?

In October, CBE made its decision to oppose the Nueva Azalea project, thereby resolving the tension that its Southern California office was experiencing. The Green Team breathed a collective sigh of relief. In mid-October, Alvaro Huerta returned to CBE as a community organizer—which in practice meant organizing adults—and Angelo Logan was hired as a youth organizer later in the month. Both had grown up in the area of East and Southeast Los Angeles. Huerta brought media savvy and experience to the campaign, and Logan brought a passion for and experience working with young people. Although Kidokoro, Huerta, and Logan, CBE's three organizers, were all in their late twenties to midthirties, they differed greatly in temperament and approach. Huerta is wiry, articulate, and intense. For him the goal was clear: prevent the Nueva Azalea plant from being built. To do that, CBE needed a clear plan, with strategies and tactics to be developed, along with a timetable for doing so, and he put his energy into that. Logan is much more oriented toward developing leadership. He came across to me as nurturing and, for an organizer, relatively quiet, but he listens intensely. In meetings he worked to make sure everyone spoke—and was heard—and that decisions came out of a democratic process.

Huerta had taken an earlier leave of absence from CBE to work with a campaign by Latino gardeners in Los Angeles. Los Angeles had passed an ordinance against using gas-powered leaf blowers because they were so noisy. The gardeners, many of whom were new immigrants working as independent entrepreneurs, argued that hand raking made their jobs more time-consuming and harder and that they could not raise their prices to cover costs. That campaign developed a very skillful and successful media strategy that forced the city to try to work out a compromise and not enforce the ban.[3] According to Huerta,

> A lot of the things that we did with the gardeners in terms of getting public support and being effective and creating a spectacle that the media will cover. By using the media, we were able to influence public opinion. Drawing from my experience with the gardeners, I knew that the media was going to play a key role in our victory. In the end, all of the media attention didn't come accidentally; I conceived it from the beginning and, with the collective effort, it worked perfectly. But the fact of the matter is that, without the community support and mass participation, we would not have won.

Angelo Logan had grown up in the Southeast Los Angeles city of Commerce and went to high school in nearby Bell Gardens. Before coming to CBE, he had worked as a millwright, a skilled manufacturing trade, at an aerospace company, as well as working in other plants and with their unions in the area. His real passion, however, was working with young people. He'd gone to Seattle to work with youth but wanted to do this work closer to home in Southeast Los Angeles:

> For a long time I have been working with young people—police harassment and education, things like that. I wanted to concentrate more on young people and young people in the communities that I grew up in. I know this area pretty well. I was keeping my eyes open and environmental justice was something I have been concerned with for a long time.

Even before Logan knew about the environmental justice movement, he noted,

> I was really aware that there was something unjust about what was going on in the communities that I had lived in. It was something that I was passionate about, so I applied and got the job. The power plant campaign [was] something that the youth group had decided before I had been hired. That was one of the campaigns that they wanted to take on, because of the Youth in Action conference.

Kidokoro credits Huerta with taking the lead in urging the Green Team to develop a clear plan for the campaign. Huerta reasoned,

> Before I integrated anybody from the community to participate in the campaign, I wanted to have at least some ideas of what we were up against—a skeleton plan as to how to integrate them. I didn't want them to commit to something chaotic, something that they would get dissuaded from doing. The idea was to deal with the youth and the adults as one unit, to integrate them into one plan of action. First do the plan of action, second, kick off the big meeting so that people are educated before they start advocating against the power plant, and give them that opportunity to ask questions and provide their input. We were very open about it. It wasn't like a closed plan of action.

On October 26, Kidokoro and Huerta presented their organizing plan to Carlos Porras, CBE's executive director. It reaffirmed the priority

of organizing in South Gate and presented a long to-do list for education, outreach, and mobilization in South Gate and neighboring cities
that was to build up to a big community meeting in December. By
mid-November, the plan had gotten more specific. They knew they
wanted to build a campaign that included nearby cities in which they
had supportive contacts, and which would also be directly impacted
by the power plant. Their outreach to adults focused on PTAs and
community groups, and they went door-to-door in selected areas. They
planned to make presentations not only at South Gate High School but
also at those of other cities, as well as at church youth groups and teen
centers. By mid-December they hoped to be able to hold a community
meeting with more than a hundred people to share information and
motivate them to become involved in a variety of ways. This meeting
was to be a keystone, the point at which CBE would evaluate whether
there was real community involvement and a base of local activists. CBE
even roughed out the beginnings of an agenda for this meeting. Forms
of potential community involvement included meeting with the CEC
and Sunlaw, circulating petitions, participating in the organizing effort,
and working on an anti-plant resolution for the city. Media coverage
on the issue and at events was important as well (Kidokoro and Huerta
2000; CBE Green Team 2000).

Looking for Community
in Southeast Los Angeles

A plan is one thing; it is quite another matter to figure out how
to make it happen and what a community-based campaign might look
like. Everyone agreed community members would be the core of the
campaign, but "community" is a slippery word that often covers not
only those who share an interest they already recognize—such as the
environmental community—but also those whom organizers believe
should share an interest that they may not yet recognize—such as a
community of color's interest in environmental justice.

Even with the best of plans, organizing is a fishing expedition—
trying to meet people who are likely to be interested and supportive, as
well as willing to take action. It is also a two-way street that demands
flexibility of organizers and openness to new ideas as well as a plan.
The key question for CBE was: If the community is composed of all
the working-class people of color in Southeast Los Angeles, how do
we reach them, and where do we focus? This experience of organizing

a grassroots campaign from the beginning was the first for both CBE and Youth-EJ. CBE's earlier work with Huntington Park residents to get rid of the mountain of freeway rubble had been with a neighborhood community already defined by its own mobilization. In this campaign, the only community was a small group of activist youth, mainly from Huntington Park. So the organizers had to ask: What specific groups of people do we want to focus on? Where and how do we meet them? And, as the organizers knew too well, three organizers and the ten or fifteen members of Youth-EJ could not carry out such a plan by themselves. It was the familiar circle of needing to involve more people to organize more people.

Initially, organizers and Green Team youth went wide and participated in a variety of venues. They went to CEC hearings hoping to bring their concerns about pollution and environmental justice to area residents who attended. Fazeli and Youth-EJ members continued to attend CEC workshops, although the youth were especially underwhelmed by their experiences. "Boring" and "useless" were the words they used most frequently to describe them. Milton recalled that "at first they had translation and then, when we saw people come, like after the first two meetings, they stopped having the translation." Alicia felt that "a lot of community members had questions but they didn't give answers." Milton stuck with the meetings, perhaps because he was "off track"—that is, his part of Huntington Park High's year-round school was on vacation.[4] He was particularly frustrated that Sunlaw never had answers to people's questions, that it

> always said they did not have information provided, but they were going to have it soon, which that day never came. The CEC never saw anything wrong with that. A lot of things like that, a lot of questions unanswered were what got people kind of like, what are they hiding? And also to the youth, they were pretty disrespectful. When another youth member went up to ask a question and she was talking about PM10 which is the smallest particle of dust—you can't see it, you just breathe it and it accumulates in your lungs. And one of the Sunlaw representatives was talking to her like she was a little girl—just the vocabulary he was using was pretty insulting.

Although the youth found CEC meetings boring, Sunlaw materials shocked Bahram Fazeli when he read them at an early meeting.

He discovered that Sunlaw had already lined up key players on the state level in the very quarters from which CBE drew its own support. Sunlaw had endorsements from the director of the Coalition for Energy Efficiency and Renewable Technology, and the executive director of the Coalition for Clean Air—of which CBE was an organizational member. Although both later told him their endorsements were for SCONOx, Sunlaw's specific technology, and not the plant, and that they had been misattributed, Fazeli felt blindsided.

Once CBE had decided on a community-organizing campaign to oppose the plant, Fazeli and staff attorney Anne Simon decided that environmentalists were also an important "community" to organize. Fazeli, Simon, Jairus Ramos, and other students gave a presentation to the California League of Conservation Voters to ask them to oppose the project, to put the people who would be negatively impacted by the plant at the center of their concerns, and to push for renewable, green sources of energy. Reflecting back, Fazeli said, "Ann and I spent a lot of energy just neutralizing them, making sure no environmental organizations support the power plant. Considering that they had the whole powerful political force behind them, that was an achievement." Still, he was self-critical about the lack of early outreach to environmental organizations. "We started this process late. We didn't pay very close attention to it until it became a crisis."

Through October and much of November, members of the Green Team were busy looking both for individuals and for community groups who wanted to participate in the campaign. Youth-EJ members were active in these efforts, and youth organizer Angelo Logan thought their organizing gave youth a new confidence to take on a bigger role in attending Green Team meetings to "make their point and say, we belong in that meeting. It's our role to be in that meeting and important to come from the bottom up instead of from the top down."

Although they went to any venue they could, like health fairs, their biggest efforts were in schools. They made contacts and presentations at South Gate's adult school and at East Los Angeles Community College classes, and then at South Gate High School. Huerta was making presentations at parent centers in South Gate, Huntington Park, and Cudahy, and to schools in Huntington Park and East Los Angeles, hoping to inform and recruit people for the December meeting, and from there to a community-based movement. "I went to an adult school in South Gate High School and made several presentations. We did a classroom presentation with one of the community college professors." Logan noted that the youth, as the major initial base of community participation, "were critical in these outreach efforts to adults." There were posted speaking schedules for the presentations Huerta and Logan had set up, and members of Youth-EJ signed up for those in which they could participate. Milton remembers that being off track allowed him time do a lot of presentations, the lion's share Logan thought. According to Milton, "It was tiring but it was really cool." Also, because Logan's Spanish was not fluent, Milton, who is fluent, often went with him on presentations to adult groups.

At the adult schools, Milton gave both pro and con arguments, otherwise, he contended, people are going to think "if they find out the pros of the power plant and they see that we just told them negative things about the power plant they will think we just want to brainwash them." He was pleasantly surprised at his reception from adults: "They were excited about the power plant, but they were also thinking I guess highly of me because I was doing something, giving up my time; but I don't see anything uncommon in that." For his part, he thought that the adults showed a lot of interest in community issues. "I did not even hear or sense any negativity [about having a teen talk to them] from the parents."

In October and November then, CBE and Youth-EJ's campaign, and the hearings held by the CEC, focused on reaching people in surrounding towns who were likely to be affected by the power plant.

Despite putting into effect its plan of speaking at any venue that presented itself, with the goal of getting enough people together for a big meeting, the CBE found that the responses were not generating the kind of independent initiatives that had to happen for there to be a true community presence. Most of the Youth-EJ activists, drawn from Huntington Park where CBE had been active longest, felt that the campaign was an uphill one, and they were beginning to become demoralized. Alicia Gonzalez said, "We wanted to get more people in the campaign. Students felt like it didn't matter, that they can't make changes in government." Jackie Amparo had a similar experience: "First it was getting the word out and I talked with my friends and tried to explain to them. And at first they were like, 'yeah, yeah, whatever.'"

Although youth activists and CBE organizers found the CEC workshops off-putting at best and disrespectful at worst, when Huerta joined the campaign, he encouraged CBE to stick with it, but to approach going to CEC workshops with a different strategic intent. Instead of trying to persuade CEC commissioners, CBE organizers should approach workshops as a platform for media exposure of their environmental justice message, as well as stepping up their efforts to recruit people who were already worried about the plant. "Since we also invited the media, many people heard about our activities via the news stations and papers. My intention was not to speak so much to the California Energy Commission but speak to the audience. Since I knew that the CEC was just going through the motions by holding these hearings, I focused my attention on recruiting more members and resources."

Despite Huerta's view, the CEC's public notification did lead to organized opposition from local governments and from a number of individuals. For example, it certainly got the attention of the Downey school system and the Downey city council early on. Downey would be directly downwind of the plant's emissions and would be impacted much more intensely than South Gate. Downey's early alarm led the CEC to expand the locations of its hearings to include the city. CEC meetings in both cities, in part because they were so frustrating to the residents who attended them, were also a forum that galvanized some to become active in the campaign on their own.

Back in early October, Rhonda Nitschky read about Sunlaw's plans in a detailed article in a widely distributed free entertainment newspaper (Catania 2000a). The article spoke about the concerns and opposition of Downey school and local officials, and brought her to a Downey CEC workshop, where she discovered that she wasn't the only one in her town to take notice of the plant. Downey city officials were upset that, being downwind of the plant, Downey residents would get all the pollution and none of its tax or revenue benefits, and they were quite outspoken about it. Early in the process, Downey hired an environmental consultant who listed some of the areas of concern, ranging from toxics in the plant's emissions and its impact on patients at the Rancho Los Amigos Hospital, a major rehabilitation hospital, to the plant's huge eight-story size, which would dominate Downey's skyline (Catania 2000b).

Downey resident Rhonda Nitschky became as worried as the consultant. Her mother had died of respiratory disease. Like Milton and Huerta, she had the impression from her first meeting that the CEC was just going through the motions, "that this project was being just railroaded through with little regard for the public's feelings." She also thought the AQMD supported the plant when she heard them "stand up and talk about how great our air quality is [in Southeast Los Angeles] compared to the air quality in someplace like Riverside, where there are a lot of cows and they have a lot of ammonia in the air. I'm thinking, the air quality can't be very good if my American flag is rotting off the stick. So it sounded like the South Coast AQMD, which I thought was so tough and interested in protecting the public, I was blown away that they seemed to be totally for the project." Rhonda recalled someone in the audience challenging the CEC by asking, if the plant is going to clean the air, "why do you need to use pollution offset credits? Someone else asked why don't you do some local mitigations, like for instance buy Downey and South Gate all new natural gas–powered school buses, cut some local emissions. And they were like no, no, that would be too expensive. We don't have to do that. The AQMD told us we can use pollution offset credits."

Nitschky lived relatively near the plant and tried to organize neighbors to come to the meetings, but without much success. "I think I probably got a whole two people to show up at the next Energy Commission meeting." Most organizers would see that as a pretty good showing for one try. That meeting was attended by a delegation of staff and patients from Rancho Los Amigos Hospital, who wanted to talk during the public comment period of the meeting, which was at the end of the long meeting, "like three or four hours into the meeting, and these people are over there with bottles of oxygen and in wheel chairs and they would get exhausted and not be able to do their two minutes that people were given to comment. Some local communities would use precious time to put in a public appearance."

South Gate resident Martha Andrade first met Sunlaw in the spring of 2000 through their public outreach at South Gate's Cinco de Mayo festival. Her daughter won a coloring contest that Sunlaw held at the festival. However, Andrade did not connect the coloring contest to the power plant until December, when she learned about the proposed Nueva Azalea plant from a CEC mailing announcing one of its public workshops at the Auditorium in South Gate Park. Andrade went to the meeting already concerned.

I know that any gas-powered plant is going to be a polluter, and to continue to focus on gas power is ridiculous in this day and age and this environment where we have so much pollution and so much CO_2. I just said right away this can't be good for South Gate.

[Sunlaw] had all the slides, presentation, the pie charts, and what was going to happen with the community, how many millions of dollars were going to come into the community, and they were going to be able to beef up the police force and be able to add money for scholarships, and we are going to create a beautiful community, we are going to add money to the community improvement, and it was a big sell basically.

By the next meeting Andrade had done some reading and made a list of questions. "I asked for more information—what kind of chemicals are going to be stored; what kind of things are you going to be using?" Finding that large amounts of sulfuric acid would be stored, she asked, "What precautions have you people taken in case of a spill? What do you have, do you have mass quantities of lime on site or what are you planning? We will get back to you. Whatever we have of a hazardous nature, there will be some sort of plan to handle it." Andrade continued to voice her concerns, correct Sunlaw's math, and ask for information. After the sulfuric acid interchange, a CEC staffer asked Martha if she would consider becoming an intervenor. "I said I don't know, what do I have to do? She said, here's the booklet for intervenors, take it home, study it, if you decide to do it, let me know. I told her I guess I could do it. I didn't know anybody from CBE; I didn't know anybody else who was working on it at all. I want to be able to say something and do something. I don't want to have to depend on the city to figure it out or council people. I wanted to do my own independent analysis."

Martha Andrade was among the few who stuck it out and went to five or six CEC workshops. Her evaluation of these meetings was very different from Nitschky's or CBE's. For this citizen scientist—Andrade had undergraduate and graduate degrees in biology—the meetings were the most exciting part of the campaign. What she took away from the process was an appreciation for her community:

At first they were very few people, but at the very end, the rooms were packed; they had to have closed circuit TVs to go through to other rooms because there wasn't enough seats in the main room, people were coming out of the woodwork to talk about particulates, there were experts in the community who were chemists who knew about microparticles and stood up and talked about their hazards and what the size of these particles that this plant was going to be spewing out would do to us. It was amazing the resources that we have in this community. You look at a city like this and you think it's just a bunch of working-class people. It's not. And the working-class people that are here are very conscientious working-class people, and even though they didn't really understand a lot, they came and tried to understand, and they tried to find out, and they talked to people afterward, and they got up and asked questions even though they had never spoken in public before in their lives, that they would be motivated enough to get up in front of a huge crowd of people and ask experts questions. It was really inspiring. I think that was the most exciting thing.

In much the way that Alvaro Huerta hoped, Martha Andrade and CBE members met one another at a CEC workshop that allowed them to see their shared concerns. Or, as Andrade put it, "I decided to glom onto them [CBE] instead of being my own intervenor. I thought, this is a really good organization, and they have a lot more resources than I do. I would like to be part of it, but I felt like I could work with them as easily as doing it on my own."

Roy Abadi also met CBE organizers at a CEC workshop. He was already alarmed about the plant and had attended at least one city council meeting to voice his concerns. Sometime in late October, city treasurer Albert Robles directed Abadi to some news articles and analyses on the brewing controversy. A CBE organizer was among the interviewees. Abadi got right on the phone and "called information, and I want to have the number of CBE, and you know what he told me, tonight there's a meeting in South Gate Park about the power plant, so show up. First time I heard that there was a public meeting about the power plant. They held them like three or four before. Nobody told me. I never knew. I was extremely interested. I show up to the CEC meeting. I remember I met this Downey resident, a lady. I then hooked up with CBE. I met Angelo [Logan] in that meeting."

Throughout the fall of 2000, word about the power plant began to get out beyond those who had heard about it through city council channels. Despite CBE's negative appraisal of the CEC process, the meetings did alert neighboring cities and a small but indeterminate number of residents, perhaps mainly English speakers like Rhonda Nitschky, Martha Andrade, and Roy Abadi, who became alarmed enough to want to become involved in stopping the plant. In addition, Youth-EJ's and CBE's speaking engagements in adult schools and parent centers reached a larger number of Spanish-speaking residents of the area.

At this point in the campaign, however, the community that the youth and CBE hoped to involve was fairly diffuse conceptually and looked mainly to adult residents anywhere they could find them in Southeast Los Angeles. This made some sense because the plant would affect the area, but it also meant a lot of organizing ground for a relatively small number of people to cover.

CHAPTER 4

Sunlaw's New Pollution Control Technology

THE STORY OF SUNLAW ENERGY CORPORATION begins in the mid-1990s, at about the time Henry Gonzalez and Albert Robles were starting to get on each other's nerves in South Gate (chap. 1), and Carlos Porras and CBE were getting acquainted with Huntington Park residents and their mountain of concrete (chap. 2). Robert Danziger and his associates at Sunlaw Energy Corporation were trying to build a better pollution control system for their small power plant in the neighboring city of Vernon. With Vernon to the north, Huntington Park in the middle, and South Gate to the south, the cities adjoined one another.

Danziger's interest in cogeneration—a way of producing, simultaneously, electric power and energy for heating—seems to have been what brought him to Vernon. In conventional power production, only about one-third of all the energy produced becomes electricity; the other two-thirds, which is heat created in the making of the electricity, goes up the stacks. Cogeneration is an efficient way of capturing and using that other two-thirds, either for heating or for transformation into energy for cooling. Cogeneration's advantage is that it recycles energy and produces electricity relatively efficiently.[1] It works well if there are markets for both the electrical power and the heating (or cooling) produced.

The city of Vernon was an ideal place to build a cogeneration system because it has a number of meatpacking plants and cold storage facilities. Vernon, however, is not your ordinary city in that almost no one lives there—only ninety-one people in 2000. It was founded in 1905 by rancher John Leonis, who decided to capitalize on the fact that three different railroad lines ran close to his land. Leonis persuaded the railroads to run spur lines to his land and incorporated Vernon, named after the dirt road that ran through it, as an "exclusively industrial city." And that's what it still is. After a brief period as a "sporting town," of bars, boxing, and baseball parks, it became known for its stockyards, starting with Leonis's own, as well as slaughterhouses and packing plants. By the 1930s Vernon was also a center of heavy industry, including the now defunct Bethlehem and U.S. Steel plants, and the Alcoa and Studebaker factories. In 1932, Vernon set up its own electric company, and cheap electric power and water, as well as low taxes, have remained powerful attractors for industry. Some of the packing plants and food processors remained after heavy industry began failing in the seventies and eighties. Through it all, the Leonis family continued to run Vernon pretty much as a private operation.[2]

In 1980, Robert Danziger founded Sunlaw, became its CEO, and began building his first cogeneration system, which was used to run refrigerators and freezers at Federal Cold Storage, and Growers Cold Storage in Vernon.[3]

Robert Danziger and Vernon are a good fit. Danziger has some of the same qualities that Leonis and other early Southern California entrepreneurs had—he thinks big, and, at least in talking, doesn't sweat the details. To understand Sunlaw and the way it operated as a business, it helps to start with Bob Danziger. He's a big man with a very healthy ego. *Los Angeles Times* columnist Robert Jones was impressed with him. "As an industrialist," Jones (1997a) wrote, "he is hard to classify. He's had previous lives as a jazz musician and scientist at the Jet Propulsion Laboratory. He is a large man, very large, and when standard golf clubs didn't fit him he designed his own. . . . After World War II, this city was full of entrepreneurs like Danziger, men who habitually poked into the margins of things, making and sometimes losing several fortunes in their lives. Now most of them are gone. But Danziger remains."

On his Web page and in the promotional videos distributed to South Gate households urging voters to support his Nueva Azalea plant, Robert Danziger presented himself as a kind of Renaissance man, a composer and musician, since 1972, of hip-hop, rap, progressive rock, funk, and ambient music, an expert in energy law, solar energy, and various kinds of cleaner and more efficient energy.[4] He did not go to college, but he received a J.D. degree from Whittier Law School in 1978. He published two articles in the *Whittier Law Review*—one on cogeneration and renewable energy sources, and another on solar energy financing—during this period. In 1979, Danziger's views on renewable energy and energy conservation were ahead of his time. His law review article on renewable energy argued for the need to conserve energy and to support cogeneration and solar technology: "If an appropriate price is paid by the public utilities, the economics of cogeneration and solar technology will become increasingly attractive. True success will not occur on a societal level, however, until there is at least a general consciousness of everyone's ability to both produce and conserve energy. . . . I believe [full energy utilization] is necessary not merely to reduce our dependence on foreign oil, or to enhance corporate economics, but rather, to begin taking upon ourselves the responsibility for our energy future" (Danziger 1979, 100).

Danziger's résumé shows few stints of employment that can serve as a guide to his formal training and background. Some people told me he was an engineer; others said he was a lawyer. For a while in the seventies, he was a data-processing manager at Cardio-Dynamics Laboratories; after that, he worked in systems analysis at the Jet Propulsion Laboratory from 1979 to 1988. It's not clear whether this job was full time, because he also consulted on energy, and tax policy as it related to research and development, and served as an adjunct professor at Whittier College Law School for two years during this period.

In other words, Robert Danziger is anything but a one-trick pony. Nor is he a linear narrative type. When I talked with him, he talked in what seemed to me to be topic sentences, and when I asked for the rest of the paragraph, I got the feeling he thought it should have been obvious to me. Danziger and I emailed and talked on the phone about this book, and I was trying to arrange an interview with him in Carmel. When I explained that this book was going to tell the story of the power plant from a variety of views, he asked if it would include those of CBE. I told him it would. He was very clear that he did not want to be interviewed for a book that included a group he considered his enemy and an enemy of environmentalism. Although Danziger chose not to be among the narrators of this book, he wanted his position—that "CBE's actions in the Nueva Azalea matter have damaged the environment and the cause of clean air immeasurably"—on the record.[5] We maintained a cordial relationship, but Danziger's own words do not appear in these pages, except where they are a matter of public record. So to reconstruct the story of Sunlaw Energy Corporation and Robert

Danziger, I took the leads he offered in our few conversations, I also talked with others to whom he directed me in order to get a better sense of what he and Sunlaw were trying to do.

This point of view is a crucial part of the story. Especially crucial is Robert Danziger's belief that Sunlaw's emission control technology was kept off the market by big energy producers who worked behind the scenes to block its adoption, and by the board of the South Coast Air Quality Management District (AQMD), the agency responsible for air quality in the Los Angeles basin, which betrayed him. Danziger gave me some clues to back up a view that seemed to him self-evident. When I followed the clues, I too came to think that big power producers indeed tried to block Sunlaw's emission control technology and, even more important to this story, that their efforts were what led Sunlaw to try to build a huge plant in South Gate. Here is what I found.

At some point in Sunlaw's Vernon cogeneration operation, the company applied for a permit to build a small power plant. Danziger was worried about the dangers of ammonia, which is a crucial ingredient in pollution control systems for power plants. Later, in testimony before the California Energy Commission about ammonia and its dangers, Robert Danziger explained how he came to fear ammonia:

> My first experience with ammonia occurred when I was having lunch across the street from our plant in Los Angeles, when we were developing the Federal and U.S. Growers Plants. The forklift operator, or something pierced an ammonia line at a refrigerated warehouse across the street, whereupon an ammonia cloud enveloped a number of us causing panic, fear. The hazardous materials unit of the Vernon Fire Department responded and addressed us behind their HAZMAT suits to find out how we were. We were all very scared. Then about four months later, five months later, an anhydrous ammonia delivery man who was brand new on the job, first day on the job, clipped the wrong hose on the inlet or outlet or whatever he was delivering to, and another spill occurred. And I was there, and again panic ensued, people were very scared; we all thought that we were going to die. A few people were taken to the hospital. The area was evacuated.
>
> Those were scary events. And I knew at that moment that ammonia, without having to do the studies, I knew at that moment that ammonia was a very bad thing.[6]

Most electrical power in California is generated in plants whose turbines are powered by natural gas. This process creates a lot of pollution from toxic by-products released into the air as part of normal plant operation. The most common airborne pollutants are nitrogen oxides (NO_x) and PM 10, or very small particles that cause respiratory diseases like asthma, and carbon monoxide.[7] Carbon monoxide is toxic by itself, and nitrogen oxides contribute to ozone and fine particle pollution, or soot. According to the South Coast Air Quality Management District (2003), "all such power plants have emission control systems to reduce the amount of pollutants they release. Since the mid-eighties when it was introduced from Japan, the prevailing technology for reducing airborne pollutants in California's power plants has been a technology called selective catalytic reduction, or SCR. Over time, it has gotten more efficient, and is now capable of eliminating more than ninety-five percent of NO_x emissions."

One of selective catalytic reduction's big disadvantages is that it uses liquid ammonia, large quantities of it, that has to be trucked in and stored at the plant site. As Danziger testified, a liquid ammonia spill is a major danger to the public, especially in urban areas, because the fumes can kill anyone in the vicinity who breathes them. Ammonia in power plant emission control systems has another downside in that not all the ammonia is used up in the process. The residue, called ammonia slip, goes up the stacks and into the air. Ammonia slip also contributes to PM 10, or small particles of soot.

So Danziger and his partners began trying to develop an emission control system at their Vernon plant that did not require ammonia. In late 1995 they completed their first non-ammonia emission control system, as a retrofit of one of the refrigeration plants with their cogeneration system (South Coast Air Quality Management District 1995). The opening of that plant, with its new emission control technology, put Sunlaw and Robert Danziger on the California energy map. Beginning in 1995, Danziger and his partners took out four patents for a catalyst technology that removed toxic by-products from the gases emitted into the air by a power plant's gas turbines; they trademarked it SCONOx. SCONOx is a technology to control carbon monoxide and nitrogen oxides or NO_x emissions by oxidizing NO and carbon monoxide, and absorbing NO_x on the surface of their patented catalyst. Not least, SCONOx uses no ammonia.[8] Since then, Sunlaw has taken on a number of different business names, identities, and global corporate ties.[9] Despite these, Sunlaw remained very much Robert Danziger's brainchild and baby, at least for most of the period of the Nueva Azalea effort. SCONOx technology is the core of Sunlaw's business and was to be the emission control system installed in the 550-megawatt Nueva Azalea plant Sunlaw hoped to build in South Gate.

The early days of SCONOx gave Sunlaw reason for great optimism. It attracted attention as a promising technology for reducing power plant pollution and as a potentially less dangerous alternative to selective catalytic reduction. The AQMD helped fund SCONOx research, and in November 1995 it put out a press release headlined "Company beats year 2010 pollution control goal with new technology." It praised SCONOx technology for being able to reduce "emissions of nitrogen oxides from 25 parts per million to 4 parts per million. It also reduces emissions of carbon monoxide and eliminates ammonia emissions normally associated with selective catalytic control equipment." The press release continued, quoting the AQMD manager of technology advancement: "We had to invest a lot to develop this new technology, but we have found it is cost-competitive with selective catalytic reduction." The press release concluded by noting that Sunlaw hoped to market SCONOx (South Coast Air Quality Management District 1995, 2). Danziger had early support from the California Air Resources Board, as well as from AQMD in 1995, when the latter helped him to develop SCONOx, and again, in 2000, when its acting head, Barry Wallerstein, wrote a letter in support of the Nueva Azalea project to the CEC (Martin 2000).

Danziger and SCONOx also had fans among prominent environmentalists. Mark Abramowitz and V. John White, both experts in air pollution, were strongly supportive of SCONOx technology. White, who is the executive director of the Center for Energy Efficiency and Renewable Technologies, wrote to the California Energy Commission in support of it. Abramowitz also has a long environmentalist track record. Back in the eighties, when the federal Environmental Protection Agency (EPA) was supporting air quality standards that favored industry in Southern California, Mark Abramowitz initiated a suit, joined by CBE and the Coalition for Clean Air, that ultimately lowered ceilings on pollutants. Abramowitz also worked for CBE in its early days, and for AQMD. Abramowitz thinks highly of Robert Danziger and sees him as a visionary, "very inspiring," someone who "always wanted to do the right thing. [He] was frustrated and angry about the compromises around pollution that he saw." Abramowitz worked for Sunlaw for about two years in the early stages of the Nueva Azalea project.

After SCONOx had been installed and was operating well at the Vernon plant at Federal Cold Storage, it began to get a little traction. A small five-megawatt SCONOx unit was set up at the Genetics Institute in Andover, Massachusetts. And in 1999, Alstom Power Environmental Control Systems (ABBES) began testing for design of a SCONOx system for larger-scale operations. Alstom has been involved with SCONOx since 1999, perhaps even earlier, and at some point after that had became a global marketer of SCONOx technology.[10] Alstom performed computer modeling and built larger installations of portions of the equipment to test what modifications would be needed to develop a full-scale operation. By 2000, Alstom was working on redesign and testing to develop a SCONOx unit that would handle an output of up to 180 megawatts (Czarnecki et al. 2000). By late 1999, the company had developed a smaller system it was marketing commercially.

AQMD, as the agency responsible for monitoring and assuring the quality of Southern California's air, is inevitably a political target. Businesses that deal with toxics want fewer restrictions on emissions, and those concerned with public health and the environment want cleaner and less toxic air. Occasionally those battles erupt into court cases, but more often they are fought in the back rooms, where rules and procedures are set, and where political appointments are made. So the fact that AQMD supported Sunlaw's technology and praised its performance publicly does not mean that everyone on the staff or the board was behind it, or that the agency would continue to offer substantive support.

AQMD works by establishing ceilings on emission rates of particular pollutants that any existing or proposed technology must meet. The agency can certify any technology that meets those ceilings as a "best available control technology," or BACT, for those pollutants. Both selective catalytic reduction and SCONOx can meet the standards for NO_x and volatile organic compounds, so both can be certified as BACT for those emissions.[11]

In the mid-1990s, however, SCONOx beat selective catalytic reduction in lowering NO_x emissions. In an ideal world, AQMD should have lowered the ceiling for NO_x emissions to the level SCONOx achieved. This would have meant certifying SCONOx's level as the new ceiling for NO_x—leaving selective catalytic reduction to get cleaner or lose its certification as BACT for NO_x—which would have been a big blow for the process. But that is not what AQMD did. Instead, it allowed selective catalytic reduction's higher emission rate stand as the ceiling, meaning there was no incentive for power plant owners to adopt the cleaner SCONOx technology. Sunlaw fought with AQMD on this.

It also fought a second battle with AQMD. Sunlaw, whose technology does not use ammonia, has been asking AQMD for a long time to set a zero emission ceiling as BACT for ammonia. If that were done, says an AQMD staff scientist, "SCONOx would be the only game in town," something that the manufacturers of selective catalytic reduction and plants with SCR systems would not have been happy about. Ammonia is dangerous, and zero emissions would be a big improvement for health and safety. Nor was Sunlaw the only force trying to get rid of ammonia. In the late 1990s, there was a big national debate about whether to do so. But to date, neither the U.S. EPA nor the state of California have a zero emission ceiling for ammonia.

Considerations of economic feasibility are where big corporations exert their pressure. None of the ceilings on emissions is absolute, largely because big companies have insisted they not be. Rather they are specified to be the most technologically and *economically* feasible under the specific circumstances of any given case. This leaves a lot of wiggle room. As a new technology, SCONOx cost much more than selective catalytic reduction to install, and companies want the cheapest technology available. In the mideighties, when selective catalytic reduction was the cutting edge of conventional gas plant pollution control, AQMD wrote the regulations and standards that supported its adoption. Since then, its use has increased dramatically, its costs have decreased, and thanks in part to cost, it has become the established technology. Mitsubishi, Johnson-Engelhard, Peerless, and many other large companies produce it. They have their own national association, called, somewhat paradoxically, the International Clean Air Companies. Big companies and trade associations commonly work to get regulations that favor them over their competitors. Sunlaw would probably have needed a similar boost to get its SCONOx technology to that point—working on a large scale, and regulatory support for its adoption so that its costs could be reduced. Power producers with an investment in selective catalytic reduction were less concerned about the costs of installing SCONOx in new plants than they were about what it would cost them to install it when they retrofitted and modified their existing plants, which they did more often than building new ones.

The political jockeying came to a head in 1995. Just when Sunlaw was patenting SCONOx and installing it on its Vernon plants, the California legislature considered and passed Senate Bill 456 (California, state of 1996). That legislation targeted AQMD's process for certifying the best available control technologies (BACT) for emission systems on new and retrofitted plants. The new regulations made it much harder for AQMD, which had supported SCONOx, to certify it. Senate Bill 456 lengthened the one-month testing period for any new technology to be considered for BACT certification to one year, added provisions requiring that BACT standards be set at a public hearing held by the AQMD board, and thus open to the selective catalytic reduction lobby, and required an environmental impact review of new technology. *Los Angeles Times* columnist Robert Jones (1997c) argued that big energy producers were working behind the scenes to block the adoption of Danziger's new pollution control system with this legislation.

Although environmentalists usually like environmental impact reviews, they did not like Senate Bill 456, which did indeed come from big utilities. Its sponsor was the California Council for Environmental and Economic Balance (CCEB), a business group with an energy producer's focus (California Council for Environmental and Economic Balance 2004), whose supporters included Southern California Edison and the California Municipal Utilities Association. Opposition came from the Planning and Conservation League, the Sierra Club, and AQMD itself. Proponents argued that it cost a great deal to comply with BACT and that Senate Bill 456 "is intended to impose limitations on BACT ... regulations to insure their cost-effectiveness and workability for affected sources of air pollution." CCEB argued that the bill allowed "discussions with the opposition and other interested parties on the central question of ensuring that incremental cost-effectiveness is properly included in the imposition of air pollution control devices for new and modified sources of emissions." The Planning and Conservation League argued that Senate Bill 456 "would virtually eliminate the ability of the South Coast Air District to require new technologies to improve air quality; this is the technique which has proven so successful in the past."[12]

V. John White and Mark Abramowitz say that this sort of practice is an old pattern with big utilities. Led by Southern California Edison and the Los Angeles Department of Water and Power, these environmentalists argue, utilities have done a lot of damage to efforts to improve air quality by blocking retrofitting efforts for pollution control.[13]

It is hard to blame Robert Danziger for feeling sandbagged and betrayed by AQMD and attacked by big power corporations. The struggle to get SCONOx technology certified was going nowhere, despite the advance's very low levels of NO_x emission and its complete elimination of ammonia. Without that certification and the pressure to install it that came with it, SCONOx was unlikely to make any sales. It looked like business interests were winning the war over Southern California air quality.

The story about regulating air pollution in Southern California takes a few interesting twists after 1995, however. First, environmental justice activists challenged big energy corporations' control of AQMD in moves that dovetailed with Sunlaw's own efforts to win AQMD certification for its system. Second, in 1996, as we saw in the introduction to this volume, the state of California began to deregulate the production and sale of electric power in the state in ways that gave Sunlaw an opportunity to make an end run around big power by providing the company with a statewide market for electric power, and an incentive to build its own plant to demonstrate its SCONOx emission control technology.

ENVIRONMENTAL JUSTICE AND AQMD

In 1995–1996, AQMD seems to have been a battlefield under fire from industry and environmentalists, and as a consequence an agency at war with itself. Recall that environmental justice activism was gaining ground in Southern California in the midnineties (chap. 2). Part of its success was that it heightened public awareness and criticism of AQMD for failing to do anything about the southland's dirty air. In May 1997, public pressure led the AQMD board to fire top management of the agency for being too business friendly.

In July 1997, SCONOx also got some help from the federal government's Environmental Protection Agency. The EPA stepped in and certified SCONOx as the federal equivalent of BACT for NO_x. They notified AQMD that its three-month test of SCONOx achieved a 3.5 parts per million (ppm) level of nitrogen oxide emission and asked pointedly why AQMD continued to allow a much higher level (9 ppm). The EPA insisted that AQMD either certify SCONOx or risk losing its authority to review new technology. Even in the face of the EPA ultimatum, AQMD continued to delay. One member of its scientific review committee spoke out publicly against the EPA action. That person also happened to be Southern California Edison's chief lobbyist at AQMD (Jones 1997b; *Los Angeles Times* 1997a, 1997b).

Almost a year of public critique, as well as media and local pressure against the general regulatory laxness and business-friendly practices of AQMD, was beginning to force changes inside the agency, however. After the top management firings, the AQMD board appointed its first African American chair, who promised to deal with environmental justice concerns, even though he had voted for some of the business-friendly regulations as a board member. By fall 1997, the agency signaled a new direction with a ten-point program to monitor and correct potential environmental injustices in low-income communities of color (Jones 1997b).

The backstory to AQMD's new sensitivity to Southern California's bad air and to its environmental justice implication was a court challenge filed by CBE. The CBE lawsuit challenged an AQMD regulation allowing oil companies to conduct marine unloading operations at the Port of Los Angeles in San Pedro without equipment to capture the toxic fumes that polluted the neighborhoods surrounding the port. The AQMD regulations allowed oil companies to pollute if they took measures to reduce air pollution in other ways. The measure the companies chose was to scrap old, polluting cars in the four-county area of the Los Angeles basin. Those reductions in polluting cars were credited against the toxic fumes from their operations at the port. However, it was the predominantly low-income communities of color in the Port of Los Angeles area that bore the full brunt of the toxics, whereas the benefits of removing polluting cars were very dispersed. As the *Los Angeles Times* (1997b) editorialized at the time, "Complaints pressed by environmental and community groups in recent months have charged that the agency pursued cleanup strategies that slighted low-income minority areas. The complaints, some of them lawsuits asserting federal civil-rights violations, have clearly pressured the AQMD to respond."[14]

CBE sued under Title VI of the Civil Rights Act, which, thanks to Warren County's pioneering activism in 1982, offered a precedent allowing CBE to argue against racial disparity in the distribution of environmental toxics. As part of this campaign, CBE began door-to-door education and organizing in neighborhoods near the port. It also set up meetings between residents affected by the fumes and AQMD officials, and conducted wider campaigns of public education, including writing op-eds and doing outreach to the press. The lawsuit was successful. It won a moratorium on this sort of pollution credit trading, compelled companies to install vapor capture equipment and to fund an asthma clinic, and forced the AQMD to be more accountable to low-income communities of color. Particularly important for the South Gate campaign in 2000 was AQMD's ten-point Environmental Justice Initiative, which was something CBE had pushed hard for. Largely as a result of pressure from environmentalists, the agency also established several environmental justice initiatives, and in 1999 adopted a Children's Air Quality Agenda as a result of legislation sponsored by the state legislator from Southeast Los Angeles, Martha Escutia. By 2000, even the California Energy Commission had its own environmental justice official, and power plant applications were also required to undergo an environmental justice review (Environmental Justice Collaborative 2004, 6; see also South Coast Air Quality Management District 2004).

Still, these environmental gains were limited. In early October 1997, much to the relief of business and industry-friendly players, California's governor vetoed legislation to include environmental justice as a consideration in California's Environmental Quality Act (Pastor 1997). Yet such changes as there were—to AQMD's decisions to clean up oil-unloading operations at the port, to adopt an environmental justice program, and to certify SCONOx technology as BACT, even if only on paper, owed much to the legal, media, and outreach efforts by CBE and its environmental justice allies.

Robert Danziger and CBE were on the same side of the struggle, even if they were unaware of one another at the time. SCONOx's ultimate certification owed a debt to environmental justice efforts and the resulting shakeup they caused in AQMD, and the federal government's EPA intervention with AQMD in support of SCONOx also helped create the shakeup in that agency and the changes that benefited environmental justice.

How effective these admittedly limited changes were is a matter of debate and perspective. The *Los Angeles Times* seemed to agree that business was more than holding its own. The newspaper pointed out that Southern California's air regulations were "still weaker than those of several other states [and] one-tenth as strict as the regulations recommended by the agency's staff but rejected as too expensive by the board. Though industry representatives supported Friday's action [monitoring air quality], any attempt to make the toxic regulations stricter will probably encounter stiff resistance, especially if the monitoring does not support complaints that minority communities are exposed to unusually severe toxic pollution" (Clifford 1997).

Robert Danziger was not alone in maintaining that AQMD in practice never enforced low emission levels of BACT because big power continued to hold sway within the agency.[15] Because the agency simply allowed retrofitting and new plant construction to proceed with dirtier emission control systems, AQMD effectively blocked the ability of Danziger's company to market SCONOx. Deregulation of electric power, however, provided the legal and economic wherewithal to do an end run around big power.

DEREGULATION AND OPPORTUNITY

Deregulation provided an opportunity for independent power producers to build their own plants and to sell power to statewide buyers at market price. Most of the companies referred to as independent producers were really big national power-marketing companies such as Enron, Duke, Williams, Dynegy, and AES. With a statewide market for electric power, Sunlaw discovered that hostility by big power to a new technology was no longer an insurmountable barrier to installing SCONOx on large plants. With statewide purchasing of wholesale power, Sunlaw found there was a market for its electricity. A market, in turn, would make it financially possible for Sunlaw to build its own plant with its own emission control system, whether big power liked it or not. When retail electricity prices were deregulated and the price of electricity skyrocketed, a very profitable market was created for power producers, among whom Sunlaw hoped to be numbered. In the summer of 2000, as Sunlaw Energy Partners prepared to move forward with their plant, all signs indicated that this was the right economic time to build a power plant.

Sunlaw's principal business was not building power plants, however; it was creating and marketing an emission control system for companies that did build and operate power plants. So, with two perfectly good plants in Vernon that demonstrated their technology, why did Sunlaw want to build such a huge plant? Danziger knew that for SCONOx to become commercially viable, Sunlaw needed AQMD to refuse to certify the dirtier selective catalytic reduction emission control systems on retrofits and new plants. Given that agency's regulatory foot-dragging, why Sunlaw chose to build a big plant was not a mystery to those I interviewed on the subject.

Part of the answer to the size question was the desire to test SCONOx's performance in a big plant. An AQMD staffer explained that testing a new technology had to be done in stages, beginning with "bench tests," then a small-scale version, and finally working up to large, commercial operations. What may work in an experimental situation may need changes to work in practice, and what worked on a small scale had to be shown to work as it was progressively scaled up. This sequence was the testing process that Alstom had begun with SCONOx technology. Although that company claimed its tests supported building a SCONOx operation as large as 180 megawatts, Sunlaw's 30-megawatt Vernon plant was the biggest that actually existed.

Both Mark Abramowitz and V. John White thought the demonstration effect a big plant would have was more important. Abramowitz pointed out that because SCONOx is a modular technology, scale should not have been the issue. White thought that the bigger issue was testing with particular turbines and having turbine manufacturers guarantee the workings of their turbines with the SCONOx emission system. Because turbines are the most expensive part of a power plant, he thought financing would be likely to rest on such guarantees. Regardless of BACT certification, White also thought AQMD would have to take financing issues into consideration in deciding whether to enforce BACT.

Whether a big plant was to test the technology or to dramatically demonstrate it, such a plant's performance would be very visible. Sunlaw was also working at about the same time with a community group that was trying, without success, to get SCONOx installed on another large plant, the 600-megawatt Metcalf Energy Center in San Jose (California Energy Commission n.d.; Environmental Protection Agency n.d.). There was a clear consensus among those on both sides of the controversy that what was probably driving the jump in scale was Sunlaw's hope to establish the new technology as a kind of gold standard for gas-fired power plant emission control. Bahram Fazeli, CBE's staff scientist, explained that if SCONOx worked as hoped, its low level of nitrogen oxide emissions would be more likely to be enforced as a Southern California–wide ceiling, which would mean that all new plants and existing plants needing to be retrofitted would have to adopt it. Because Sunlaw held the patents on SCONOx, and because so many gas-fueled power plants were getting old and were in need of updating, this process would prove very profitable for the company. Mark Abramowitz explained that "Danziger saw opportunity. He foresaw the rising power needs and envisioned 3000 megawatts of new power in the LA basin, all low polluting. Then when less efficient 'dinosaurs' [old, inefficient gas-powered power plants] needed replacing, they would be replaced with SCONOx emission controls. He was scouting locations [for a big plant]."

If Sunlaw wanted to install its technology on a big, visible, demonstration-sized plant, then Sunlaw would have to build it. Deregulation made it financially possible. It promised to end the monopoly of the big three (PG&E, SDG&E, and Edison) over the wholesale energy market by forcing them to buy their wholesale electricity from other producers and marketers in a free market. For Sunlaw, this meant there would be a wholesale market for the energy it produced (assuming it could produce the energy at a competitive price). Southern California Edison, the local electricity retailer, would not be able to shut Sunlaw out.

Sunlaw and CBE came close to meeting one another before they found themselves in conflict. When I interviewed Carlos Porras in 2001, he recalled Mark Abramowitz telling him about something like Sunlaw's plant back in 1997. Porras had high regard for Abramowitz.

[He's] an environmentalist, a lawyer who was largely responsible for forcing South Coast Air District to have to do a state implementation plan. It's a significant achievement and accomplishment. He used to work for CBE as a matter of fact. So just to say that we are talking about somebody who was very much in a public position and arena arguing on the good side of stuff, and he was the first one to approach me and said that there's this new technology available and could we talk about the matter a little more because people were considering where to put this thing now. And I said, sure, we can talk. We had a conversation and he wanted my support. And he said, will you support this project if we are proposing to do it in South Gate? And I said, well, I would have to have more information and just off the cuff, I can't say that I'm going to support the project. You got to show me what the impacts are going to be, who is going to pay, who is going to benefit.

Porras remembered not hearing from Abramowitz again, nor did he hear any more about the plant until 2000, at which point, he remembered having that conversation. "And so I knew right away there was a connection to the environmentalists and the South Gate power plant, and so I was very cautious always to make sure that we would be objective in looking at the impacts of whatever the project would have."

Mark Abramowitz remembers things somewhat differently. He began consulting for Danziger sometime around 1997, and urged Danziger and Sunlaw to meet with environmental groups to get their input before the permitting process even began, and before South Gate was a site. Abramowitz believed that these groups would be very favorably disposed to SCONOx and that CBE was by far the most important environmental group to involve. Danziger agreed, and Abramowitz proposed holding a full and open discussion between CBE and Sunlaw staff and consultants. He talked with Porras and thought they had set up such a meeting. When Abramowitz called Porras the day before the planned meeting, he says, Porras was out of town and never returned Abramowitz's phone calls. He had to cancel, and that ended his involvement in the project and his consulting with Sunlaw.

Sunlaw continued to develop its plans to build a large plant showcasing its new technology. Among the Southeast Los Angeles County locations the company explored were parcels in the cities of Bell and South Gate. The consensus among those I spoke with is that Sunlaw was attracted to Southeast Los Angeles, especially the area along the concrete ditch called the Los Angeles River, because that area had easy access to the gas and electrical power lines, and the recycled water the plant would need. South Gate is not the only city along the river, and South Gate was not the only city Sunlaw approached.

Sometime in the middle of 1999, Sunlaw met separately with the city councils of South Gate and nearby Bell to discuss leasing or buying specific parcels owned by each city, as a possible site on which to build the plant. Bell city councilor George Cole said the property in question was about fourteen acres of land zoned for industrial use. At the time, Cole believed that the city of Bell was quite far along in negotiations with the company. When Sunlaw discovered that Bell had a 10 percent utility tax on the use of city gas, electricity, and water, it asked the city to waive the tax, but the city refused. Bell also asked Sunlaw for certain commitments to the community. At the same time that it began negotiating with Bell, Sunlaw also approached the South Gate city council about a similar parcel, also an industrial-zoned piece of city-owned land, this one at the juncture of the Los Angeles River and the Rio Hondo. Cole thought that South Gate had no utility taxes and was not asking for any specific local commitments at the time.

In 2000, however, when Sunlaw applied for a license to build in South Gate, Bell officials were still under the impression that their city was in negotiation with Sunlaw. They continued to think so until the California Energy Commission announced Sunlaw's application to build in South Gate, and they heard that people in South Gate were protesting those plans, about which more in the next chapter.

Sunlaw also continued to seek support from environmentally friendly allies in the legislature, from among clean air activists, and from labor. Progressive Democratic local legislators from Southeast Los Angeles seem to have been among its early supporters. CBE's Carlos Porras reasoned that state senator Martha Escutia was probably an early and crucial supporter, because one of Escutia's staffers who had been supportive of CBE's work in Southeast Los Angeles in the nineties turned up on Sunlaw's staff in 2000. As part of its environmental justice protocol when Sunlaw applied for a license to build a plant in South Gate, the California Energy Commission set up a meeting between the Sunlaw officers and CBE staff. So, according to Porras, "when we met with Sunlaw, who do you think they bring with them? None other than this woman—who now works for Sunlaw. Immediately it hits me, okay, Mark Abramowitz was talking to me. I couldn't have been the only one he was talking to. And so I knew they already had Escutia in the bag, and if they had Escutia, they had [Marco] Firebaugh [California Legislative Assembly member for this district] in the bag." Both Escutia and Firebaugh were influential members of the California legislature's powerful Latino Caucus and could be expected to be essential in getting active support for Sunlaw's Nueva Azalea power plant in South Gate from that body.

Then there was support among environmental activists. Mark Abramowitz was not the only environmentalist to support Sunlaw's technology. We saw that when CBE staff scientist Bahram Fazeli and CBE staff attorney Anne Simon began attending CEC workshops and saw Sunlaw's literature, they were shocked to find it contained endorsements from Martha Escutia and from some of CBE's environmental allies, most notably from V. John White, director of the Coalition for Energy Efficiency and Renewable Technology (CEERT), and Tim Carmichael, executive director of the Coalition for Clean Air, of which CBE was a member. All of them—legislators and environmental organizations—had worked together on environmental issues, especially a zero emissions effort for automobiles. In short, it looked as though Sunlaw's new technology had substantial support from CBE's friends.

By 2000, Sunlaw had also gotten significant labor support. The pipe fitters' union understandably was among the early supporters. It had a direct stake in the plant jobs that Sunlaw promised them would be union jobs. Sunlaw approached the South Gate city workers' union, Local 347 of SEIU, to ask them to support the plant. That local's officials thought it was a good opportunity for a municipal union and a building trades union to work together. Probably more important in determining SEIU support was the request for their backing from state senator Martha Escutia's office. Both the pipe fitters' and the city workers' locals, independently or at the urging of Escutia's office, most likely asked the Los Angeles County Federation of Labor to support the plant, which it did unanimously—and its president, the late Miguel Contreras, sent a letter endorsing the plant to South Gate voters.

Not least, Sunlaw had its own publicity campaign up and running early in the game, in the spring of 2000. In what was probably not the wisest move, although some speculated that this was a quid pro quo, Sunlaw hired a public relations firm headed by Leo Briones, the husband of state senator Martha Escutia. Predictably, this move eventually drew plenty of fire from plant opponents.

Most important, people were hearing Sunlaw's case directly from Sunlaw. Its campaign was extensive. Not only were many mailers sent out about the plant, but every house in South Gate received a fifteen-minute video cassette featuring Robert Danziger. Sunlaw's efforts were designed to persuade South Gate residents that the power plant would be clean—indeed, its air quality would exceed that currently at the site—and that Sunlaw was a pro-union, socially concerned company determined to be a good corporate citizen in South Gate. Sunlaw's booth and coloring contest at the city's Cinco de Mayo celebration (chap. 3) were part of its demonstration of good citizenship, as was its publicity about how much the plant would contribute to city revenues—anywhere from $3 million to almost $8 million. So too was its claim that Sunlaw would only build its plant in South Gate if the people wanted it. Press and anti-plant activists picked up on this promise pretty late in the game, and it would turn out to be a big mistake.

Still, if the goal of Sunlaw's public relations campaign was to make everyone familiar with Sunlaw, the Nueva Azalea power plant, and what it could do for the city and its residents, the campaign was a smashing success.

Until sometime in the middle of 2000, Robert Danziger and CBE had been pursuing their own versions of environmentalism independently. Both continued to frame strategies to address political dynamics at the state and regional levels. CBE began to build a base in Southeast Los Angeles County for regional grassroots environmental activism and was having a modicum of success among youth. It looked for and found allies among California's clean air environmentalists, Southern California state legislators, and Los Angeles County labor unions. Sunlaw's battle with big power and its supporters at AQMD and in the state legislature led the company to seek new ways to demonstrate the value of SCONOx for generating cleaner electricity and new support for it from the same quarters as CBE.

Looking back on the battle that was to come, smart money might well have bet on Sunlaw. The stars seemed finally to be lining up for Robert Danziger and Sunlaw's pollution control technology. They had outflanked CBE and garnered support from powerful and popular legislators, labor, and environmentalists, who were CBE's usual allies. They had a proactive and professional publicity campaign in high gear that presented Sunlaw and its Nueva Azalea power plant as a wonderful opportunity for South Gate residents. And they did it before any criticism surfaced.

But Sunlaw and CBE were relatively clueless about the local political climate in South Gate. Indeed, Robert Danziger's troubles were only beginning.

CHAPTER 5

The Perfect Storm

SOUTH GATE POLITICS AND THE MAKINGS OF A PRO-PLANT COALITION

They're against the power plant; they just don't like
Robles, so anyone with Robles they'll boo.

—Comment by an older white man
at a city council meeting

A THIRD INTERPRETATION of the struggle over the
power plant is seen through the lens of local politics. In it, the struggle
is not about the power plant at all but rather about South Gate residents organizing to get rid of a corrupt politician—one who happens
to oppose the power plant and who is effective in manipulating naïve
voters. In this interpretation, South Gate residents and public employees
support the power plant in no small part because their allies in fighting
corruption support the plant and their enemy opposes it.

Although Sunlaw had a broad base of support for its technology
and its proposed plant, most of that support came from outside South
Gate, indeed outside Southeast Los Angeles County. Even within the
union local representing South Gate city workers, arguably the most
local pro-plant base, enthusiasm for the project came from the leadership, who admitted that their members were not initially enthusiastic
about supporting the plant. Sunlaw's legislative and labor support might
have carried the day for Nueva Azalea at a time when conventional
wisdom held that building power plants was an obvious necessity. But
in addition to opposition from environmental justice activists, there
was local political opposition in the person of city councilor Xochilt
Ruvalcaba and city treasurer Albert Robles. Ruvalcaba was a new face,
but Robles had been making local political enemies for years. By 2000,
those enemies reached critical mass and began to coalesce into a local

movement to oust him. The marriage of the anti-Robles movement to those supporting Sunlaw's power plant created something of a pro-plant coalition with local South Gate legs.

This chapter tracks the brewing storm from its beginnings inside South Gate's city hall to its public coming out and its transformation into an anti-Robles movement that also became the local base of support for the power plant. Local support for the plant such as there was seems mainly to have been a correlate of opposition to Robles— "the enemies of my enemy are my friends" reasoning—and much less deeply felt than was anger at Robles' corruption.

CITY HALL BATTLES

In chapter 1, we saw signs that Albert Robles, well supported by his $69,000 salary as city treasurer and his $23,000 salary as a member of the Water Replenishment District, was beginning to ruffle feathers in city hall, not least those of his former mentor Henry Gonzalez. Subsequently, he began to engage in more unsavory kinds of politicking. He owned a ten-line automated phone dialer that could send out recorded messages to the city's electorate. He also is said to have created his own database of registered voters, which he and his allies used to send birthday cards and candy to voters (Quinones 2001).[1]

From the time he was elected city treasurer, Albert Robles also began to create a workplace climate at city hall that earned him the enmity of SEIU Local 347, which represented South Gate city employees. In 1997, the then vice mayor sent a memo to city officials detailing Robles'"threats, tirades, screaming fits, interruptions and general . . . improper behavior." She noted that "his behavior is not only frightening to me but harassing" and went on to sue on grounds of sexual harassment. The city manager testified in his deposition in the suit (which was settled out of court) that several women city workers also complained of Robles' harassment (Marosi 2002b). Union officials also accused Robles of firing and replacing managers with his own people, moving departmental offices around, generally disrupting space, and creating a climate of fear, heightened by alleged threats to the graffiti unit that he would subcontract out their jobs if they didn't support the city budget he proposed.

Robles helped to bring his enemies together. By 1997, the union joined with Henry Gonzalez to get Robles out of office. Local 347 began to oppose Robles and candidates aligned with him and to support those whom Gonzalez supported. Despite all this skirmishing, Local 347 manager Julie Butcher said that Robles was good to the city workers' union and the police union. Local 347 officials noted that although Robles fired managers and city workers who were in non-union jobs, he did not attack unionized workers. Indeed, the local's contract gained things like civil service for middle managers and longevity pay. They also noted that the police got bilingual pay, even those police who didn't speak Spanish. Butcher thought all this was because Robles had higher political ambitions and hoped for union endorsement.

People point to the March 1999 municipal election, which the *Long Beach Press Telegram* (1999) described as "the most vicious in memory," as a harbinger of things to come. Gonzalez and Local 347 fielded one slate of candidates and Robles another. This campaign was the first of several to be dominated by "hit pieces," or unsigned negative campaign mailers, from both sides, which became emblematic of South Gate elections.[2] The most vicious hit piece, aimed at a Gonzalez-backed candidate, falsely accused him of being a child molester. He lost. The most dramatic event associated with the campaign happened after the election. On the night he was chosen mayor by the new city council, Henry Gonzalez was shot in the head when he returned home from the council meeting. He was only grazed and recovered, but no one was ever caught or charged.

In the end, the Gonzalez/Local 347 forces controlled the council, but that did not last long. Their majority consisted of continuing councilors Hector De La Torre, first elected in 1997; reelected Henry Gonzalez; and longtime Gonzalez ally Bill DeWitt, who had been on and off the council since 1980. The remaining councilors were Raul Morial, first elected in 1997, and new councilor Xochilt Ruvalcaba. Although some believed Ruvalcaba and Morial were supported by Robles from the outset, Ruvalcaba denied this.

Labor Democrat Henry Gonzalez and Republican small businessman Bill DeWitt were already South Gate political allies. During his long tenure on the South Gate city council, Henry Gonzalez tried to combine his union perspectives with economic development efforts. In the late eighties, one of his ideas, to start a South Gate electric company, put him in the crosshairs of Southern California Edison's big guns. Gonzalez recalled, "They put $60,000 in a campaign to beat me [for reelection to the city council], and they beat me by seven votes in 1988." DeWitt had supported Gonzalez's effort, and the two had worked together as city councilors and civic activists for a long time. Hector De La Torre, when he was elected in 1997, allied with Gonzalez; subsequently he worked with Bill DeWitt after the latter was elected in 1999. Gonzalez and DeWitt were by then old opponents of Robles. By 1999, Hector De La Torre came to share those feelings.

Hector De La Torre was of a much younger political generation. He grew up in South Gate, and his parents and grandparents live in South Gate. He entered politics in college, interning with his congressional representative, and then worked on Gloria Molina's campaign for Los Angeles County supervisor. Subsequently he was appointed to a position in the Department of Labor under Robert Reich during Clinton's first term. When Reich resigned, De La Torre, married and the parent of a toddler, returned to South Gate, took a job with Southern California Edison, and in 1997 entered electoral politics, winning a seat on the city council.

The other two councilors were Raul Morial and newly elected Xochilt Ruvalcaba, who emerged not too much later as Robles' allies. Raul Morial was of the same generation as Henry Gonzalez and Bill DeWitt. Born in Mexico, he grew up in Texas, moved to South Gate in the seventies, and became a businessman. "I must have been about thirty-eight, thirty-nine, when I stopped working because I had been in business for myself." Morial, who had invested in rental properties and did some of his own maintenance, was supported by the properties' income. He seemed to have backed into politics more than aspired to it. When he learned that the city had instituted an ordinance against overnight street parking, he attended several city council meetings to try to change it, but "I realized I was getting ignored, and subsequently helped out in the campaigns of some people who did one of the elected positions in South Gate, and was appointed as the planning commissioner," where he was able to help "a lot of people, business people. Then along the way there was an opportunity to for me to run for city council. I spoke to a few people and asked them what they thought. And they all encouraged me and I ran, and I won." Unfortunately, I interviewed Raul Morial before I knew enough to ask him who some of the encouraging people were.

Xochilt Ruvalcaba was of Hector De La Torre's political generation. She had attended UCLA and had no political experience before she ran for city council. After her first unsuccessful attempt in 1997, she worked for Los Angeles city councilor Ruth Galanter and then ran again, successfully, in 1999. She was proud of being "the youngest elected official in the history of South Gate, the first Latina." She added, "I hope to be the first Latina mayor." She saw herself as part of a new generation of young candidates who were raised in the community. She emphasized that she wanted to focus on needs of those living on the poorer, western side of the city and to expand social services and economic development programs for them.

Morial and Ruvalcaba, who came to be most closely allied with Robles, were both political novices and largely unconnected to any political network. Like Robles, they were not part of Los Angeles labor-Latino political networks or the local chamber of commerce and Rotary Club networks. Nevertheless, both Xochilt Ruvalcaba and Albert Robles asked for endorsements from SEIU Local 347, according to its officials. In Southeast Los Angeles, a labor endorsement carries a lot of weight. Local 347 is a large and influential local, and SEIU is even larger and even more powerful in the Los Angeles County Federation of Labor and in California Democratic politics.

It is unclear whether Morial and Ruvalcaba were elected with Robles' help and were his allies as far back as 1999. Arguing against the likelihood is the fact that they did not always act in support of Robles in 1999 or early 2000. Arguing for it is Hector De La Torre, who said that even in 1999 Robles was "telling Xochilt and Raul what to do. Over time, it turned into a three to two—Henry, Bill, and I versus them." Xochilt Ruvalcaba denied accusations that she was elected with Robles' help. She argued that she won because she campaigned by precinct walking and speaking to people directly.

This was the city council Sunlaw encountered in early July 2000 when the company asked for a meeting to discuss its interest in buying a piece of city-owned property, at the confluence of Rio Hondo and the Los Angeles River, on which to build a 550-megawatt power plant. Xochilt Ruvalcaba was outraged that the meeting was in closed session, and then outraged at Sunlaw's presentation.

> They were claiming that this power plant was actually going to clean the air. How could it be cleaning the air if they are going to be producing electricity? I thought they were in the business of producing electricity, not cleaning the air. They invited us to tour their [Vernon] plant. I asked if they had another plant that was closer [in size] to what they were planning to build in South Gate,

and they said yes, somewhere in South America, and they offered to fly us there. I thought to myself, wow, the plot thickens. In closed session there is no public input, and I thought this was outrageous that the council would think that they are above everyone else to make a decision that would impact, not only our lives, but our children's lives.

Henry Gonzalez and Hector De La Torre were irritated at this charge. De La Torre saw Sunlaw's proposal as exploratory, as just "just a request to negotiate with the city to purchase that property." Gonzalez felt that a closed session was both legal and entirely appropriate, and didn't think "that there were too many people that wanted to give the site up at that point." Raul Morial, despite being thought by De La Torre to be a Robles person, stood with Gonzalez, De La Torre, and DeWitt on this issue.

Although she was outvoted on the council, Xochilt Ruvalcaba was determined to make the power plant a public issue. She broadcast a phone message, most likely on Albert Robles' automated phone dialer, "letting them know the council wants to make a decision on bringing the power plant to our community in closed session. I think you should know about it and you should show up at the council meeting and let the council know exactly how you feel." Many South Gate residents also received a leaflet with the same message. Although Ruvalcaba claimed the phone call, she said she had nothing to do with the leaflet.

South Gate resident and community activist Celene Leyva, who later became active in opposition to the plant, recalled, however, that "Xochilt Ruvalcaba came [to my house] very upset, she told me, Señora Leyva, they are going to put in an electric plant. Back then it wasn't called Nueva Arcelia.[3] And I told her, Xochilt, I need flyers to notify the people." Leyva explained that Albert Robles, as city treasurer, helped get the flyers made, that he "helped the community a lot. She recalled leafleting until very late at night, we distributed flyers in the community, especially at the place where they were going to put [the plant.] We alerted them to the plant and we talked a lot with the neighbors."

Roy Abadi, who lives close to the site of the plant, got one of the flyers and remembers it as captioned "Do you want a power plant in your backyard?" "I realized it was from council member Xochilt

Ruvalcaba. [It had] smokestacks and black smoke coming out of it, and do you want to have it because that's what they are planning for you. Please show up in the city hall tomorrow night." He was not able to do so, however.

The power plant was not Celine Leyva's first experience of community involvement in South Gate. Several years earlier, when a policeman was shot on her street, she invited a priest to hold Mass for him, on the spot where he had been killed, and brought out many neighbors. After that, she became the chairperson of Community in Action/Comunadad en Acción, in partnership with the South Gate police department. Her ongoing passion, however, was the school situation. Leyva's family lived in the western part of South Gate, in an area where the high school students were bused to Jordan High School in Watts. Like many parents on the west side, she wanted her children to go to South Gate High School because it was academically a better school. When I interviewed her, she was working with her neighbors to change school district boundaries so that all of South Gate could attend South Gate High School.

Leyva attended and spoke at the city council meeting. She remembers that two hundred to three hundred people were present, "and they all brought flyers. And we began to speak to city hall, to tell them that we don't want the plant in this city, that we don't want our children to be sick. We have a lot of children with asthma. I have a son who has asthma. If you put this plant in without the consent of the community we are going to protest against you, to vote against you." Leyva believed that the strong showing of popular sentiment against the plant was what stopped it.

To De La Torre—an employee of Southern California Edison, and Gonzalez, a former opponent of same—Ruvalcaba was "grandstanding." They claimed that the furor around Sunlaw's proposal at the July 1999 city council meeting was unnecessary because no one was disposed to sell that particular parcel of city-owned land.

De La Torre also believed that Ruvalcaba was in league with, and acting at the behest of city treasurer Albert Robles, who was against the plant for reasons that had nothing to do with health or safety issues. Like many others, De La Torre believed that Albert Robles came to oppose the power plant because Sunlaw would not make financial deals with him for his support. An observer of Southeast Los Angeles politics who shared this view suggested that Robles probably first encountered Sunlaw early on, in his capacity as a member of the Water Replenishment District (WRD), and that Robles was likely to have asked Sunlaw for a political contribution in exchange for support. When Sunlaw refused and went around him in talking with the WRD, Robles is reputed to have begun opposing the plant in South Gate.

The belief that Robles was indeed a key behind-the-scenes player developed traction later. As evidence for that connection early on, Hector De La Torre pointed to the automated phone messages Xochilt Ruvalcaba sent out, noting that "it's a sophisticated campaign mechanism that costs something like $80,000. Nobody else in the city is a full-time politician that way." Celine Leyva's recollection about Ruvalcaba's and Robles' roles in publicizing the power plant, "that Xochilt and Albert Robles did a lot. I didn't think that they were so concerned with the community," suggests that they were already working together, at least against the power plant, although at whose initiative is not clear. Leyva's surprise at their interest in community issues, however, is consistent with my inability to find evidence of direct community involvement by either Robles or Ruvalcaba. As best I could tell, the power plant was the first community outreach for either of them.

A behind-closed-doors fight between city councilor Bill DeWitt and Albert Robles was the catalyst for making the wider divisions in city hall a public matter. Recall that there was already enmity between the two. Bill De Witt had twice gone after Robles in 1997, over the latter's possible conflict of interest (holding two elected positions simultaneously), and in his suit against the city for hiring an economic development consultant without public posting of the opening. According to Hector De La Torre, in December 1999, in the midst of a quarrel with Robles, DeWitt threatened to cut the city treasurer's annual salary—from $69,000 to $7,200, the amount that city councilors, as part-time officials, earn. De La Torre recalled, "Albert went through the roof. That full-time salary is what allows him to do politics full time, so within a week or two, the recall against Bill started. That's what triggered it." An official recall petition against Bill DeWitt, to appear on the November 2000 ballot, was circulated for signatures.[4] DeWitt carried out his threat to cut the city treasurer's salary. His measure passed the city council unanimously, with both Xochilt Ruvalcaba and Raul Morial, alleged Robles allies, voting in favor. Still, before the summer of 2000, the South Gate public was largely unaware of just how dysfunctional their municipal government had become.

MAKING CITY POLITICS PUBLIC

Two things happened that summer to change the public's attentiveness to their local government. First, Sunlaw returned to South Gate in a way that showed publicly that not only was it serious about building a power plant in the city, but it was much farther along with its plans than anyone thought. Second, Albert Robles gathered enough signatures to put the DeWitt recall and an election for his possible replacement on the November 2000 ballot. The recall of city councilor Bill DeWitt would become the missing link connecting city hall's Albert Robles problem to the power plant.

City officials learned of Sunlaw's return to South Gate from the California Energy Commission (CEC). Having found a willing seller of a private site with appropriate industrial-use zoning, Sunlaw had applied to the CEC for a license to build the plant. Even before the application was complete, a fair amount of information about the proposed plant—now named, in Spanglish, Nueva Azalea, after South Gate's city flower and festival, became available to the city and to the public through the CEC. The proposed site, the J. D. Hunt truck depot, a privately held 13.5-acre parcel, became known. So too did Sunlaw's plans to build a one-mile natural gas pipeline from the existing gas lines to the plant, to purchase water for the plant from the city of South Gate, and to sell its electricity "in the deregulated electricity marketplace" (California Energy Commission 2000a). The site was not far from the original city-owned parcel that Sunlaw had offered to buy. People discovered just how big the plant was going to be, 550 megawatts—capable of generating enough electricity for half a million houses, and about the size of Dodger Stadium, as its opponents put it. The CEC planned to make their licensing decision within a year of receipt of Sunlaw's completed application, which was ultimately filed in August 2000.

By applying for a license to build its plant, Sunlaw thereby submitted itself to CEC protocols, including public outreach and hearings. Also, the CEC was required to consider whether minority communities would be overburdened by the addition of a power plant, a protocol created in response to environmental justice activism during the nineties. The

CEC quickly sent formal notification of Sunlaw's application to the city government of South Gate in March and to CBE's director in May.

From Sunlaw's point of view, the timing of its application couldn't have been better. As the energy crisis unfolded and electricity prices skyrocketed, the state of California did everything it could to get more power plants on line. In early 2000, Governor Gray Davis's state of emergency declaration included new regulations for speeding up the process for licensing new power plants. Environmentalists long pushing for alternative, green sources of power were pretty well silenced by the immediate need to focus on generating enormous amounts of electricity and to produce it by building known types of plants on a massive scale.[5] Judging by the pace of CEC approvals of applications, mid-2000 through 2001 was the best of times to apply for a license to build a power plant. Few plants were licensed before the price of electricity began to skyrocket, but twenty-three plants were approved in 2001, which was the peak year for approvals, and the year in which South Gate's plant would have been scheduled for its decision.[6] It was also the right timing in terms of the state's political climate, which, as we have seen, was a familiar context for both Robert Danziger, from his struggle with big power and regulatory agencies, and for CBE, from its environmental justice lawsuits and activism in the nineties. South Gate's local political climate was another matter.

CONNECTING THE POWER PLANT
TO LOCAL POLITICS

Almost as soon as Xochilt Ruvalcaba discovered that the issue of the power plant had returned, she urged her colleagues to block it by any means possible. The same disagreements that divided Ruvalcaba and her fellow councilors the previous year remained. Hector De La Torre and Henry Gonzalez both felt that Ruvalcaba was premature in her opposition. Gonzalez expressed confidence in the CEC process and felt the city should take no position until its hearings were complete. Raul Morial, who later came to oppose the plant and to align himself with Ruvalcaba and Robles, was also neutral and, like his colleagues, "felt that the process should be played out in its entirety."[7]

Ruvalcaba had better luck by again going directly to South Gate residents. She managed to put a citywide referendum about the plant on the city council agenda for a meeting in late July. She automated phone messages to tell residents about the meeting, urging them to turn out and insist the city council approve the referendum. This action made a significant number of South Gate residents aware of the power plant issue, and it turned out to be a crucial strategic move.

Already worried about a power plant so near to his house, Roy Abadi listened to "one of those annoying recorded phone calls" from Xochilt Ruvalcaba. This time he went to the meeting, as did Celine Leyva. Abadi remembered about fifty people in the audience, but Leyva remembered it as larger. Both of them spoke in support of the referendum. Saying "money corrupts," Abadi urged the council to "give [the decision] to the people." Leyva recalled that a Sunlaw representative spoke "about all they were going to bring and inviting people to join with them and sign a paper that said 'We want this plant here.'" She too warned of corruption. Sentiment at the meeting ran strongly against Nueva Azalea and in favor of a city referendum on the issue. The council was also unanimous in its agreement that a citywide referendum was the appropriate path to take.

The councilors were sharply divided about when to hold the referendum, however. Ruvalcaba's proposal for a November referendum would link the power plant to the recall of councilor Bill DeWitt, which was also on the ballot for November, along with an election for a seat on the city council to replace DeWitt should the recall succeed. Hector De La Torre was among the council majority who wanted to separate the power plant issue from the DeWitt recall. "I made the motion to put the issue on the ballot in March because, by then, the CEC application [would be] complete. And clearly it was [Ruvalcaba's and Robles'] intent to have this advisory vote happen at the same time as the recall so that they could tie the two issues together." Xochilt Ruvalcaba confirmed De La Torre's view that she wanted to link the power plant and the recall. She said she "tried putting this initiative on the ballot for November at the same time as the recall election, letting people vote whether or not they wanted the power plant or not."

Ruvalcaba lost the vote, with the council majority trying to decouple the two issues by voting to hold the referendum in March 2001. But she and Robles succeeded in making themselves known publicly as opponents of the power plant, their first high-profile stance on a community issue. Still, Albert Robles and Xochilt Ruvalcaba were not exactly political twins at this point, given that Ruvalcaba voted with the other councilors to cut Robles' salary.

In the run-up to the November 2000 recall of Bill DeWitt and the election to replace him, talk of Robles' behind-the-scenes machinations became more than vague rumors. The press began picking up corruption stories. Susan Carrillo, Albert Robles' sister and, handily, also president of the WRD, wrote a letter on WRD stationery urging South Gate voters to recall DeWitt for "picking the pockets" of South Gate residents by failing to distribute a two-million-dollar rebate from the WRD. It was a false accusation.[8] Anti-DeWitt literature also claimed that DeWitt had supported an "English-only" law in 1985. As we saw in chapter 1, what had been proposed was a signage regulation; it had failed, and the then mayor Bill DeWitt had opposed the directive.

When one of the candidates running for Bill DeWitt's seat on the city council, Maria Benavides, a total unknown, built her campaign around her opposition to the power plant, it began to look as though the recall campaign involved more than Robles' personal vendetta against DeWitt. Roy Abadi loves the machinations of politics, and he got it right away. But he also learned that word about Robles' corruption was becoming more well known. "I got involved. I talked to some people. . . .I called people I know. I said listen we need to recall DeWitt and put [Benavides] in. . . . Maybe I'm responsible for fifty votes. [But] whenever I talked about it to some neighbors, they said, this Robles is a crook."

Word of Robles' corruption wasn't public enough. In November, South Gate voters recalled DeWitt and elected Maria Benavides, who ran on a platform opposing the power plant, to replace him. This election changed the balance of power on the city council. Widely regarded as a Robles person, Benavides confirmed that opinion by never saying a word at council meetings and voting in lock step with Ruvalcaba, who was later joined by Morial.[9] By winter, it became clear that Robles' supporters were now in control of the South Gate city council.

While this drama was unfolding, still another, even stranger conflict began to develop at city hall. City workers began to notice that Albert Robles was interfering with the police department. According to Local 347 sources, Robles had maintained good relations with the police until he decided to attend the Fullerton police academy and become a policeman himself. The South Gate police command was said to have agreed because they did not believe Robles would make it through the training. According to a variety of sources, Robles not only got the city to fund his academy fees, but he also persuaded South Gate's police chief to accept him as a policeman with gun and police badge even before he completed the course—perhaps because, as city treasurer, Robles had a fair amount of power over the police department budget.

When Albert Robles took on the police department, he made a very powerful enemy. Al Lopez, the president of the South Gate Police Officers Association (POA), told me the organization had gotten involved because Robles was trying to get rid of the current police chief, to create a position of deputy chief, and to force the city to hire Robles' own choice for it. The South Gate POA got a preliminary injunction and temporary restraining order against the city to block the firing of the police chief and to keep the position of deputy chief within the POA bargaining unit. Others told me they believed Robles' intent was ultimately to hire his own person for the deputy chief position, to have that person promoted to chief, and then to have this new chief appoint Robles as deputy policy chief.[10] With police funding equaling almost two-thirds of the total city budget, the police department was at the top of the food chain, and the stakes were large indeed.[11]

When the police protested Robles' actions, he tried to disband the department and bring in the county sheriff's department to police the city. The police were outraged. Working through the union in the sheriff's department, the SEIU city workers' union, which we have already seen had a long-standing beef with Robles, intervened and persuaded the sheriff's department to stay out of South Gate. The struggle between Robles and the police department was bubbling under the surface just as the struggle over the power plant was heating up publicly.

This police situation added to the growing sense that Robles' agenda was, as Henry Gonzalez put it, to use the city of South Gate treasury as his "private piggy bank." Robles held a post on the WRD, served as city treasurer (albeit now at a much reduced salary), and, not least, was throwing his weight around in the police department. Robles' move on the police department was a credible threat, given that the November 2000 election gave him a majority on the city council, which in turn had control over city finances, including the police department.

By fall, Albert Robles' opposition to the power plant became stronger and his enemies list longer. In South Gate, the city workers' union and city councilors Gonzalez, DeWitt, and De La Torre, and the South Gate Police Department all wanted to get rid of him for corruption. In turn, Robles' opposition to the power plant earned him the enmity of the area's state legislators Martha Escutia and Marco Firebaugh

and the statewide pro-plant coalition they helped build, which included
the Los Angeles County Federation of Labor and the Latino Caucus of
the State Legislature. It was an obvious step for the legislators to support
their South Gate allies' efforts to get rid of Albert Robles and for local
anti-Robles forces to support the plant.[12] Although Gonzalez and De La
Torre maintained their position of neutrality toward the plant throughout
the process, they were nevertheless central to this larger, emerging anti-
Robles coalition.

By late fall, the police, city workers, and state legislators began
actively organizing against Albert Robles' actions, and they began
to garner support from a growing number of South Gate residents.
Together these forces constituted the local base of the coalition in favor
of the power plant. Nevertheless, the passion that brought South Gate
officials, unionists, and residents to activism was really to get rid of
Albert Robles. The power plant was minor, significant mainly because
Robles supported it. Indeed, in journalist Sam Quinones' engaging story
of the anti-Robles movement, at least its local base, there is almost no
mention of the power plant (Quinones 2007, 65–116).

The resulting coalition that emerged to support Sunlaw crisscrossed
the political spectrum from labor and progressive Latino Democrats, to
the police, who did not have a historic reputation for liberalism, and to
a mix of older white and younger Latino/a residents. It was a coalition
of people who had different priorities but who agreed to support one
another. State legislators from Southeast Los Angeles provided the initial
impetus for supporting the power plant, and they helped to generate
labor support. The city workers' union was predictably the intersection
in joining the anti-Robles and pro-plant strands of this emerging movement. They had an independent interest in both issues—promoting the
good union jobs Sunlaw promised, and their own real beef with Robles,
which they shared with the POA. Most likely they were instrumental in
engaging legislators' influence in the wider political landscape to bring
the law down on Albert Robles.

Although my interpretation of the local anti-Robles movement
shares much with that of Sam Quinones (2007), we interpret its racial
dynamics somewhat differently. Quinones argues that the movement to
get rid of Robles and his allies brought together whites and Latina/os
and groups that had formerly mistrusted one another, and that working
together allowed them get to know one another as people; it also helped
overcome distrust of the police among new immigrants and anti-

immigrant sentiments among white seniors. According to Quinones, "South Gate had become an unashamedly teary-eyed, heartwarming Norman Rockwell painting, updated to the twenty-first century. Young shaved-head Latinos and blue-haired ladies stood shoulder to shoulder during the campaigns and ate from the same box of donuts" (2007, 111). There was indeed a great deal of cordial cross-ethnic cooperation around their shared views by people on all sides of the issue. But there was also a not so sunny side to some of the cross-ethnic dynamics that neither Quinones nor the anti-Robles city councilors addressed. Especially in the coalition's local anti-Robles base, there were people with very different views about immigration and immigrants. Some of the anti-immigrant sentiment became public in the last months before the referendum on the power plant and remained public after the March referendum.

XENOPHOBIA IN THE ANTI-ROBLES COALITION

I got a firsthand view of xenophobia in the anti-Robles movement when I attended several city council meetings with CBE after I was well into my research. It was in fall 2001, after South Gate voters had defeated the power plant in the referendum. Between March and that autumn, CBE continued monitoring to see whether Sunlaw would keep its promise not to build the plant once South Gate residents showed they did not want it. In October, when Sunlaw's application still had not been withdrawn, CBE organized two large community delegations to the South Gate city council, which I attended. Worried that the application would be reactivated, the organization planned to ask the city council—which had an anti-plant majority—to rezone the proposed plant site to prevent its development as a power plant. While in attendance, I saw what people had told me about city council meetings. At the two meetings I went to, power plant business had to take a back seat to the real focus of the anti-plant coalition, the now very large and very angry movement to get rid of Robles and the three councilors—Morial, Ruvalcaba, and Benavides—widely regarded as his puppets.

That effort brought some of South Gate's latent ethnic divisions back to the performance of city politics. I arrived early on October 9 as people were filing into the council chambers. The South Gate Police Officers Association had a table outside with donuts and sodas. Many attendees were older and white, but there were also Latino/as who were wearing Support Your Police Department T-shirts. Many also held signs saying "We want truth, get rid of corruption" or "Raul and Maria, this ain't Kansas, go home." The crowd was big.

I heard drumming outside and followed the sound. On the lawn in front of city hall I counted about seventy-five people from CBE and other anti-plant activists, joined by a troupe of Aztec dancers. Alvaro Huerta and Celine Leyva both spoke to the group about the fact that Sunlaw had not yet withdrawn its licensing application and that the city needed to do something to prevent the company from coming back. The police came out and shut down the drumming, I thought somewhat provocatively. The group on the lawn then went into city hall.

Between the very sizable pro-police, anti-Robles crowd already inside and the fairly large CBE crowd, there were more people than room in council chambers so that the hallway outside was also packed. Inside, the anti-Robles forces and the city council majority tangled over the real issue (Robles) by proxy. Anyone or any comment the audience thought supported Robles generated loud booing. Any speaker whom Robles' allies on the council opposed, or who disagreed with them, got cheers and support from the crowd. Although the people holding anti-Robles signs and wearing pro-police T-shirts were both white and Latina/o, the active booing came from a small number of older white men and women.

During the public commentary period, several CBE speakers asked the council to downzone the proposed Sunlaw site, but even though the council majority was friendly, CBE speakers perceived the audience as unfriendly. Indeed, Alvaro Huerta prefaced his remarks with "I know you don't want to listen to me." Celine Leyva then spoke in Spanish, and a city interpreter translated her speech into English (council meetings are conducted in English, with Spanish speakers as the main constituents using translation). Leyva had people listening attentively until she praised Xochilt Ruvalcaba and then there were boos—which must have come from Spanish speakers, because I did not see headphones on the whites who had been booing.

At that point, an older white man sitting next to me leaned over and said, "They're against the power plant; they just don't like Robles, so anyone with Robles they'll boo." I thought that described the anti-Robles dynamic across ethnicities quite accurately. The crowd was not friendly to CBE, but it did not treat the speakers with the hostility reserved for city councilors Morial, Benavides, and Ruvalcaba. If the crowd was pro-plant, it was not obvious.

Race was an issue in two ways—as part of the Police Officers Association lawsuit and as an animating factor for a number of whites in the anti-Robles coalition. The POA lawyer argued that Robles forces wanted a Hispanic (their word) for the position of deputy chief because the police needed diversity. The POA argued that this prospect violated the 1996 California voter initiative Proposition 209, which bars affirmative action anywhere in California. It looked to many as though Robles was using diversity—and its presumed appeal to Latino/a residents—as a cover to take over the police department. Both the POA head and its lawyer were Latino/a, and a significant number in the pro-police coalition were Latino/as. The irony is that by supporting the POA lawsuit, the anti-Robles forces were taking a public stand against affirmative action.

White xenophobia was more visible at the next city council meeting, when the anti-Robles issue generated an even bigger crowd: between 100 and 120 people were seated, another 60 were standing, with more outside the chambers. Again the police department was the central issue. The POA had a table outside with donuts, pizza, water, and coffee. By the time the council entered the chambers, perhaps 200 people were tightly crammed into the seating, and more were standing several deep along the sides and outside the chambers. The television cameras and press were out in force. The signs this time were even more explicit: "Albert Robles: the party's over"; "We're taking back our city"; "Stop the corruption"; "Change is good so be careful what you ask for"; and "No juntas las lunes/No Monday night meetings."

Mayor Raul Morial tried to clear standees, but police wanted them to stay, so they asked people to leave a path and assured them they were in accord with fire regulations. The police were visibly irritated when Morial cleared the aisles. At this meeting Morial appointed his son to the police commission, over objections from Hector De La Torre that this was a conflict of interest. Every item of business brought catcalls and booing from the audience, and insistence on decorum by the mayor, who called two recesses when people continued. Several people in Support Your Police Department T-shirts stood up and asked the audience to stop acting out so they could get to the important items on the agenda.

Much verbal abuse directed at the three pro-Robles Latina/o councilors felt racist to me. It came from a few large white men and older white women and men who were getting angry and visibly agitated. When they were yelling at the council, the Latino/a supporters of the police were very quiet. Latina/o members of the pro-police contingent were also taking and reading the flyers being handed out by CBE and students about the power plant. The emotional intensity was coming from older whites and police both in and out of uniform, most of whom were white. I did not see much contact or conversation between white and Latina/o supporters of the police inside the chambers.

Although this broad coalition was united against Robles' corruption and corruption of South Gate's civic life, corruption itself seemed to represent different things to different people in the coalition. The police, most of whom were white, and the city workers, most of whom were Latina/o, had their jobs, budget, and working conditions at stake. For the actively angry white residents, however, Albert Robles seemed to represent their worst nightmare of what a Latina/o government was like. For this group, anti-Robles activism became a target for their anti-immigrant sentiment, which became clear on the eve of the March 2001 power plant referendum.

CHAPTER 6

Finding Traction
at South Gate High School

I remember looking through my mail [back in 1999]
and a lot of the teachers got them. It was my first
year of teaching. I was leafing through the flyers and
there was an organization Communities for a Better
Environment, and I said, this would be great, maybe
I can have them come and do a presentation on air
quality issues and things that I thought were relevant
to the people that live here. I thought this would be
a good organization. Yuki [Kidokoro] came and did a
presentation, and then I told them, you should hook
up with Ms. Martinez and Ms. Ortiz and do presentations. And they did. And that's basically how we
first decided that—we all decided it would be a good
organization to support because we had thought of
supporting—getting involved in other organizations,
but we decided that would be a good organization
to work with. So that's how we first started with
Communities for a Better Environment.

—Veronica Sanchez, South Gate High School teacher

WHEN CBE AND YOUTH-EJ RECONNECTED with a
group of socially engaged teachers at South Gate High School, things
began to change. The teachers brought together activists in search of a
constituency and high school students who were looking for something
they couldn't yet name. Until this point, most of the Youth-EJ activists came from Huntington Park, where CBE had been active longest.
Hoping to engage students from other schools, the students and Angelo
Logan began following up on Yuki Kidokoro's contacts and put flyers
in teachers' mailboxes about bringing environmental justice workshops
to their classrooms. Because she felt that "a lot of kids are not aware

of the political and environmental issues that are relevant to them, and there is a lack of information, communication about what is going on," Leticia Ortiz invited CBE to her classes.

Ortiz was the most senior of the group of social studies teachers who came to work most closely with CBE on the Nueva Azalea plant campaign. When she started teaching, she was one of two women in her department, but with the addition of Veronica Sanchez, Sylvia Lozano (a pseudonym),[1] and Claudia Martinez, Ortiz said, "I really felt like I had important colleagues and people that I could really talk to the most." She jokingly calls them the bloc of four. They regularly work together in planning courses and thinking about their curriculum. "We talk about things we wanted to do in our classroom, or lesson plans or certain perspectives that we wanted to introduce; we're definitely on the same page where we wanted to go with certain things." Her colleague Veronica Sanchez added that "although we don't agree on everything, we are—I guess you could say we are on the left. We have similar goals, and we all want to see our students be active citizens in the community. So we all kind of gravitated toward this project as well because our students did have the opportunity to be leaders." Although they made up the core, other teachers, including science teachers, also invited CBE to make presentations, especially after students began talking about the group and several teachers popped in to see what was happening.

In November and early December 2000, when these presentations were going on, knowledge about the power plant being proposed for South Gate was still spotty. A feature article in late October in a widely read entertainment newspaper was the first many heard about the plant (Catania 2000b). The four social studies teachers used it as classroom reading, as part of their unit on industrialization, for understanding the arguments on both sides and the nature of the debate, and for encouraging students to develop their own opinions.

Because he was off track at the time, Milton Hernandez was able to participate in all the classroom presentations, which was a pretty grueling schedule. "Every single period we had a workshop to do. One day it was one teacher and another day it was another teacher. All their classes. It was tiring too because I was supposed to be here at 6:50 in the morning because first period started—back then it started at 7:30."

My mental image of a workshop as a combination of informative talk with a question-and-answer session did not map onto what

Youth-EJ members thought a workshop should look like. They thought the most effective approach would be a workshop run by students, for students, that had lots of room for the class to participate. They didn't want South Gate students to be talked at, either by adults or by Youth-EJ members. Milton explained: "We said we want to have a presentation on what we are doing, and we need for it to be proactive, and we need for it to be interesting for youth and for everybody else. But in order to be interesting, you have got to be interactive with the audience. And so we met several days for preparing and organizing this presentation and workshop."

The key concept they wanted to explain was environmental racism and the need for environmental justice. To do that, they focused on the toxic environmental situation facing residents in Southeast Los Angeles County. They also believed that their presentation needed to go beyond what is and allow people to see what could be. So Youth-EJ members wrote a dramatic skit. Milton explained:

> The skit showed how if the community organizes and unites, they could change their situations, they could change the community. I was representing a community member and Angelo [Logan] was Sunlaw Corporation, and he had a tie with money signs on it. Whoever was the third person was CEC, and then we had some people made of cardboard, and they were the council members because back then the council members were saying they were neutral, they did not have an opinion on the power plant, and they were not saying anything or hearing anything, and not seeing anything, basically the three monkeys.
>
> We also gave out cards for people to be a character in the skit. One of them was Joe Schmo; they were my friends. There were a few people who had that card, just to show how one community member organized and so he got a few people. And then the other people were Tia Canuta. We made up funny names just to get people's attention. The skit went like this. You saw Angelo driving down the street and saying this looks like a good place to build a power plant. He went to the person representing CEC and said I want to submit an application and I want to build a power plant. So CEC went you have to fill out this application and you got to do all the process, and you are going to be set. And he went to the council members saying I'm going to build a power plant here so

I'm sure you are going to support me. And the council members did not say anything or do anything.

After that, I came into the picture with a flyer saying, there is a town hall meeting; you should go. And then Sunlaw is talking, and I was trying to ask questions and they were ignoring me. And so I would like say, hey, they are not listening to me, why? I should go tell all my friends, and so that is when I called Joe Schmo, and then we would chant. I would say what is the solution? And then the people who had Joe Schmo [cards] would say, no more pollution. We were in the meeting according to the skit, and no one was paying attention to me. And I was like, Joe Schmo, do you think that is right, do you think that is right to ignore people in the community, so that is when I called Tia Canutas, and all the class said the chant with me—to show people if the community unites we can be powerful and change the situation, to demonstrate what could happen with the power plant.

After the skit, they discussed the concept of environmental justice and how it related to the power plant. They spoke of the concentrations of industrial pollutants in the air of Southeast Los Angeles and other places where communities of color were concentrated. "We were talking about cases that have happened, about elementary schools open, but they're on toxic landfills or next to the toxic facility, and people reacted to that." They spoke about the power plant, circulated Sunlaw's information and their own, and passed around flyers announcing a big December community meeting to be held in the school cafeteria.

The South Gate students who were on track, or in school during the campaign against the plant, were the ones who heard most of these presentations. Because school tracks are also based on perceived academic ability, they also segregate students academically. The college-prep track at South Gate High, including students whom teachers described as "the alternative kids," were on track, in school, in the fall of 2000, and the most active participation came from this group.

In addition to these classroom presentations, Milton also did presentations for Project Cool, a rap group of young men of color who were not on the college track. Organized by a Human Services counselor, their meetings were regularly held in South Gate High School (as well as some other Southeast Los Angeles schools). Project Cool dealt with health and social issues, like responsibility in sex, personal relationships, and community life. In this group Milton saw his main point as convincing students that they too were members of the community, and that being socially engaged with community issues was also a way of exercising responsibility. This group of students feared being targeted by the police if they were to get involved in community protests, so Milton stressed that they had a right to be there. Many Project Cool members participated in later events around the campaign.

TEACHERS AND TEACHING

Although high school students became the public face of the community movement that ultimately developed in South Gate, that movement's roots lay in a more complicated local landscape centered in South Gate schools. It included teachers and a supportive principal, as well as parents who were deeply concerned and involved with their children's education. By all accounts, from the time that the PTA switched to Spanish in 1990, schools and their quality and accessibility engaged widespread parent participation in South Gate's PTA. In arguing that the power plant was not an issue that galvanized the South Gate community, Hector De La Torre contrasted low turnouts at CEC meetings with huge turnouts, sometimes of a thousand people, at meetings concerned with school issues. These meetings included those of Padres Unidos, a parent group formed in the nineties to combat overcrowding in South Gate schools, especially in South Gate Middle School, by getting more schools built. Its efforts succeeded in getting funding for five new schools in South Gate (Quinones 2007, 102).

Like many of the Los Angeles high schools that are in working-class and minority neighborhoods, South Gate High School is severely overcrowded. Unlike most of those schools, South Gate High seems to do an extraordinary job placing its students in top colleges and universities. My sense of its success was confirmed when three students in my introductory anthropology course told me they were among twenty-six from South Gate who had been accepted to that year's freshman class at UCLA, and that they thought about the same number had been accepted at UC Berkeley.

South Gate High was also blessed with a cadre of idealistic and socially engaged teachers, many of whom were children of immigrants and the first of their families to attend college, and with a principal who encouraged their educational initiatives and welcomed community participation. The environmental justice workshops would not have happened without their active support. Teachers brought the power plant debate into their classrooms, and they felt supported by their principal in their varied educational efforts on the issue. Some teachers were opposed to the plant and others supported it, but they agreed that the best pedagogy was one that engaged students with issues that affected their lives.

South Gate's activist teachers were beneficiaries of the social movements in the late 1960s and 1970s that opened up higher education in California to students of color. Those movements opened the University of California and other universities to working-class students of color, and created new programs and courses, such as Chicana/o studies and women's studies, that put these students' priorities and experiences at the center of analysis. South Gate's activist teachers were part of a wider college cohort out of which had also come a goodly share of California's Latina/o politicians, such as Hector De La Torre and Marco Firebaugh, the district's state assemblyman, as well as teachers. Veronica Sanchez went to the University of California at Berkeley, and Leticia Ortiz attended UC Santa Cruz. The teachers in the cohort identify with their students and their students' families: they too are for the most part children of immigrants, and perhaps the first generation in their family to attend college.

South Gate's activist teachers share a sense of teaching as giving back to their own Southeast Los Angeles Latina/o community. Social studies teacher Emilio Macias (a pseudonym), although he is older than this group, could well have spoken for them with respect to local roots. As he explained to Sylvia Zamora, a South Gate High School graduate who interviewed him for a study she conducted while at Smith College, "Well, I grew up in the City of Vernon, Lynwood and South Gate. I come from a family of twelve, three died so I'm the tenth one. I have five kids and I've lived in the City of South Gate since 1973. I left for one year to move to Hawthorne and I came back in 83 and I've been here since 83. I've been teaching since 88, I graduated from SGHS in 1978 and this is my community."[2]

Others, like Leticia Ortiz, feel that they have a responsibility to their communities: "I also feel like it is my responsibility because in these kids I see myself, and when I was in high school I connected to a lot of my teachers. I feel like I needed to come back and do something.

But it wasn't just South Gate. I would have come back anywhere in LA and worked."

Southeast Los Angeles also continues to be home for many of the school's teachers and for their families. Sylvia Lozano attended Roosevelt High School, where Mexican American students began the Chicana/o movement thirty years earlier. She lives in Boyle Heights, "which is right across the other side of the city of Vernon. It's part of the community to me regardless of whether it's the community I grew up in or not. To me it's the same so I want to help the kids to know what's going on in their community, to do something about it. That's why I became a teacher."

Veronica Sanchez lives in Cudahy, "right next door to Southgate. I don't know why they let people live there because there's factories. I live inside a factory practically [but] it was just really convenient, because I only have a five-minute commute and in ten minutes I drop off my kids; one is in school and one is in daycare, and then I'm here in ten minutes; that's one of the things I like about it, but I don't like the air."

Leticia Ortiz's family moved from South Central Los Angeles to Compton and then, when she was in fourth grade, to South Gate in the late 1970s. Her parents live in South Gate and are retired. They care for her daughter—their first grandchild—while she works. Her sister teaches in the South Gate adult school. Ortiz recalls,

> I grew up in South Gate. I went to South Gate High School, class of '86. I went to South Gate Middle School. I was always one of those people I just didn't ever really quite fit. I didn't want to fit. So I went away to [the University of California at] Santa Cruz. My parents always wanted us to have an education. My dad had very little education but he's really an intelligent man and very proud and has a lot of good values. They have two sons and four daughters. I'm the middle. They always encouraged the girls and boys to go to school. My dad has lived here since the '50s. He was on the bracero program.

This cohort of teachers grew up in the era of plant closures and deindustrialization. They have seen the gradual shift from white-only political rule in Southeast Los Angeles towns to the emergence of Latino/a political officials, largely of their own age cohort, and in some cases, from among their friends. This experience has shaped their perspectives, but they are also aware that South Gate is a nicer city, an upwardly mobile step, for many of the families who live there.

It is important to recognize that South Gate High's teachers were not of one mind on whether the power plant was a good or a bad thing for South Gate. Sylvia Lozano, who teaches world history and economics, opposed the plant on health grounds, also the main reason given by other teachers who opposed the plant. "The day they [CBE] presented they asked if we have or know somebody who has asthma, and that's when I started to pay more attention. I realized how many kids had other problems too, and every year since then I've been noticing still that it's a lot. To me it was a good reason to get involved." Since the power plant had become part of her unit on the Industrial Revolution, she connected this plant to the larger picture of industrial pollution, and South Gate's industry to the poor state of respiratory health in the area.

Social studies teacher Emilio Macias has been paying attention to South Gate politics for a long time, but he did not see the power plant as being clearly good or bad. Although he opposed it, he wasn't sure later that he had done the right thing. He was especially frustrated at the lack of solid information on which to base an opinion. The vice principal told him that

> he has [a power plant] real close to his house; he says, you guys were stupid fighting it. He says, it doesn't pollute; it pollutes less than most of the places we have here. In actuality you guys would have been better off if you had been able to work, that money would be set aside for jobs and then money would be given to the schools. So you fought for the wrong reasons. I said, I don't know enough. But I was suspicious about them sending all kinds of information. Maybe it's true. Maybe if they had been willing to work with the community and the community had said well we want jobs for the people, we want to make sure that we control what happens, we want to be able to get the money set for scholarships and nothing else, then maybe it could have been. I think if the people had been honest and approached the community without using so much propaganda.
>
> I got pissed off when they sent that candle. The candle really bothered me a lot. If they hadn't sent the candle I think I would

have said well you know, maybe it's okay. Because Henry Gonzalez was in favor of it. Martha Escutia, regardless of her husband being able to get a job with them or not, I respect Martha's opinion; I think Martha is an honest person, she's always been honest with us. I said so maybe it would benefit, because Martha wouldn't want to screw up her own community.

Biology teacher Carmen Avalos, who was teaching environmental science, supported building the plant. Her decision also came to be linked to her engagement with South Gate electoral politics:

Before I started to become a candidate, we got beautiful, beautiful literature. As a matter of fact the building looked so damn nice, I wanted it built the next day. They had a beautiful design, which I think would have been aesthetically pleasing to the area. I think they had wanted to make major improvements in that area which would have been great. Speaking as a mother, we could have actually had life in our park where my kids could play. But it was very interesting to see how as the progression of the campaign moved forward, how views went from yes, we want it, it's going to be fiscally good for our city, to no, we don't want it, it's going to be harmful and detrimental for health reasons. One of the things they were quoting during the campaign was cancer rates, asthma rates. Anyone who understands environment knows that our diesel trucks [that] come off our freeway were a larger polluter than the power plant.

In trying to explain it to her class, Avalos likened the plant's SCONOx emission control technology to the fastest running computer—both were the best there is at the moment, but with more research there will be better computers and cleaner power plants.

ENGAGED PEDAGOGY

Regardless of their views on the plant, Avalos, Macias, and the four social studies teachers agreed that the most important part of their teaching mission was to give students the skills and encouragement to be informed and involved, because they believed that the best education is a socially engaged one and that people need to be involved in the decisions of their community and society. As Sylvia Lozano put it,

"I wanted to help the kids to know what's going on in their community, to do something about it."

Veronica Sanchez explained how studying and engaging the power plant was connected to her curriculum. "The thing about Communities for a Better Environment [is] the issues they bring up—issues of industrialization, globalization, and how companies want to save money, how people are impacted, and how the rights of companies supersede the rights of the environment. What better way to understand historical events like industrialization and imperialism?" The power plant concern was an excellent issue because it encouraged students to do research about their city and to develop their leadership skills. She continued, "Not only do they learn something, but they put it into some kind of practice. Because I majored in Chicano studies, we did paradigms and theory, but we also did these practical components. One of the things I love about CBE and Youth Action is that they do the same thing. It's alive, it's active, and the only reason that we should be looking at history is to understand our present."

Emilio Macias agreed with most of what his younger colleagues said.

> Just living in South Gate, you have to get involved because either you're part of the problem or you're part of the solution, so I'd rather be part of the solution. We hoped to get students involved, and more than anything else I kept emphasizing and telling my students that by getting involved they could make a difference. By not getting involved then they can't complain. We just talked, and we read the articles, and we let the kids decide. I said the bottom line, as the teacher, we're not there to indoctrinate them [but] to expose them and then have them make a decision. Because if you just try to manipulate them, they don't know. They're impressionable so you don't want to tell them this is what's wrong with the world. [You tell them] here are some issues and you determine whether there's a problem or not. They have to make a choice, otherwise you're cheating them out of freedom of choice.... A lot of them were in favor, quite a few of them were skeptical about both sides. They were like I don't know, I think both of them are full of crap. And that's what has happened in most places, you have voter apathy.

Comparing the differences between Sanchez's and Macias's descriptions of engagement suggests there were some real differences among teachers about exactly what engaged pedagogy meant.

Carmen Avalos wound up modeling the kind of engagement she advocated when she decided to run against (among others) Xochilt Ruvalcaba's sister for the position of city clerk in the March 2001 election. Angered by the mudslinging of anti-plant politicians seeking to recall Bill DeWitt from the city council the previous November, she decided to run for city clerk herself. As she explained,

> Our city was going through a recall, and at the time, they were trying to recall the only Caucasian man on the city council, Bill DeWitt. Like the average person who lives in the city, I was too busy trying to take care of my life. I was naive and ignorant about city political turmoil. I had no clue who the mayor was, no idea what a precinct was, no clue that I could get voter information. So, when this teacher stopped me in the hallway and said to me, did you vote? And I said, no not yet, his question to me then was are you going to vote yes or no on the [DeWitt] recall? And I told him, I don't know. Those things that come in the mail look pretty legitimate and what a horrible person to not want people to speak Spanish, especially in a community—and then he had this funny look on his face, and he said, you too? I said what do you mean, me too? You have allowed them to fool you too. And he started telling me what was happening politically in our city. I became infuriated to think that somebody [used] my ignorance to trick me.
>
> Having come to this country as an immigrant undocumented, having struggled for an education, having gone through the bilingual system, or ESL as they called it back then, and knowing what it was like to feel inferior, I felt that way again and I hated that feeling. If they are doing this to me and I have gone to school, what are they doing to our blue-collar workers who have to have two jobs to support their families to be able to provide a roof over their head and do the basic stuff.
>
> It infuriated me that they were using our hardworking community and taking it for fools. That infuriated me so much that by the time I got to my class I told my students I need ten minutes because I'm really upset right now, and they said could you share that with us?

She explained that DeWitt was attacked

not because he was a bad man, not because he did all they were accusing him of, just because he was a Caucasian man in a mostly Latino community. It upset me more so because this is the way that I think many people are perceived. I said I'm so upset because nobody has the right to judge you based on the way you look. They should judge you based on your character and what you have done or not done, on your commitments, things that have some substance.

And so the kids were like, who cares? Look at all the things the white people have done to us. And I said, has this man ever done anything to you and their answer was no. Do you know this man? No. Then how can you judge him based on what kind of person he is? And the kids were like, well, I mean they have it all so we should try to get what we can. And I said, let me ask you this: Why should your parents have health insurance? After all, they are only immigrants and probably undocumented; who the hell cares if they die in the factory? So how would you like someone saying that about your parents? They said that's wrong. I said what you said was wrong; you don't know this man. You're basically saying he's white, he's bad, and you don't even know him. And so the kids realized it was wrong and they said, you are so mad, you should run because we know you really care.

And I said you're right. So that's how my political career started. My students held me to it. The kids said, well, if you do it, we will help you and I said do I have your commitment, and they said yeah, and I said, then we are going to do this, and their next question was do we get extra credit, and I said it's part of your free education. It costs nothing. It's free. They walked and talked and called and cried, and we did it all together.

The four anti-plant social studies colleagues differed among themselves about what exactly was involved in a pedagogy of social engagement, especially in how they approached discussions about the plant in their classrooms. Veronica Sanchez was probably philosophically closer to Carmen Avalos than to Emilio Macias in that she tended toward modeling the kind of engagement she wished for her students. "In my classroom, yes, I encouraged them [students]. I would make the announcements a lot. We would talk about it, talk about the issue of the power plant and get into detail about it, because after CBE left there were a lot of questions. But the students themselves were interested, and we kept talking about it because they kept asking questions. And then I would always remind all my classes there is a meeting today." For Sanchez it was also important to challenge the idea of objectivity as neutrality or as a truth that exists regardless of the perspective of the analyst. Rather, for Sanchez, truth and honesty meant calling it as one sees it. "If anybody pretends that teaching is an objective exercise, they are fooling themselves. I finally realized when I got to college that it's not, that it's subjective. I'm not going to hold it against anybody for disagreeing with me, but the truth is the truth."

Her colleague Leticia Ortiz preferred a pedagogical approach more like that of Macias: give students tools to think with. She emphasized the ways perspective and interests on all sides shaped people's views on the power plant. "I wanted to provide information for the students. I knew what my position was, but I didn't want to have it one sided. As a teacher I mean I obviously have my point of view, but I like to present both sides, at least both sides, and the students make up their own minds in the process. My involvement was that I provided a space for students to find out about what was going on."

Ortiz worried that students might not speak out in class if they feared she did not agree with their point of view. "I don't want to indoctrinate people—that you have to believe what I believe, although I think what I believe is true. I think the process of arriving at your ideas is just as important. It is a real process. I have to really wrestle with things, with ideas; [students have to do the] same things to become independent thinkers. I tried to do a point of view–type thing, you know, get them to question who is saying what, what kind of interests they have at stake to determine where people are coming from. I have never been attracted to sloppy politics."

But Ortiz also recognized what her colleague emphasized—that there was no such thing as objectivity in the sense of being free from position, interest, or values. The best one could do was to be fair and create space for debate and disagreement.

Like Veronica Sanchez, Carmen Avalos believes in calling it like she sees it. "I told my students that, if they were going to rally for or against the power plant, I would support them as their teacher, and they did rally from the South Gate High School to city hall. It was quite a spectacle. And I let my students do it because I wanted to teach them a lesson. I said I would support you if you believe in what you're doing. The students rallied, and they came to city hall that night." About half her class attended. She then told those who attended, "you were used yesterday and you didn't realize it. And once I started to explain the issue and what was really happening, they felt humiliated, embarrassed, and angry. My point was that you need to really understand the issues, but they were being given only one portion of the entire picture."

Teachers on both sides of the issue gave accounts of teachers as well as students who ultimately were persuaded to their position. Leticia Ortiz noted, "I know that my students would make other teachers feel uncomfortable because they would talk about these issues, especially my seniors, in other classes. They would even engage other teachers. One teacher, a math teacher, was for the power plant. He was like we need energy, we need a power plant, and he and a couple of students would get into a debate. They made him feel uncomfortable. I guess he thought about what they said and later on he changed his opinion."

In speaking about Carmen Avalos and her views on the power plant, Veronica Sanchez described how students became confused when teachers whom they respected differed. "During her campaign, [Avalos] became ambiguous on the power plant issue, and it was interesting because she had students who were my students, and they really admired her, and they would even work for her during her campaign. And then they told me, well, she doesn't know. And I'm like, how do you feel about it? And my students were like I don't know either. And you see the power that teachers have on the students."

Sanchez also illustrated the constraining power of consensus in the classroom on those who disagree. When stories about the power plant started appearing in the news,

> We had to talk about it. And the students who were ambiguous or for the power plant were uncomfortable about expressing their ideas. That had never really happened before. I know students are uncomfortable about expressing their ideas because they might feel like they are not valid or not intelligent enough, but they have never been uncomfortable about expressing their ideas because somebody would strongly disagree. So it's wonderful to have them passionate about something so much to the point that some

students even felt uncomfortable. And I told the students, I hope I'm not making you feel uncomfortable. You should know that your ideas are important and if you have a differing opinion, you're welcome to express them.

Although both Avalos and Sanchez reported classroom interactions that seemed to discount the influence that their knowledge and position gave them over students, they were nevertheless grappling with ways to encourage and model the kinds of critical thought, social engagement, and civic responsibility they wanted students to learn. All these teachers experienced a double bind that activist teachers perennially struggle with. Negotiating between modeling the engagement they hope for in students, and teaching students to think for themselves—and finding a reasonable balance—is like steering between a rock and hard place. These teachers are part of the same community as their students, so to be silent about their views or not to participate in a campaign they found important would have sent the wrong message. But because they are in positions of authority, their stand on an issue could put a chill on students who had contrary views. Veronica Sanchez and Carmen Avalos steered closer to putting their own views into the mix and participating in politics themselves, whereas Leticia Ortiz and Emilio Macias seemed to keep their own views in low profile and emphasized training in critical thinking.

What happened when students got different messages from different teachers? I suspect one consequence was that they were less likely to think of the power plant issue as academic. Another was that it caused discomfort. Newly energized students wanted to debate the issue with teachers with whom they disagreed. It also turned out that some parents who felt one way were not altogether happy to find that their kids' teachers felt differently and said so in the classroom. And there were students who felt shut down by other students or by other teachers who did not share their views. Although it is impossible to compare their impacts, it is safe to say that students who had classes with both Sanchez and Avalos had to think pretty hard about the bases for their own positions.

I suspect there is no "right balance" between modeling the engagement one advocates and teaching students to do their own critical thinking. Teachers who nurture activists and model activism have helped some students to find meaning and direction in life, just as teachers who nurture critical thinking regardless of where students take it, while keeping their own conclusions to themselves, have helped others to find their way .

STUDENTS

This campaign resonated with things South Gate students had already been feeling. When Abram Ruiz heard the presentation by CBE in class, he immediately became active in opposing Nueva Azalea "because I wanted to get more involved," even though it was the first time he'd heard of the power plant. Marco Martinez heard about the power plant and about the concept of environmental justice first from his history teacher. When he read some of the literature she distributed, he remembered that he'd seen flyers in the mail about two years earlier about clean electricity. Because he worked after school in the engineering department at city hall, he tried to find information about it there. "I got an engineer's point of view, Technically it should be cleaning the air, but it would be on a very polluted trucking site." After hearing all sides, Marco "was kind of neutral about pollution. But the big question was why here, not Beverly Hills? It's like Southeast LA has lots of pollution, more than other cities. When I figured it out I was devastated, mad." He got involved in the campaign and did some public speaking, "in Spanish for the Spanish-speaking people, [which was] that the power plant shouldn't be built and that there's many schools around the power plant where it's going to be built. If it wasn't for CBE, it would have most likely passed because a lot of people thought that the power plant was going to be a positive thing, and we never thought about the toxins that it was going to give out."

Marco told Jorge Dueñas about the plant "and also about a meeting that was going to be on that night at the cafeteria at the high school, and he told me go check it out." The concept of environmental justice put a name to something Jorge already felt. "I grew up thinking that it was like this all over the world, like train tracks and freeways and buses and trash." As he grew up, he discovered that these things were not evenly distributed. "It's not right, this culture. I thought, when I heard about [the power plant], we are being used like guinea pigs as an experiment. There are so many trucks, airplanes, freeways, and trains that are here in Southeast LA and still they want to put a power plant. And I thought it was totally racism, environmental racism, building a power plant here."

Like Ramos several years earlier, Dueñas was already on a reading quest to understand why things were so unjust and what one could do to change them. He'd read Howard Zinn and a book on anarchism. "My teacher suggested like I should read a book called *Che: The Making of a Legend*. I read the whole thing. It was pretty thick." What stood out for Jorge was that when Che saw people in poverty, "he feels like he has to do something about it. It was a good book." Before he got involved in the power plant, he had been among the demonstrators at the Democratic National Convention held in August 2000 in Los Angeles. Jorge recalled, "It was on Monday I think. I went to see Rage [Against the Machine]. I heard a cop say, 'five minutes to disburse,' and then I started walking. And with all the cops surrounding me, and it was like a trip. I have been in other clubs like poetry club. I draw political images. I do art, music, and writing."

If their teachers were the beneficiaries of the Chicana/o student movement during the late sixties and early seventies, these South Gate High students are successors to the high school students who created that movement. Those earlier high schoolers were also drawn from among the students regarded by their teachers as student leaders and the seventies equivalent of "alternative kids" (Acuña 2000; Bernal 1998; Briegel 1974; Muñoz 1989).

COMMUNITY MEETING AT SOUTH GATE HIGH

Recall that the centerpiece of the organizing plan that CBE's Yuki Kidokoro and Alvaro Huerta developed was a large community meeting in South Gate in early to mid-December—they hoped for about a hundred people—to gauge the state of community sentiment on the plant. The plan was pretty specific. Its goals were to share information about the power plant, to get people from South Gate involved in meetings with the CEC and Sunlaw, to take around petitions, to form a Nueva Azalea campaign committee, and to participate in a city council resolution effort. By the time the meeting took place, on December 13, the city council had already voted to include a referendum about the power plant on the upcoming March 2001 ballot.

The turnout at this meeting exceeded CBE's expectations. Between two hundred and three hundred people, half of them students, showed up. And the sentiment of those attending was overwhelmingly opposed to the plant. Students in the social science and history classes in which

Angelo Logan, Milton Hernandez, and others from CBE had made presentations were the core of the attendees. Many students brought their parents. What is more, the meeting had plenty of drama, and it drew television coverage.

The four social studies teachers encouraged students by offering extra credit for attending the meeting, a decision that was criticized by some. Veronica Sanchez countered that their decision made good pedagogical sense: "This is a history class, this is government, and this is the most perfect government experience. But they tried to use that reward to de-legitimatize the concerns of the students."

All the workshops, role-playing, and skits at the high school had gotten the message about the power plant out to a large number of South Gate students, and through them to their parents and neighbors. The meeting was held at the school cafeteria, which was packed, and those who couldn't get in formed a crowd outside. Angelo Logan thought that more than three hundred would have attended except that a last minute change of venue (from the larger high school auditorium to the smaller cafeteria) probably lost them some folks who couldn't get in.

This meeting marked a turning point in the campaign. Previously CBE's public events, such as speaking at PTA meetings and at CEC hearings, had been small, and the discussion had been limited in scope and time. This meeting was the first time that Youth-EJ was able to present its message in a manner of its own choosing to a specifically South Gate audience of students and adults. Again, in true Youth-EJ style, political theater was part of the political message. While people were having coffee and donuts, and milling around before the meeting began, a South Gate resident, played by Milton Hernandez, ran into the cafeteria, screaming that there was a poison cloud over Tweedy Elementary School. The play and Milton's narration were in Spanish so that the parents would be able to engage fully. Youth-EJ members had written it in English, and Milton translated it into Spanish.

The skit dramatized an incident at Tweedy Elementary School in 1986, when a chlorine cloud released by a ruptured pipeline from the nearby Purex plant caused injuries, forced evacuation of the school, and sent seventy-one people to the hospital (Bansal, Bacon, and Davis 1998, 15). Students playing people with cancer, asthma, and other respiratory diseases portrayed the consequences of environmental pollution. As the skit shifted to the issue of the power plant and its impact on air quality, it asked for what was becoming a Youth-EJ tradition—audience partici-pation. Yuki Kidokoro and Angelo Logan played Sunlaw presenting its proposal to a sympathetic CEC, while a Youth-EJ member got the audience to chant "Si, se puede" loud enough to force the CEC char-acters to back down. Here, as in the classroom skits, a key message was that people could change things they did not like if they acted in concert.

After the skit ended, Alvaro Huerta did a presentation on the environmental impact of the plant and the meaning of environmental justice, before opening the floor for discussion. Logan remembers that halfway through Huerta's presentation, Hector De La Torre walked to the front and tried to talk. He said that Huerta held him off until he finished speaking and opened the mic for discussion, whereupon De La Torre dominated the meeting and spoke for ten minutes.

Hector De La Torre's remarks provided another kind of dramatic focus. The way Robert Cabrales remembered it, "he spoke—he hadn't said yes that he was in favor of the power plant, but it seemed obvious that he was in favor of the power plant, talking about the benefits of the power plant and how there was no such thing as a health impact. Of course, people didn't receive him very positively. A lot of the people were really upset. They started yelling I think obscenities to the council member, and he decided to leave the room."

Youth-EJ members and some of the South Gate High students felt De La Torre was rude in hogging the mic, and that he insulted them by saying they were there only because their teachers made them.

Roy Abadi was also at the meeting, having heard about it independ-ent of the student network. He added his own bit of drama by taking on De La Torre:

Hector De La Torre was there. He grandstanded and he stole the— he was talking to Spanish TV saying that these are only kids. Hector De La Torre tried to highjack the meeting. He's a politician. He took the mike and explained to people why it's not a bad thing, it is a good thing. He was speaking Spanish, and I was listening to the translator. I got up and I said, so why did you hijack our [referendum] and move the vote from November to March, tell me that, and I got up and I told everybody? My neighbor, he likes Hector De La Torre, he said, shhhhh, sit down. And I said, no, you don't understand, I'm doing it on purpose. Then there was another guy asked his wife to translate, and he was telling people how good [the power plant] will be. So I start heckling him too. Are you here on behalf of yourself or somebody else paying you? Who are you working for? So he called me a moron, so I just almost got in a fistfight with him. Sometimes you have to do that. You have to steal people's attention, and usually altercation is what people remember.

Hector De La Torre was apparently the only city official who attended the meeting. It seems that neither Xochilt Ruvalcaba nor Albert Robles, both opponents of the plant and known to CBE organizers, was present.

Hector disputed the CBE account:

> I don't see the patronizing the kids thing. I see that "in favor of the plant" [charge by CBE] is the same thing that they said about me the whole time because I was unwilling to take their position. That's what I went to say to them. Roy Abadi was there and made an ass of himself. What I didn't like about that meeting was that a lot of the people who were there, the adults, were not from South Gate. [They were from] neighboring cities, people who do stuff with CBE—Cudahy, Huntington Park. Another thing that bothered me was that I knew going in that teachers had offered extra credit to students to attend that meeting. I think somebody took a pot shot at the Edison thing. I want people to make decisions based on the facts so their perception was that I was challenging them and advocating the power plant, which was not the case.

Beyond the School

This meeting was also attended by several members of Padres Unidos. They had already begun to look into the power plant issue. One member dated her interest in the issue to attending a CEC hearing at which Sunlaw, when asked why it wanted to locate in South Gate, answered, because there was room. "How can we find property for a power plant, yet not for new schools?" she asked. According to members of Padres Unidos, the power plant became an important concern in the community. Several felt bombarded with information on both sides. Those who attended CEC meetings to hear Sunlaw's presentations thought the company did not present a clear argument, nor did they give Sunlaw's argument much credibility. Padres Unidos members also attended this meeting and city council meetings to learn more. At the cafeteria meeting they learned that the power plant would replace the truck depot. They pointed out that this move would wipe out jobs already held by many South Gate residents in that the trucking depot was South Gate's largest employer. Ultimately, however, they were most worried about the health impacts on their children. They knew about the elementary school in Cudahy that had to be closed because it was built on a toxic dump and about the chlorine gas at South Gate's Tweedy Elementary School. Padres Unidos members felt that the community gave most credence to information that came from someone they knew and trusted. So they became active in spreading the word, person to person, among family and neighbors. Several held house meetings for neighbors and family, but mostly they saw themselves as getting the word out to overlapping personal networks (Barraza, Gutierrez, and Martinez 2003).

The sentiment in the cafeteria during the meeting ran strongly against the plant. Attendees felt the council wasn't looking out for the community. Angelo Logan felt that Hector De La Torre's comments encouraged many of the South Gate students who attended to become more actively involved.

Jorge Dueñas was one of them. This meeting was Jorge's first contact with CBE and Youth-EJ, and he liked what he saw. "They did a role play, and they talked about it. Most of the people were against the power plant, and I was too, of course. After they did their thing, they gave out papers to people who were interested in like creating a club in school and helping in the campaign, and so I signed up, and that is how I got involved."

Marco Martinez knew many of the families at the meeting. "It was a great experience. And my mom, she was against it." He was energized. "I convinced my dad, and he went against it. So pretty soon, the neighbors, I also convinced them. I convinced a lot of people to vote against it. At first [my friends] were skeptical about it, and when I showed them the papers and about the pollution, then they went against it too. I also got teachers involved against the power plant. It was a great experience. It helped me—now I can actually give public speeches."

At some point, the meeting moved from discussion to action. Here, CBE's plan had four options for people who wanted to participate:

attend meetings with CEC and Sunlaw, work on a petition drive, join a community anti-plant committee, and work on urging the city council to pass an anti-plant resolution. CBE seems not to have known about the city council's decision to put a referendum on the power plant to the voters in March. At the meeting, Huerta proposed a follow-up meeting and asked people to sign up if they wanted to be involved in planning it. People signed cards volunteering to help, and there was sentiment for some kind of march to make local opposition to the power plant public and visible. This meeting showed CBE that there was strong interest in and substantial opposition in the city of South Gate to Sunlaw's proposed power plant.

All that time-consuming, face-to-face organizing was beginning to bear fruit. In addition to finding public support, activists learned more specific things they needed to know for organizing an effective campaign. First, they learned that South Gate High School was an important institution in the city, and that it was likely to be the organizing center of community support. Many of its teachers were local; its principal supported socially engaged pedagogy; parents took a great interest in the school and the education of their children; and there was a core of activist history and social studies teachers who helped bring students together. Second, they discovered that Youth-EJ's classroom presentations and CBE's meeting at the school had created a strong buzz beyond South Gate High, to the parents, and perhaps beyond. It showed that face-to-face organizing around the issue of the plant could be self-reinforcing. Third, they learned that they could attract media attention to South Gate. The fourth thing was something that CBE and the students took for granted, and hence did not mention, namely, that those most interested and engaged were the children of immigrant parents—among the teachers as well as the students. The next challenge was to help build leadership or ownership of the campaign within South Gate, starting at the high school.

Like most people in South Gate, CBE organizers had not paid much attention to the November recall and replacement of Bill DeWitt, and they were beginning to become wary of Albert Robles. They were also about to get their first lesson in South Gate politics.

CHAPTER 7

Going Public

ENVIRONMENTAL JUSTICE ACTIVISTS were about to encounter one of the wild cards that are facts of life for popular social movements, namely, that the playing field of grassroots politics is shaped by political forces that have little to do with their concerns. Between December and January, two separate fights were developing among local constituencies. The first battle pitted Albert Robles against the coalition of his enemies (which included Sunlaw). The other battle was that of environmental justice activists against Sunlaw. By January 2001, these battles began to commingle.

ROBLES AND MEASURE A

Unbeknown to the students, there had been a great deal going on behind city hall's closed doors since the November election when Bill DeWitt was recalled and replaced by a councilor regarded as a Robles loyalist. The center of attention seemed to be the referendum on the power plant, which was to appear on the ballot for the March 6, 2001, election. Measure A, as it was called, would ask voters to say yes or no to whether they wanted a power plant in South Gate.

The state of California requires that all ballot measures have written arguments, one pro and one con, published in the official voter information booklet that is mailed to all registered voters before each election. But when the booklet for the March election was mailed to voters, surprised readers discovered that there was only one argument about Measure A. Martha Andrade showed me her ballot booklet. The page labeled "Arguments in favor or Measure A," read "none filed." "How stupid is that? They [Sunlaw and supporters] didn't even file any kind of an argument for themselves to get their measure passed." How did this happen? Did Sunlaw and its supporters forget, or was there chicanery to keep a pro–Measure A argument from appearing in the voter information booklet? Almost all signs point to the latter.

According to a lawsuit filed by supporters of Measure A, they and the full council attended a December 7 city council meeting at which there was no talk of a schedule for submitting ballot arguments. They were led to believe a date would not be set until after the holiday recess, which ended January 9 with the first city council meeting of 2001.

The lawsuit charged that between December 8 and December 22, several city council meetings were held without public notice, at times when opponents of the plant knew some council members were out of town and when city hall was officially closed, and that this was done deliberately to exclude councilors not in the anti-plant bloc, and to set the timetable for submission of ballot arguments secretly so as to exclude arguments in favor of Measure A (Superior Court 2001). On December 8, the city council, which included newly elected anti-plant council member Maria Benavides, held a special meeting at which it selected a new mayor, Raul Morial, and vice mayor, Xochilt Ruvalcaba. The council held more special meetings on December 14, 18, and 22, during which it discussed the language of Measure A and who would file arguments, and it set deadlines for submission of ballot arguments. At the December 14 special meeting, there was enough of a "hubbub," as the lawsuit put it, to end the meeting for lack of a quorum and to prevent council action on anything related to Measure A.

Roy Abadi was one of the individuals named in the lawsuit. He agreed that all was not on the up and up with the new city council majority of Morial, Ruvalcaba, and Benavides: "Usually council meetings are Tuesday, and they had council meetings on Friday morning when city hall was closed to the public. Even Gonzalez and De La Torre, so they claim, they did not know when there were council meeting votes."

The Friday meeting Abadi referred to was held on December 22 at 10:00 a.m., in council chambers in city hall—a time when the building is closed and locked. The following is an account of what happened, from the court papers filed by those who had been seeking to file an argument in favor of Measure A:

> Upon arrival at 9:50 a.m. on December 22, 2000, City Manager [Andrew] Pasmant and Councilman Gonzalez noticed people leaving City Hall and, themselves, discovered it to be locked up and closed. Pasmant attempted to open the doors to City Hall, but

was unable to open the main front door. City Manager Pasmant entered through a security door and was then able to open two side doors to City Hall. However, he did not have the appropriate allen wrench the custodian uses to open and unlock the front main entrance. Since a custodian was not in the building and no one had given him notice to appear that day, the door remained locked during the entire meeting. Attempts to prop the door open failed repeatedly throughout the day. (Superior Court 2001, 5)

How did the city manager and city councilor Henry Gonzalez happen by city hall when they knew the offices were closed? It turns out that Measure A was only the tip of the iceberg. When officials of the SEIU local representing South Gate municipal employees complained about Albert Robles' mistreatment of city officials not protected by the union (chap. 5), they were probably referring to the treatment of city manager Andrew Pasmant. Pasmant, who had worked for the city some twenty-two years, had given a deposition in a 1997 city employees' lawsuit attesting to Robles' abusive and harassing behavior toward employees. A week after Morial, Ruvalcaba, and Benavides began to work together in 2000, at the same December 14 special city council meeting held to discuss Measure A, there appeared an agenda item for closed session consideration, "Consider the appointment, employment, evaluation of performance or dismissal of a public employee." The positions of city attorney and city manager were listed. Mayor Morial told city manager Pasmant he would be put on paid administrative leave for wrongdoings, which then and subsequently were not specified. The city attorney did not appear and was fired in his absence. A new city attorney, John Raynor, who was also said to be Albert Robles' personal attorney, was hired. Pasmant argued that the meeting had no status because he never received any complaints or charges and because two councilors were absent. After Pasmant's attorneys intervened, the meeting was rescheduled for December 18. At that meeting, Hector De La Torre refused to recognize Raynor as the city attorney, and he and Gonzalez left.

Back to the Friday morning meeting of December 22. Its agenda contained another closed session attempt to get rid of Pasmant and hire Raynor. Andrew Pasmant fought back. He challenged the city's case, arguing that council members Morial, Benavides, and Ruvalcaba acted illegally and in concert with Albert Robles and that they opposed him because he "stood staunchly between the overreaching interest of the bare majority of the City Council and the City Treasurer." Pasmant claimed that their political behavior was all about taking control of South Gate's growing municipal budget.

Pasmant and Gonzalez went to the December 22 meeting loaded for bear. Hector De La Torre was out of town and unable to attend, but Gonzalez conveyed both of their objections to the meeting going forward. He was outvoted.

If they had keys to city hall, why were Pasmant and Gonzalez trying to unlock the front door and to prop open other doors? It turns out that it was because they had already generated significant community opposition to Robles and his supporters on the council. Pasmant's attorneys and "a large group of the assembled public" managed to attend the meeting, and they were angry enough that they "demanded a citizen's arrest of the council members who insisted on proceeding forward with the illegal meeting" (Superior Court 2001, Exhibit D).

This meeting seems to have been the first event in the generation of what grew into a large public movement to oust Albert Robles (discussed in chap. 5). At this point, it was announced that a formal charge was being filed against Maria Benavides for not being a South Gate resident and for falsifying her election materials. During the public comment period there was "a long line of citizens wishing to speak," only a minority of whom had the chance before Mayor Morial ended the meeting.

There are also indications that the anti-Robles forces, most probably with leadership from state legislators and Police Officers Association lawyers, had begun to set in motion a number of city and state investigations into Robles' behavior as a public official. Andrew Pasmant was cooperating with this effort, and Robles was reputed to have been trying without success to get information from Pasmant about these investigations (Superior Court 2001, 14).

Roy Abadi got caught up in some of the machinations around Measure A because he did not have high expectations of the anti-plant councilors and worried about the way they would present Measure A to voters. He kept after the council and city clerk Nina Bañuelos to make sure there would be a clear argument against the measure:

I put a [written] request with the city clerk to write an argument. Monday after the New Years vacation, I'm calling the city clerk, and I asked her, what is up with my argument because I want to submit it. She said no, don't submit it because then they will see what you are writing and they will answer. Just have the letter [the argument to submit for the voter information booklet]. She tells me the mayor decided to write an argument. I remember less than a month before, the mayor [Morial] asked the city attorney to reserve the right to write an argument against the power plant and to write an argument for the power plant. This is a joke. The city attorney tells him, you cannot do that, you can write either/or. So the mayor, tells him, so I'm just going to write an argument against the power plant.

Abadi felt he was instrumental in pushing to get an informed argument against the power plant into the ballot booklet, although he didn't bargain for the way it was done:

Every council meeting I was mentioning the power plant—and you know what, he [Robles] looked at me one day; we went to his office, and he said you know what, I like you because you represent thousands of people. Then he tells me, today at 5:30 is the deadline to file the arguments, and what is going to happen will be the mayor requested to write an argument. What you can do, even though you wrote one, you can bring it over to the mayor, and he will combine what you wrote. So I took an argument that I wrote, and also my neighbor wrote one too, and I took those two copies, and I gave it to the city attorney. I talked to Robles and Robles said, come over at 5:30, if you want to sign it. So I gave them everything and I came at 5:00. They got a fax from a special service that rewrote the whole thing and Robles added more stuff, and that's a problem. He added stuff that shouldn't have been there; would you sign this? I said, sure I would. I read the argument, and it was a little bit tougher than what I wrote. So the mayor signed it, I signed it, and Robles said, I have a permission to sign it for Ruvalcaba [and Benavides], and I looked at him and I tell him, I said—no, what about Ruvalcaba going to read this? He said, you know I can sign it for them, and but that's between me and you. And he signed for himself, but somehow it did not have his signature on it.

Although it made him uneasy at the time, Abadi really did not want to know too much about what was going on. But he soon learned just how amiss things were when he was named as a defendant in the lawsuit brought by supporters of Measure A, arguing that city clerk Nina Bañuelos and council members Ruvalcaba, Morial, and Benavides had prevented those in favor of the plant from submitting their argument for the ballot. Robles was not named.

It looked as though Sunlaw and its supporters were not stupid, as it had appeared to voters like Martha Andrade, but rather, as their lawsuit charged, "the actions taken by City officials evidence a manipulative process in which the City Council rushed the measure through the process and cleverly arranged for deadlines to be set in a manner that prevented the proponents of Measure A from having their position heard."

SUNLAW'S CAMPAIGN

If the lopsided voter information booklet favored anti-plant forces, the rest of the playing field seemed nevertheless to favor Sunlaw, with one big exception. Sunlaw's Robert Danziger had made a public promise that Sunlaw would leave South Gate if people did not want the plant. It is unclear when that promise was first made. Danziger's statement "If the city of South Gate does not want us there, we will leave. I guarantee it" was first quoted in the *Los Angeles Times* on January 10, 2001, after the bruising battle over Measure A and before the students marched to the city council meeting. Another Sunlaw executive gave almost the same statement to the press again on January 25 (Martin 2001b, 2001c). Was this the move of a good corporate citizen or was it a sign of confidence in the persuasive power of their campaign and the strength of their endorsements?

That campaign was intensive and expensive, perhaps made more so as a result of Robles' machinations. It was directed toward registered voters and included a video as well as many, many mailers. Sunlaw-supported Friends of Measure A spent well over $300,000 on full-color mailings, videos, canvassers, as well as advertising on Spanish-language television (Quinones 2001, 23–24; Catania 2001).[1]

State legislators also appealed to Los Angeles County and state officials to oversee the election and to block the city clerk, whom they saw as a Robles ally, from conducting it. They held her partly responsible for excluding the pro–Measure A argument. Groups working to get rid of Albert Robles began to mobilize a slate of candidates who were in favor of the plant to run against Robles' candidates. The statewide Latino Political Action Committee contributed $18,000 to the campaign funds of several of them. Members of Senator Escutia's and Assemblyman Firebaugh's staff took vacation time to campaign for them. City employee union members campaigned as well. Two South Gate pastors who had not been active in politics became involved on behalf of Robles' opponents and against Robles' corruption.

Sunlaw's bilingual mailers portrayed Sunlaw as a good corporate citizen and emphasized the benefits that the Nueva Azalea plant would bring to South Gate—cheap electricity, four hundred union construction jobs, and somewhere between $3 million and $8 million in revenue—the numbers rose as the election neared. Sunlaw's mailer suggests the latter number would be equivalent to 30 percent of the city budget.[2]

One mailer urging a yes vote on Measure A warned that "big out-of-state polluters and their political operatives" were trying to block the plant's new technology with disreputable tactics and urged anyone who experienced such tactics to report them to the appropriate state agency. Several pro-plant, anti-Robles people told me that CBE was working for or paid off by big power producers. Rhonda Nitschky remembered that one of Sunlaw's mailers said that "somebody is trying to scare you. And on the last page it alleged that it was big out-of-state power producers who didn't want to see this new environmentally friendly technology used on a power plant because it would force them to have to spend the money to upgrade their facilities."

Several mailers took a "keep the lights on" theme. One from Theresa Gonzalez, who identified herself as a South Gate grandmother and former PTA president, said that the plant would be good for working families and stressed cheap electricity. This same cheap electricity, "keep the lights on" theme was struck in another mailer. It had a map showing municipal power plants in affluent cities with the caption "Why them and not us?" It asked why rich cities had their own utilities and quoted the late Miguel Contreras, head of the Los Angeles County Federation of Labor, as saying, "Every community deserves to be energy independent. Affluent areas have always taken care of their own electricity needs." However, the Nueva Azalea plant was to be privately owned. According to *La Opinion*, Sunlaw said that it could not initially guarantee below-market-rate electricity because, under deregulation, Sunlaw would have to sell on the open market. In its promotional video, Sunlaw said it supported pending legislation (by state senator Martha Escutia) that would keep a percentage of the energy produced by power plants in the community where it was produced. Later in the campaign, it promised to sell power to residents at lower than market rates by the summer of 2003 (Martin 2001b).[3]

Sunlaw's fifteen-minute video "The Energy Puzzle: One Man's Solution" (2001), distributed to South Gate residents, made a personal case for the power plant. The problem it presents is that deregulation isn't working as it should. The huge price jumps consumers experience are caused by a shortage of plants, which in turn is because of NIMBYism, which rests on the fact that these plants pollute. "Enter Bob Danziger," an "unconventional energy producer." We learn that Danziger was student body president of Fairfax High in Los Angeles around 1970, when it was newly integrated. There is footage of civil rights and anti–Vietnam War demonstrations, of Richard Nixon, and of Danziger describing himself as aligned with the progressive forces of the time. "I marched with Cesar Chavez," he tells us, and was inspired to believe that people could change things. We learn he injured his back in a roofing accident and became a blues, then funk and jazz, musician; we see him in a home music studio. The voiceover tells us that Danziger is a self-made man. He never went to college, but did go to an unaccredited law school and published two "important and revealing" papers on energy that landed him a job at Jet Propulsion Laboratory in Pasadena, and somehow to the invention of SCONOx.

The video shifts to SCONOx and its benefits. The Coalition for Clean Air's Tim Carmichael explains that the technology eliminates the need for dangerous ammonia; we see the Vernon plant and AQMD and EPA's support for it, and there's an award presentation in 1996. More to the point, the video continues, SCONOx would not cost much to install in existing dirty plants—of which there are a dozen in the Los Angeles basin alone—only about ten cents for each one hundred dollars of a monthly utility bill. But big energy companies are greedy and don't want to be forced to clean up their plants. And they've bought the politicians. Danziger quotes a legislator who told him, "Southern California Edison is a thousand lunches ahead of you."

The scene shifts to show Danziger's support for Vernon Elementary School: a school lunch program for farmworkers' children, free musical instruments, and field trips—all accompanied by glowing testimonials from school personnel. Danziger is presented as a businessman who takes community responsibility seriously.

The closing segment focuses on the plant's cleanliness and ends with a direct appeal from Danziger: "We are the people who are trying to do the right thing, who have invented the technology and proven that it works and brought the money to the table. And lived in the community. We are they, and we are reaching out to the community now. And we need the community to reach back to us."

I wish I knew how this video came about and more about how it played in South Gate. I heard about it and got a copy from anti-plant people, who, not surprisingly, panned it. To me, the celebration of Bob Danziger's genius and caring seemed over the top and undercut the intended message of a clean, safe plant and Sunlaw as a public-spirited corporation. Video aside, Sunlaw's public relations campaign did not seem to have its intended effect in that people with a variety of positions on the plant reported that mailers and gimmicks roused their suspicions more than a positive interest. Still, the overall effect of the publicity was to bring the power plant issue into all of South Gate's homes.

SOUTH GATE STUDENTS

Neither CBE nor the Youth-EJ students knew about the Measure A ballot controversy, or even about Sunlaw's public relations blitz, when they reconvened after the holidays. They looked at the sign-up sheet from the December meeting at South Gate High cafeteria and discovered that over a hundred South Gate High students had signed up to attend a follow-up meeting to decide the campaign's next steps. In the days after the meeting, teachers who had sponsored CBE presentations in their classrooms underscored the point by calling CBE to say that their students wanted to do something. At this point, Youth-EJ decided to focus all its organizing effort on South Gate High. Its members went back to the classrooms where they had given presentations. Now they wanted to help start a South Gate environmental justice club like the one that had been in existence since 1997 at Huntington Park.

CBE and Youth-EJ also decided to organize another big meeting about what to do next. They made posters for that meeting, which was to be held after school at South Gate High. CBE brought pizza and soda, figuring that there'd be about twenty students, but the classroom where it was held overflowed, and, Angelo Logan remembered, "the pizza went immediately." Students brainstormed and decided to take their case to city hall and demand that the city council take a stand against the plant. Youth-EJ members thought there might have been about a hundred students at this and a follow-up meeting to plan the march from South Gate High School to city hall, where they would make their case at a council meeting. They set the date for January 23, a Tuesday and the evening of the regular city council meeting. Milton Hernandez pointed out that this whole part of the organizing effort "was really well organized by youth, 90 percent with only a little help by CBE."

Alicia Gonzalez explained that they wanted South Gate students to plan and lead the march because they were also trying to educate and train potential activists, who could form their own environmental justice club. She described how Youth-EJ members set up training sessions at a second meeting for South Gate students to learn the skills they needed in order to take leadership of the march. "We have been through trainings, and we have done trainings. Everyone in Youth-EJ did trainings based on whatever you liked to do or have done. I have always done public speaking and media workshops, so we did the first training on public speaking and media." Another Youth-EJ member and Angelo Logan taught students to make art and the giant puppets on sticks that attracted a lot of media attention. Someone else led a workshop on making up chants. Jairus Ramos and Jackie Amparo led a security workshop that planned the route and figured out people and traffic control. In the media workshop, Jorge Dueñas, one of the new South Gate students in that group, drew a flyer for the march: "7 Good Reasons to March against the Power Plant/Siete Razones Buenas para Marchar contra la Plant Electrica" (Dueñas 2001). And CBE added its bright yellow, red, and black poster of a skull, captioned "Would you let your child play near a power plant?"

Part of the reason the second training meeting was so well attended was that students who already knew something about the plant brought friends, some of whom had not yet heard about it. South Gate student Norma Velasco (a pseudonym) was among those who came along because she got caught up in the general excitement. "I ran into my friend one day and she is like are you here for the protest? and I'm like what protest? There was a meeting going on, and I went along with her and found out. Actually I was confused in the meeting until I started reading newspaper articles and flyers they were passing out and fact sheets about all the pollution it would bring. I was sitting in the back right there with the media [committee]."

Norma had ended up in Alicia's public speaking workshop. So did Abram Ruiz, another South Gate first-timer. In all, there were about fifteen students in that workshop. Alicia explained that they taught them the

> do's and don'ts of public speaking, and showed them video exam-
> ples of the good and bad speeches. And then we made them write
> their own speech, and practice it with each other. We told them
> how to deal with the reporters and tips on how to always repeat
> your message, like conservation, solar energy, like no more polluting
> in communities that are already overpolluted—and always have the
> message in your head so they don't mess you up.
>
> I remember we had a little exercise with the message. Me and
> [another Youth-EJ member] would do a little skit where I would be
> the reporter and I would try to get her off and she would always
> try to bring it back to the message.

Abram remembered that part, "what to say and what not to say, because they can be kind of tricky if they get you to say something you don't want to. [So it would] look like we were wrong for going against the power plant in the middle of a power crisis and we are dumb for doing it."

Students also wrote their own speeches, which were videotaped and discussed. "The last thing we did," Alicia explained, "we had a camera, and people would volunteer [to give their speech], and I would be the reporter and try to get them off message. They did a pretty good job. And then we would play it back, and we could say what could have been done better? After that, people signed up to go to [one of the subgroups]—the message committee, the media committee, and the committee that was going to speak at the meeting."

By the end of the workshop, Abram said, "we all knew what to say, we practiced and went over all the facts and [learned to] just stick to the point. We wore badges that said media and that way we attract the media, but it didn't work."

Jairus Ramos and Jackie Amparo led the security workshop. Jackie had joined Youth-EJ after the summer training, and this was her first major time commitment to activism. At this workshop, Jairus said, they planned "the logistics of the route, and what we would need because it was going to be at nighttime, and if approached by the police, how to handle that." Jackie pointed out that in addition to leading the workshop, the security committee was "to help out with the march not to get out

of hand, to keep them on the sidewalk—and where we move and stop."
But, Jairus added, "the students were really excited and basically were
very intelligent about what to do. If situations came up, they did them
themselves. They didn't need my help. I was there if they had questions. I
was one of the people asking questions like if situations would come up
like how to handle this. I was facilitating the security people."

In addition to security, Jackie also helped lead the outreach workshop.

> We had a group of students; we had flyers and told them this is
> what we do to get the word out to the people. But they were all
> excited. We [asked] them what kind of ideas you have, and they
> were saying, go to supermarkets, go to stores and outside of school;
> they were enthusiastic about it right away. We helped them pass
> them out outside of school and to neighbors. After maybe two
> meetings, we decided that we can make handmade flyers, also word
> of mouth. We didn't meet again, but each person that participated
> in different committees also did their own outreach by getting their
> own friends involved. And I talked to my family about what was
> going on and my neighbors.

Once committees were formed, they were self-starting. They met
on their own and carried out their own work. By the night of the
march, South Gate students felt well prepared and ready.

RALLY AND MARCH

The night of South Gate city council's regular meeting was also
school night. Students and parents began to gather by six in the evening
in front of South Gate High School. Milton arrived with noisemakers,
T-shirts, and a bullhorn. The puppet committee had made two giant
puppet heads, one of pollution and the other of a skull that could be
seen above the crowd.

Jackie was one of the early arrivals. Seeing television news choppers
above, she worried how they would look, because "when I got there
it was not that many people. But then, people kept coming and kept
coming, and a lot of people went."

The crowds and the energy built quickly. The marchers, whom
students thought numbered about 200 or 300, rallied at the school, then
divided themselves into four groups, one on each corner of Firestone

Boulevard in front of the high school, all chanting. Teachers who came to the rally were impressed by their students' leadership and energy. Veronica Sanchez loved that her students were telling her to "stay on the sidewalk and to go this way and go that way. It was good that they were the leaders and I was following their directions." Leticia Ortiz came with her sister. "We marched from here to city hall and you could feel the energy. It was the chants, and it felt really powerful, like we could really do it." Norma remembered that when she arrived, "people were already picketing and people had banners, and there was a lot of people, and I was like, wow, I didn't think a lot of people were coming to this. I was really happy there were a lot of people there. And we started walking and chanting, and then we got people honking at us and that would pump us even more. We would start screaming more." Jorge was one of those on the bullhorn who led the chanting. "Like 'What do we want? Justice'; that was one. Another was 'Sunlaw, hear us; we don't want you near us.' Or 'Do we want a power plant in Southgate?' And the crowd would say no!"

Teachers at the rally pointed out another important thing: student participation in the march transcended segregation by tracks and students' own subgroups. It wasn't just the college and "alternative" group of kids who participated. Veronica Sanchez noted, "Right now our core group [of activists] is an alternative group, but for the protest it was everyone, all the subcultures, everyone. All the students were involved, which was really wonderful." Another teacher expanded:

> It was a mix of all the different classes, a handful of kids who actually wanted to go to the next step, not all of them obviously, but enough from all the different classes and then they told people so it got big, our group of kids who wanted to get involved.
>
> At the beginning of the meetings, you go into a room, because in some groups you have like a certain type of people here and a certain type of student here and a certain type of student here. But this, because everyone has lungs I guess, it was everyone.

Although to Marco Martinez those participating in the march seemed to be mainly students, some of the activists brought their parents. The march also brought out some new faces, among them Rhonda Nitschky, who came from Downey after having seen a flyer for the march at a CEC meeting.

The march was Rhonda Nitschky's first contact with CBE or Youth-EJ, and it was a bit of a culture shock:

> There's maybe a hundred people, and they are all teenagers except for Alvaro and Angelo and [CBE's] lawyer Anne. Where are all the parents? There's all of these like disaffected youth dressed in punk rock regalia—some had huge Mohawks, hair dyed purple and black clothes—and I was wondering how that was going to come out with all this media coverage, and people were filming it from the air and from helicopters. It's not going to look very impressive because it wasn't parents with little toddlers and the thing that you would expect to see.

Maybe because they didn't look to themselves the way they looked to Nitschky, some of the students thought there were more parents in the crowd than Rhonda did. Abram thought that at least by the time they got to city hall, "there were lot of older people too, they brought their kids, and people told their parents about it."

Even though she thought she was "the only white person out there with all these Latino kids," Nitschky stayed and got caught up in the spirit of the demonstration:

> They were well organized; they had group leaders, and chants in English and Spanish that were scripted. And everyone was totally obeying the laws. There was also like this great spirit of fun, to voice our opinions about something like this and create a public disturbance out in front of the school. I liked the whole atmosphere. So I grabbed a sign. It felt really good to get out there and march. You feel like you're doing everything that you can do by just speaking out. All these kids lived miles away from where the plant is going to be. It fascinated me that they were so upset about it. And I could not believe the media turnout. There were helicopters hovering overhead, media events, people running up and down from every major network with cameras. And we caused major traffic snafus, everybody was honking.

South Gate resident Martha Andrade also came to the rally, and brought her son. "How did I get wind of it? I think they must have sent out a flyer. I did not know it was going to end up at the city council meeting but that's where we went."

AT CITY HALL

When it was time to march to the city council meeting, all four groups, at each of the corners, merged together into a single march. The city council meeting had already started when the march arrived. Robles' opponents and power plant supporters were already there, and with the march, there were more people than could fit into the council chambers, so the crowd, whatever its numbers, overflowed onto the lawns outside.

Supporters of the power plant engaged the demonstrators in debates. The first thing marchers encountered was a large delegation from the pipe fitters' union, who had a direct stake in jobs the plant would provide. Rhonda Nitschky remembers them standing outside the council chambers "with their picket signs kind of blocking the way." But Martha Andrade thought that no union pipe fitters lived in South Gate and that Sunlaw's current employees would fill most of the jobs the plant would provide.

Although the students found the unionists both threatening and disrespectful, the adults seem to have been minimally intimidated. Rhonda Nitschky, for example, saw unionists as trying to persuade the students with promises and telling them about the importance of unions.

Jairus Ramos, however, heard disrespect. He remembers a unionist "heckling the students about why don't you get a job, and this is going create jobs, and he's telling the students go to college and be somebody."

This event was most marchers' first experience with a city council meeting. Leticia Ortiz told me, "I lived in South Gate since I was in the fourth grade, and I had never been to a city council meeting, and I know my parents have never been to one. And I think most residents of the area have never been."

When the marchers finally got inside, they found most of the seats already taken by pro-plant, anti-Robles people, whom they identified as unionists and Sunlaw people. Marchers stood around the perimeter of the council chambers. Nevertheless, the students managed to get time to address the council about their concerns and to have their request for a council vote placed on the agenda. They had to march in and demand it, though.

The students, who were unaware of the political warfare going on among their elected officials and between some of them and the growing anti-Robles movement, were shocked by the behavior of the city councilors toward one another. Jackie Amparo described the lack of respect her elected officials showed: "When we got inside city council, it got really ugly. Instead of dealing with the issues, they would actually be mudslinging, talking to each other, talking their background, talking about personal stuff to each other that only they would know. Rhonda Nitschky was equally disturbed at council members trading insults: "They are wrangling back and forth among themselves and accusing each other of taking money under the counter from Sunlaw." But then she got into the act too, shouting down the mayor and Sunlaw's representatives. When Mayor Morial praised the kids and spoke about how the power plant

> is going to bring money into the community and how he wants to build a skate board park for the kids and this is the first thing he says; at first the kids were ecstatic. They are high school kids, and some were junior high kids, and the kids are applauding because he is praising them and saying all these great things about the youth. And I'm sitting there going, they don't know that he is trying to bribe them. And I just started saying booo—We want clean air. We don't want a polluting power plant, we don't want a skateboard park if it means—I started being totally disruptive, and the kids got it, and they started booing the mayor.

Nitschky also took on Sunlaw's representative when he got up to speak:

> I wondered if the kids even knew who he was. He had been saying such outrageous things at some of the CEC meetings, and there was no chance to respond to him publicly. So the minute he got up and headed for the podium, I started—I had this big yellow poster, right. I'm like putting it out in front of my face and scrunching down in the seat because the seats were long benches filled with these union guys, and I was in the very middle of all these people. As he got up to the microphone, I started yelling "Sunlaw hear us, we don't want you near us." And the kids all started in right away, and it got very loud and very rowdy. And he was really upset and

really rattled by it. We shouted him down, which wasn't very polite, but the fact was the city council just had no control. They didn't bother to try to gavel the meeting to order or to stop the protest. They just let it go on.

All this took place before the public comment period. When the meeting was opened for public comments, things got even wilder. South Gate resident and anti-plant activist Robert Cabrales felt that the anti-council speakers were equally disrespectful of the anti-plant speakers. "Mostly the older representatives and the voters for the plant were making bad comments when we had something to say in front of the council meeting. They were being very disrespectful and treating us like outcasts and people who are stupid, ignorant."

Despite the civic theater, the students were determined to have their say. They got up one by one, and there was a long line out the door of kids wanting to speak. South Gate high student Norma Velasco summed up their collective message:

We were explaining to them this is not good for the city and it's not good for the world. We have too much pollution already, and that was obviously the main issue, getting the word out to people because I'm pretty sure a lot of people did not know about this power plant. Once people know both sides and not [just] maybe the city is going to get money, but in the long run it's going to be affecting our health, they are going to start thinking more about health and forgetting about the money. That's what we hope for.

Martha Andrade spoke for others who were moved by the students:

Most of them were talking about the health problems that they already had in their homes, the amount of asthma, allergies, the smog problem we have here. There were people from Huntington Park who had been dealing with La Montaña, which was that huge cement pile of waste. It seems like everything that had to do with toxicity is centered in this neighborhood, so to have anything else here is just overload. They figured we will flip it in here; these people are too stupid to do anything about it. Even the president of the South Gate High student body spoke.

Speaking publicly to the city council was a powerful and frightening but heady experience for the students who did it. A number of students told me that Norma Velasco's speech was the most memorable one, and that even though she is shy, she did it. One of her teachers told us she's a really good speaker.

Norma herself remembered it as being pretty scary before—but that she was euphoric afterward.

> It was the day before [the march], and we had another meeting in the cafeteria, and everyone was like okay, we have to put up these posters and pass out flyers and make sure people go to this rally, and I was helping out by passing out flyers throughout the city. And then there was a meeting before at the park, and they were talking about what people were going to say at the city hall, and I have an idea what to say and not just be there. And then Angelo was saying everybody write a speech, so I wrote one. And then the last minute, I don't think anybody had written one, and I was like I still have a speech. I still didn't know I was going to talk. And then he's like, so are you going to speak and I'm like no, somebody else can read it for me. So it was done by accident. I'm not one of those speaker types, especially in city hall.
>
> I was nervous. I was trying to bribe my friends into doing it for me. Even at the rally, before we went into city hall, I told my friend, the one who had told me about this, you read my first paragraph, and I will read the last. Well, the good thing is that the whole crowd was cheering, even if you didn't understand anything the person was saying. And at the beginning you were really into it, and your voice would become stronger and much more powerful. [My Mom] was there. She was in the corner, and then after I finished my speech—I looked at her. She was right there. I felt really good. I'm glad I went through with it. She said that people still come up to me and say I saw you on TV. I was on Channel Two.

Martha Andrade also spoke, and talked about carbon dioxide (CO_2)—long before its contribution to global warning was the hot topic it is today:

> So I stood up and I told them my background—I had graduated from South Gate High School, valedictorian, went to UCSB, got

a degree in biology, went back and got my master's degree in biology, went to UC Davis, got a degree in veterinary medicine. [She went on to point out that] you need to consume a whole lot of oxygen, and you are going to be pumping out a whole lot of CO_2 and you don't have any way of the eliminating the CO_2. You are going to be putting more greenhouse gases into the air, which is the major pollutant causing global warming. So how do you propose to deal with that? And they didn't have anything to say. I was mainly talking to the city council and saying I thought it was a really bad idea, that the city council should not in any way back this process up at all. It's not a good idea for the area, and thank you very much.

Rhonda Nitschky also spoke about her health concerns and "that I lived close to the project. I told them I was from Downey but that I grown up in Maywood and Bell and that I went to church for ten years in South Gate so I was familiar with the area and the issues that affected it. I left after that. I thought we had done everything that we could. I thought the vote would go against us." Still, she thought that Sunlaw might make some concessions to mitigate local pollution to appease the opposition, "like buying natural gas school buses. And when [Sunlaw official] Tim Smith saw the opposition at the meeting, all of a sudden when he got up to the podium he started saying we will give South Gate lower energy costs."

Youth-EJ activists Milton, Jackie, and Jairus couldn't even get inside the council chambers because there were so many people there. Being from Huntington Park, they decided to stay outside, figuring it was more important for people from South Gate to be inside. Jairus said, "It got very late, and these were students who had school, so some of them went home, and there was still a good crowd who stayed and endured. We had some Aztec dancers come out and do their ceremony before we went inside and then, while we were waiting outside, people were drumming. Some dancers invited some of the people to join them and they did. And they did this snake line and went around the police officers and the little park area. Like a mambo line."

Late into the night, the city council voted three to zero, with two abstentions, against building the Nueva Azalea power plant in South Gate. Councilpersons Ruvalcaba, Morial, and Benavides formed a majority opposing it, and Gonzales and De La Torre abstained. Mayor

Raul Morial later attributed his opposition to the power plant to this outpouring of community opposition at the council meeting: "I was overwhelmed. I didn't expect that. I don't think we really had debated the issue of the power plant. I was really impressed with the different approaches that our young people had and their sincerity, the purity and their conviction. This really was the pivotal point for me. I had already decided that I was going to oppose the plant, but when I saw this demonstration, I knew that our community didn't want this power plant."

The mayor was being less than frank. As we've seen, perhaps a month earlier he had asked to write the argument against the power plant that was to be printed in the voter information booklet for the election, although initially he'd asked to write both arguments. This first request could be chalked up to indecision. Nevertheless, Morial apparently had been a willing participant in the secret city council meetings that resulted in a biased information booklet.

In any event, students were exhilarated by the meeting and its results. Jackie stuck it out to the end, "even though after everyone left, it was like 11:00 o'clock. I had to go home and it was a school night, and I was tired, but it was worth it." Jairus added, "After the vote, everybody just went nuts! There was a lot of noise inside city hall, the city council meeting room."

Students were surprised that it was so quick and seemingly easy. They might have been less surprised had they known what their city council had been up to in the last months. That they did not know was in part the result of CBE consciously avoiding electoral politics because, as a tax-exempt educational and advocacy organization, it was legally limited in this arena. Their surprise was also an indication that city hall was, as Leticia Ortiz had said, not a part of the lives of most South Gate residents.

If students were energized by their success at the city council, they were almost equally energized by the media coverage, particularly television news, which turned out in force. The students, their signs, the Aztec dancers, the giant puppets, as well as clear sound bites made for great footage.[4] If there was anyone in South Gate who did not already know of the plant from Sunlaw's publicity campaign, they and the rest of Southeast Los Angeles learned about it in Spanish and English in a way that highlighted what looked like massive popular and city council opposition to it. Robert Cabrales thought that the angles from helicopters watching all those people, that whole big block full of people—it must have been a great impact for a lot of residents who were home and tired, watching [television]. It was one of the biggest things for me. I watch TV and you see this big crowd of people, and of course I know about the campaign. But the really big thing—inside the meetings and then reporters were also there doing reports and you can see large groups of people just standing in the hall or in the actual room where the meetings are held and outside—that was the greatest impact. People saw a big group of concerned residents who were opposing this project—the helicopter shot from the street, when you see the whole group, the helicopter above them. It was cool.

Participants saw their movement as more significant for having been reflected back to them through television and the next day's newspapers. Alicia Gonzalez thought there was a real sea change after the march and city council meeting. Before the march, she said, "students felt like it didn't matter, that they can't make changes in government," but afterward, students were empowered by the leadership roles taken by their peers. Activists began to believe that they really might be able to stop the power plant. Jairus echoed the student consensus when he said, "the high event was most definitely the march to the city council, because that's when we were out on the streets and demonstrating. It was planned by young people, and we had a lot of numbers out there, and we showed community power."

How did the parents of these activists feel about what their kids were doing? Although I did not interview parents, students told me that their parents responded to their involvement with a mixture of pride and concern. Parents took seriously their children's involvement in the power plant issue not least because the kids were learning about it at school. Parents were also worried about activism cutting into the teens' attention to schoolwork. As one student told me, they were concerned "about [me] being stressed out and what was I involved in and everything, and why I was involved. But I basically told them it was my school work and my grades would not drop. And they [agreed to my participation] as long as I keep my school work up."

This campaign was also an opportunity for some parents to share their own past activism with their children and to support their efforts fully. One student captured a more general ambivalence among parents who had been activists in their own youth, about their children's role.[5]

> My parents were happy. They were like that's what you are supposed to be doing and you get up there and you make a difference somehow. I think my dad was [an activist] in Mexico during the '60s because he was always warning me, like I don't want you to get too involved, because he thinks I'm going to get shot. I think I always wanted to be an activist. If it was something like human rights or things like that, I would be there helping out. You know what is funny though, my parents they don't really agree with me being an activist, but when a family member comes or a neighbor comes, it will be like oh, yes, my daughter, she's an activist and she cares about the world; so they just contradict themselves.

Although most parents were on balance more supportive than not of their children's activism, some parents who had been activists in Mexico and El Salvador worried for their safety.

In sum, with the high school students' decision to march into the city council, the campaign against the power plant went public, and so did the campaign in favor of the plant, even if its passion was focused on Albert Robles. The mudslinging and disrespectful behavior students observed among councilors and between members of the audience and the council had their roots in Robles' corruption and support for it by city councilors Ruvalcaba, Benavides, and Morial—a prime example of which was excluding a pro-plant statement from the voter information booklet. Although students did not know it, Robles' enemies saw the students and environmental justice activists as Albert Robles' enforcers, which may account for some of the hostility the students experienced at the city council meeting.

Participants on both sides felt directly that this was their own South Gate issue, a feeling amplified by the media. More than any previous effort, this council meeting attracted the attention of television reporters and brought the issue to people in neighboring cities.

From this point forward, youth became the public face of the campaign against the power plant. They orchestrated the events that put the Nueva Azalea power plant on the nightly news in Spanish and in English. They spoke in public meetings and became visible to their neighbors, both face-to-face and through television exposure. The publicity they generated created a great deal of talk around the issue of the power plant. Far from least, the Youth-EJ and CBE ways of thinking about environmental justice and the health consequences of industrial pollution became part of a public discourse that South Gate residents appropriated as their own to explain to themselves and others why they opposed the power plant. Even those who supported the power plant had to address its possible health impact in their arguments, even if only to dismiss it as scare tactics.

CHAPTER 8

Sudden Death

BEFORE MID-DECEMBER, CBE and Youth-EJ's primary effort was to publicize the plan to build a power plant—explain its health dangers and explain Sunlaw's choice of site as part of a larger pattern of environmental racism—and to discover whether there was significant community opposition to the plant. By the time South Gate High students led the march to the city council, it was clear that community opposition did indeed exist and that a grassroots movement was taking shape. By this time too, a locally based anti-Robles movement had also emerged, if not in the streets then in the kinds of confrontations that the students witnessed at city hall. Thus, by mid-January, South Gate was the scene of two grassroots movements: one against the power plant and the other against Albert Robles. The opponents of each movement had not in any way constructed social movements. Robles and his supporters manipulated voters more than they educated or mobilized them. Sunlaw was the central player in the pro-plant campaign. It had allies aplenty but not much in the way of outspoken, active campaigners inside South Gate. Such support for the power plant as existed in South Gate was catalyzed by anti-Robles sentiment. Both on-the-ground movements won their respective battles: the anti-plant movement in 2001 and the anti-Robles movement two years later.

In this chapter I put the power plant movement in the foreground and analyze the activities of both sides in the six weeks leading up to the city election and power plant referendum of March 6, 2001. I examine what the environmental justice campaign looked like and the factors that helped it to succeed. I also consider what success looks like for a social justice campaign. Is winning everything? Doing the right things (in the sense of messages, organizing strategies, and tactics) is a necessary but not a sufficient condition for social movements to win specific battles. Much also depends on what the opposition does: here, Sunlaw and the pro-plant activities of the anti-Robles movement.

Much too depends on wild cards, on the unpredicted and serendipitous ways that larger social circumstances affect a social movement. Albert Robles was one of those wild cards. The racial discourses and silences and how they played out at the interface of the two movements was still another. Some wild cards are just that—lucky or unlucky happenings that may play a big role but do not give us a general understanding of factors that make for social movement success or failure. Sunlaw's announcement that if the people of South Gate did not want the plant, they wouldn't build it was one of those; Albert Robles was another. Other wild cards that influence the outcome of a particular struggle also give us a deeper understanding about dynamics of success and failure of social movements more broadly. The silences and speaking about race was one of those.

The Environmental Justice Campaign

Thus far, both the students and CBE had been developing a grass-roots approach to their outreach and activism. By January, environmental justice activists discovered they had solid community support, and the campaign was developing real momentum. As they worked to create an organizing and education plan for the next phase of the campaign, they discovered that the political playing field was already structured for them in less than ideal ways, not least of which was the advisory city referendum on the power plant scheduled for less than two months away. The first decision activists needed to make was how much, if any, emphasis to place on the referendum. Then, in light of that decision, they needed to figure out the next stages of their grassroots campaign.

A Strategic Decision

Even though CBE could see that a real community-based movement was developing outward from students at South Gate High, there was still the question of where to put its strategic focus. The CEC had the power to stop or green light the plant, but its meetings had thus far proved a chilly climate for community participation. And Sunlaw was reachable mainly through those meetings. Roy Abadi kept pressing CBE to get more involved in the referendum, but the organization was understandably uneasy about jumping into South Gate electoral politics.

Abadi recalled, "Angelo told me we are not involved in politics because we are a [501(c)-3, nonprofit] organization, and we cannot be, according to the rules and stuff." It is true that nonprofit organizations are limited by law in their ability to engage in electoral politics. If they step over the line, they can lose their tax-exempt status. Nonprofit organizations cannot endorse or campaign for candidates. But they are allowed by law to educate and advocate on issues, which would allow CBE to take a stand on the power plant.

If Abadi was eager to engage in South Gate's increasingly notorious politics, CBE's Alvaro Huerta was just as uneasy. Only part of Huerta's discomfort was about dirty politics. He also worried, reasonably, about focusing anti-plant energies on the referendum because it was a high-risk, and potentially low-return, strategy.

By late January, when the power plant referendum, Measure A, and the upcoming council election were beginning to make headlines, CBE wrestled with whether it wanted to go in this direction. Would involvement in electoral politics help or hurt its grassroots education and organizing effort? With 20/20 hindsight the answer is obvious, but at the time there were real drawbacks to putting all the eggs of a grass-roots effort in the electoral basket. CBE had been implicitly working with a longer time frame for its campaign, and this decision was hardly an easy one. It was difficult in part because the CEC had stipulated that it would make a decision on Sunlaw's licensing one year after the company filed a completed application. That put the drop-dead date for an anti-plant campaign, and the date CBE had been working with, into August 2001. That gave CBE time to organize—and organizing takes time. Too, this referendum was an advisory one; real authority still lay with the CEC. By focusing their hopes on the March referendum, environmental justice forces would lose five months of outreach time they'd counted on and badly needed. That would mean a lot of scrambling to figure out how to organize, and to find and motivate registered voters to turn out in two short months, all without any money to speak of. Putting all their effort into the electoral arena and its referendum also carried the risk of sudden death to a movement that was just beginning to grow real roots in the community.

Also on the down side was the fact that although CBE had met with Xochilt Ruvalcaba and Albert Robles in the spring and summer of 2000, by the end of the year the organization was distancing itself from increasingly obvious dirty city politics in general, and from Robles in particular. Its reservations about getting involved in South Gate's politics also made CBE uneasy about getting involved in the March 6 referendum and election.

Yet the arguments for involvement were more powerful. First of all, everyone else—Sunlaw, Robles, and those opposing Robles—were focusing their efforts on the March elections and the referendum. "Because the power plant was sending out flyers and calling people and hiring people to go door to door," Veronica Sanchez said, "we were disseminating our information to counter that, and the *LA Times* and *La Opinion* were doing stories about it. It was almost surreal because at one point you didn't know what was true and what was not true."

Second, Sunlaw gave opponents of the power plant a neon target at which to aim when it announced more than once that if the residents of South Gate did not want Sunlaw to build the plant, the company would leave. The press circulated these announcements at least twice in January.

Third, the press and television reporting also kept the referendum visible in their increasingly frequent coverage of South Gate politics. In the weeks right before the election, the press and television coverage of South Gate events—the power plant and Albert Robles both—was intense by any standard, all the more so against a backdrop of almost no reporting in previous years. In the two-week period between February 20 and the March 6 election, in addition to regular Spanish- and English-language press coverage, every Spanish- and English-language network television station carried at least one story, and some carried five, about the power plant controversy.[1] All this activity, and the media circus that covered it in the six weeks before March 6, made it hard for people not to know about the power plant referendum and its importance for South Gate residents. Consequently, the referendum was on everyone's mind as a significant demonstration of public opinion.

Given that there was no way to avoid entanglement with South Gate's dirty politics, the challenge became how to maintain a grassroots campaign within an electoral framework. As CBE and those working with them weighed all the factors, it looked as though there was no real alternative to focusing their community education and mobilization work on defeating Measure A. To avoid the referendum would be to ignore the neon target offered them by Sunlaw. The referendum also provided an obvious focus for direct outreach and an education campaign in that it gave activists a concrete reason to talk with people, and possibilities for concrete ways that individuals could become active in mobilizing others.

Not least, South Gate High School students had already begun their own Vote No on Measure A campaign shortly after making their presentations at the city council meeting in January. Weighing all these factors, CBE recognized that there was no way a grassroots anti-plant movement could avoid engagement with South Gate electoral politics, despite the risks it posed.

What the Grassroots Campaign Looked Like

CBE urged all the students from Youth-EJ and South Gate High, and voting-age residents of both South Gate and Downey who were already working to stop the plant, to work together in a No on Measure A Committee that would formulate a plan for low-budget ways of mobilizing visible support, getting their message out to new people, and carrying out traditional electoral-style phone banking. Robert Cabrales served as the committee's treasurer. He remembered there being about fifteen regulars on the No on Measure A Committee, some individuals and some whole families, and split about evenly between student activists and adults. Not everyone participated in all events. It fell to a few of the adults to deal with the daunting set of bureaucratic hoops involved in forming an issue advocacy group that would also be involved in electoral politics. Sonya Brown (a pseudonym) was the point person on several of these thorny topics.[2] She handled filing for nonprofit status, registered the group, and raised funds from the Downey board of realtors.

The strategy of the No on A Committee was to conduct a decidedly person-to-person campaign. Adults and students went door to door with flyers, to both neighbors and local businesses. Students urged their parents to vote against Measure A. Marco Martinez recalled that "we all tried to get people involved, and we did get other people involved. Basically it was through word of mouth. We made flyers and passed them all around my block." Students also put up CBE's yellow, black, and red posters on telephone poles on Tweedy Boulevard, South Gate's main business street, and urged businesses to put them in their windows.

Conducting a grassroots campaign that involves a lot of personal contact means figuring out how to deal people who disagree with you. Youth-EJ members met disagreement in various forms. Jorge and Jairus were part of a team putting up posters one Saturday on Tweedy Boulevard. To get them high up on the telephone poles so that passing cars could see them, Jorge climbed on another student's shoulders. By the time they got to the end of their route, they were pretty psyched, but when they walked back up the street, they discovered that their hard work had been undone. All the posters were gone. People told them that "a guy in a white van" had been ripping them down. "We never saw the person or the van," said Jorge, "I was bummed." Jairus thought they were city workers or people on the pro-plant side.

As a way around this sort of interaction, the students went to merchants personally and asked them if they would put the students' flyers and posters in their store windows. This method met with mixed success. Milton had one business owner tell him, "See that gutter; throw it there." Although Jairus reported a similar experience, he had an upbeat evaluation of talking directly to business owners. "I think the fact that we actually went business to business asking people for support—put it on your window that you are against the power plant. Some of them were sympathetic. I think what worked was going out to the community and talking to people and giving them an opportunity to participate and letting them know what is really going on."

To Rhonda Nitschky, who was walking up the street later in the day, the results looked very good. "In every single business at the intersection as far as you could see along the street are the posters that the kids from CBE had put. I couldn't believe that the business community let the kids do that."

Anti-plant activists also hit the streets regularly to hand out flyers to passersby. Nitschky found that people were already interested. "Normally when people try and hand out anything on a street corner, people avoid them and don't really want anything to do with it. People were literally driving by and they would see that poster with the skull on it and they would pull over to the curb and want a leaflet."

By being visible in the community's streets and stores in this way, the students also became points of contact for adults who were looking for opportunities to help stop the plant from being built. Two women from Downey, who, quite independent of one another, became active members of No on A, did so as a result of chance contact with Youth-EJ activists.

The committee brought together people who had different understandings of what the fight was about. The high school students and CBE organizers were largely children of Latina/o immigrants. They knew one another from school and their recent activism. They also shared an environmental justice perspective on the campaign—that the power plant was another instance of putting polluting industries in already overburdened low-income communities of color. The adults on the committee were a mix of whites and Latina/os from South Gate and Downey who did not previously know one another. They joined the committee because they were concerned about the health consequences of plant emissions.[3] With the exception of Luis and Robert Cabrales, they had no exposure to environmental justice ideas. It rapidly became clear to the white adults that the campaign they had joined had a distinctive ethnic and racial subtext—on both sides. They were not altogether comfortable with the racial injustice dimension of environmental justice politics, but they were even more unprepared for the raw and thinly veiled xenophobia that they experienced during their leafleting and phone-bank efforts, which came from whites on the pro-plant side.

Nitschky described her first unpleasant experience with the ways some white South Gate residents understood the power plant debate. One Saturday, she joined Sonya Brown and several members of her church to leaflet in a neighborhood near the proposed plant site.

> We were talking to people on the street about the issue. Several people had really disturbing experiences. This one woman was talking to an older white man, and he started making racist remarks about Latinos. He was for the plant because he thought that the Latinos were against it. All he knew was that Albert Robles was against it, and this guy was corrupt and he was corrupting South Gate city hall, and when the Latinos took over running everything, the whole city became corrupt. And he was using racial slurs, and this woman was really, really upset. This is a religious group of people. Everyone stood in the street and prayed before going out and distributing the flyers. This woman was so upset that she did not want to do that in the future.

Nitschky had her own conversation with "a friend, a retired cop who was against the plant, but he thought that the plant would win at the election because he thought the Latinos were for it. And then here's this other guy who was for the plant because he thought the Latinos were against it; that kind of dynamic seemed to be influencing people's decisions for or against in a white community."

PHONE BANKING. The sense that displaced xenophobia animated white voters who supported the power plant became clear to No on A Committee members as they began to work the phone bank in earnest as the election neared. Phone banking probably pulled ahead of leafleting as the focus of No on Measure A Committee's person-to-person effort. The CBE office in Huntington Park became what Angelo Logan called a phone-and-pizza marathon in the last two weeks before the election. Students and adults showed up every evening to spend several hours calling as many registered voters in South Gate as they could reach. Robert Cabrales estimated that twenty to thirty committee members and their friends participated in the phone-bank effort. Nitschky went directly to the office from work most nights. Abadi was another regular. Despite the fact that Alvaro Huerta had told them not to waste time trying to persuade people who were in favor of the plant but just to phone the next person on their list, Rhonda noted that "people were so intensely involved in this thing, that if people said they were for the plant, everybody tried to argue with them." Nitschky recalled that she had phone conversations with people that lasted a half hour: "As long as they were listening and talking about it, I would talk to them and try and change their mind. Every night we would work until it got too late to be calling and bothering people."

For the high school students, the idea of calling people their parents' age was intimidating, but they too got into arguing. Alicia and Jorge both noted that some people, especially those in favor of the plant, were rude to them because they were kids. Alicia recalled,

> A few times I got people who were for it, and they insulted us, but I didn't get angry, but I felt sorry for what they are thinking about because they're only thinking about the money that the city was going to get. They are not seeing the negative side of the power plant. Some people happen to be undocumented; they are not eligible to vote, and they would tell me, well, I don't have no voice. I was like, no, that's not true, you have a voice. That you cannot vote does not mean that you cannot fight. Talk to your friends, talk to people who you know that can vote; you still have a voice. It was just one occasion, and that man was older than me; I guess that he felt that why should a youth tell him that. But at least I tried.

Through their practice these activists treated phone banking as one more opportunity for direct, personal outreach, education, and persuasion. Their emphasis differed from the more conventional agendas of electoral phone banking—to mobilize one's side to vote, get a sense of opposing sentiment, and persuade fence-sitters. To underscore her point about how deeply committed everyone was to personal engagement, Nitschky pointed to the pizza that Angelo Logan ordered every night "to sustain the morale of the troops," but which got cold and went uneaten because no one wanted to take a break. "Every night Angelo would be going, what are we going to do with all this pizza?"

As they worked the phones, both students and adults began to notice an ethnic pattern to voter responses, which was that Spanish-speaking and Latina/o-surnamed voters were usually against the power plant and welcomed the callers. This wasn't at all what Nitschky had been expecting. Her last phone effort had been to recruit Spanish-speaking employees to work as census takers for Census 2000. As an English speaker whose Spanish was limited to "I'm from the U.S. Census, and I want to offer a job to ___," she was suspected of being from La Migra (INS) or another hostile government agency, and people would hang up. So when phone banking began, Nitschky picked out all the Anglo names from the voter lists and called them first. Much to her surprise, she said,

> I got total hostility from the Anglo voters. They would say, how I'm going to vote is none of your damn business. At the end of calling all the Anglo people on the list, I was so depressed, I thought this is never going to work, and I just said these stupid white people, how can they think like this. Don't they understand this issue. They won't even talk to me about it. And I hear this laugh. Alvaro had come by and walked in, and he heard me, and he said just for that we are going to make you an honorary Mexican.

So she started calling Latinos:

> The minute I would say I'm calling on behalf of the No on Measure A Committee, we are trying to stop this power plant from being built, we need you to vote no on the Measure A, they wanted to talk about how upset they were. They all made it very clear

that they were against the project. There were only a couple of people that I talked to who said they were for it because they were union members or they thought it was going to bring jobs to their community.

Robert Cabrales told me that the response pattern from evening to evening was very consistent: "It was always two to one" against the measure. It turned out to be an accurate reflection of the actual vote.

SPEAKING AT OTHER CITY COUNCILS.   Anti-plant activists did not completely restrict their efforts to South Gate's voting population. They also visited the city councils of neighboring towns to help build opposition to the power plant. Their agenda was to persuade the councils to pass resolutions opposing the power plant. With the exception of the city of Downey, which took an active stand against the plant very early on, other city councils in the area had not engaged publicly with the issue. In the last weeks before the election, several members of the No on A Committee and CBE organizers made up delegations to speak to city councils on the issue.

As a Huntington Park resident, Milton Hernandez had asked his city council to put the power plant issue on the agenda for their next meeting, which CBE organizers, students, and No on Measure A members attended. That meeting rated news stories on Spanish- and English-language television, which featured interviews with Huerta and dramatic visuals of CBE's yellow, black, and red skull posters. Sunlaw's Spanish-language spokesman also appeared, and visuals of Milton Hernandez and Roy Abadi addressing the city council were shown on English-language television.[4] Despite council support for Senator Martha Escutia, council members nevertheless voted their opposition to the power plant.

So too did the Bell city council. Some of the environmental justice activists were surprised that the council consisted of white men, but any expectations they may have had of a hostile reception were quickly dispelled. After No on Measure A members made their presentations, the vice mayor told them that the council would vote on a resolution then and there, which they did. The Bell city council went on record as unanimously opposed to the power plant. The activists did not know that there were longtime progressive advocates in Bell's city government, nor did they know the city of Bell's prior history with Sunlaw. That city had believed they were in exclusive negotiations with Sunlaw over a parcel of city property near Bell's border with Vernon. They too had reservations about pollution and, as partial mitigation, had asked Sunlaw to pay the city's 10 percent utility surcharge. When Sunlaw made its South Gate plans public, Bell officials thought Sunlaw may have dumped them to avoid paying the utility charges; South Gate had no equivalent surcharge. Latina residents attending the council meeting were delighted with the vote and "went up to the microphone, one after another, thanking their city council profusely," said Nitschky. They knew about the plant but until then had no way to express their opposition. Several volunteered to work on the No on Measure A campaign.

YOUTH CONCERT IN SOUTH GATE PARK.   Three days before the election, the student activists held a rally and concert in South Gate Park. This event was completely student driven, and its appeal was mainly to young people. Students who told me about it were excited, especially about the fact that they were able to put on a concert with a sound system that was solar powered. The centerpiece was music—a number of local bands played—but there were also speakers. Robert Cabrales was the percussionist in one of the bands, a seven-member musical and social justice group named Yaksi, after a Hindu goddess of fertility or prosperity. Norma Velasco, the reluctant speaker at South Gate's city council, was drafted to emcee the event. One of her friends did the political speaking, in Spanish. Milton thought that the event "turned into a little gig for youth." Although it didn't get the turnout that the rally and march to the South Gate city council had, students thought it was a success—and it got media coverage.

Although some of the CBE organizers were less than happy about the timing of the event, some of the younger members of No on Measure A thought it was a fine experience. For Luis Cabrales, a musician himself, it was the most exciting part of the campaign because it was youth organized. "I am sure that under other circumstances it would have been impossible to think of all those kids as community leaders. What is most important is that they kept their cool even under police pressure. We had police cruisers patrolling the park ready to stop the rally because some posters and banners were located outside the permitted perimeter."

Perhaps because the concert was a youth-oriented event, and its spirit seems to have been to rally the troops, there was more environmental justice race talk there than at other events such as working the phone bank and speaking at city councils. This discourse was not always easy for some of the white troops. Nitschky recalled it as one of the few times that

> CBE's rhetoric really turned racial. They started discussing the environmental racism issue as though it really was like just white against brown and painting the people of South Gate as being kind of oppressed victims of big corporations and their industrial pollution and stuff. And a couple of people got up and said they disagreed with that point of view, like Sonya did at the rally in South Gate Park. She got up and said, now look I'm a Christian, I'm here because I believe in God, I believe he has given spiritship over the earth, and as human beings, it's our duty to take care of his creation. And I'm white. I'm here in solidarity with you. I don't believe that this is just a racial issue, and I don't like hearing that kind of negativism.

Environmental justice activists—CBE organizers, high school students, and the adults of South Gate and neighboring cities who worked with them—ran a campaign that was based on direct, person-to-person dialogue. This approach was in sync with perceptions by community activists, like those in Padres Unidos, that for residents the most important source of information on the plant came from talking with people they knew. Putting up posters brought activists into contact with businesses, phone banking engaged them with registered voters, and leafleting in residential and commercial areas put them in contact with a random mix of South Gate residents. Speaking at other city councils gave activists a sense of how officials in neighboring cities saw the issue. The campaign was not designed to preach to the choir. One of its strengths was that it gave activists a remarkably accurate assessment of popular sentiment about the power plant. The phone bankers quantified it correctly: two to one against the plant. They also learned, because they engaged a cross-section of city residents, that race played a significant role in the ways people felt about the plant. When they occasionally spoke about race with their own white supporters, they found that race talk and aversion to it were facts of life among friends as well as opponents.

Environmental justice activists were not the only voices raised for or against the power plant. Albert Robles and his allies on the city council ran their own anti-plant campaign that was the antithesis of the environmental justice campaign. Where the latter maximized personal contact and dialog, this one minimized it. Instead of phone banks, Robles' forces relied on the famous phone dialer to leave recorded messages—for giveaways and for Robles-supported candidates. It became clear in the last months of the campaign that the Robles forces were more liability than help to grassroots anti-plant efforts. Robles' many enemies were in the process of creating their own grassroots movement against him. Because some of those enemies were also supporters of the power plant, that movement had something of a pro-plant plank. The pro-plant campaign, however, as waged by Sunlaw and by the anti-Robles forces, was largely a top-down one with little person-to-person contact.

The Anti-Plant Campaign of Robles and His Allies

On March 1, five days before the election and referendum on the power plant, Xochilt Ruvalcaba, her sisters Flor and Daisy, and Mayor Raul Morial went on a hunger strike in front of South Gate city hall that lasted until the election. That event generated probably more television news coverage than any other. Clips were shown on all three channels of Spanish-language television and all seven English-language network news programs almost every day. Spanish-language Channel 34 gave it eight stories in six days. All told, there were thirty-four television news stories, all of which included visuals of the hunger strikers, and most had interviews as well. In form and timing, the strike was a brilliant move to keep an anti-plant message in the public eye.[5] For Flor Ruvalcaba, who was a candidate for the position of city clerk (running against biology teacher Carmen Avalos) and a complete unknown, the strike was also a brilliant campaign move. She was interviewed more frequently than her incumbent sister, Xochilt.

With the caveat to me that he did not remember exactly how it came about, Mayor Raul Morial described how he came to be part of the hunger strike. From conversations with residents, Morial felt that there was widespread opposition to the power plant. "I remember, one day we were analyzing the situation. Somehow in our discussion, I think

Xochilt may have been the one who said, 'I think what we have to do is come out with a strong answer to their financial resources and, since we don't have any money, a hunger strike might be the way to approach that.' And I didn't participate very much in that conversation because, that is a good idea, but at my age, do I really want to participate in a hunger strike?"

Xochilt Ruvalcaba seemed the most deeply invested in the hunger strike, and she was key to sustaining it. In 1994, when she was a student at UCLA, she had been moved by and participated briefly in a successful tent city and ten-day hunger strike that won formation of a Chicana/o studies department. Ruvalcaba explained: "As we got closer to the election, we saw that the power plant had millions of dollars, and our resources were very scarce. So we decided to go on a hunger strike to bring some national attention to this, letting the world know it's not about politics, it's a struggle for our health and our lives." They sent out a press release, set up two tents (one for the women, the other for Raul Morial), and held a press conference. "Channel 7, channel 5, channel 2, channel 9, 34, 52 [were all there.] They all interviewed us. *La Opinion* was there, *LA Times* was there. I think they were all there. Then we went on the hunger strike. My sister Daisy lasted two or three days; she had to leave because she had a final. Then it was just my sister Flor, who is two years younger than me, and the mayor, and myself. I was on a hunger strike for six days and seven nights. I know that much. But the whole thing is kind of meshed together."

Both Ruvalcaba and Morial said that the hunger strike affected their memories, so that their recollections are spotty. Morial did remember its beginning: "I was having an interview with Channel 22 or 52 in my office, and Xochilt walked in and said, Raul, the media is out there. We are ready for the hunger strike. So I went out there and I made a short statement indicating our reasons for having the hunger strike in opposition to the power plant. The tents were already set up. Who set them up, I don't know. But believe me, it was really uncomfortable in those tents, and we didn't have any sleeping bags, no phones, air bags, nothing like that in the beginning." The day before the election, Raul Morial collapsed and was taken to the hospital for dehydration, and had to end his participation in the hunger strike. But Xochilt and her sister Flor lasted until Election Day.

Both Ruvalcaba and Morial recall supporters coming by their tents and offering encouragement. Xochilt explained that "people would go to the tent and say, thank you for doing this, God bless you, and they would cry. They would even say prayers for us. They go in and hold hands and say prayers for us to make sure that we were protected."

Morial felt that he and other people saw it as not quite appropriate for a sixty-year-old man to be engaging in a hunger strike, but he was also pleased with people's support. Some of the visitors offered them food. "And some said, can I bring you a burrito? No, thank you. That would defeat the whole purpose of the message that we are trying to put across."

Ruvalcaba had a less charitable but probably more accurate interpretation of those offers. "We had members of the community running for city council who had gotten contributions from the power plant, I believe, sent students to eat Doritos in front of our tents to taunt us. Hector De La Torre's wife drove by snapping photos and just taunting us with a sandwich."

Although there was a great deal of television coverage, it is unclear how many people in South Gate actually knew directly about the hunger strike. Celine Leyva, an early anti-plant community activist, joined the hunger strike for a day but worried that no one knew they were there. "I felt sad seeing them, being among them, and we were alone in that moment. People didn't leave. No one knew they were hunger striking. No one knew there was a hunger strike. Then, one man said he thought that the Boy Scouts were camping out here. Then I said, No! nobody's going to know; we're going to die here and no one is going to know we're on a hunger strike!"

Leyva's worries seem reflected in television stories. Until perhaps the day before the election, all the visuals show no one around the tents. Spanish-language Channel 52 coverage a day or two before the election featured Leyva speaking in front of the tents to about twenty teens, and another showed a bank of *velas*, candles burning near the tents. Anti-plant teacher Leticia Ortiz heard about the hunger strike from her students.

At least some No on Measure A members knew about it but stayed away. Nitschky remembered that after a night of working at the phone bank, "Angelo did his whole thing about what are we going to do with all this cold pizza. And somebody said, well, I know somebody who is hungry and could probably use some cold pizza. And I guess they made a midnight run over to city hall where those guys were camped out and delivered the cold pizza—and the message that they had better stay out there in those tents and not embarrass themselves by ending the hunger strike before Election Day."

Less surprising was the criticism from Ruvalcaba's and Morial's enemies on the city council. Hector De La Torre, who saw the hunger strike as a "goofy" electoral ploy by Robles forces, told me that "a very reliable witness who knows Raul" saw Morial at a Japanese restaurant in Downey during the hunger strike.

The pizza story, like Hector's restaurant story, became part of the city rumor mill. Teacher Emilio Macias believed that "the hunger strike was symbolic because I heard they were eating pizza whenever they got a chance." But such stories were grist for the mill that Ruvalcaba and Morial were Robles allies and part of the general corruption that was attributed to him. Macias continued, saying, "especially the three *que andaban* [go around together] because what I heard is that they went against them because they [Sunlaw] weren't willing to give them a lot of [makes signs of money with his fingers]."

Nevertheless, Macias had a far less cynical and more supportive overall evaluation of the hunger strike. He found it interesting "because there you saw local politicians in the media and basically telling the people they were willing to starve myself for three days or four days. Most interesting was that we had so many young kids get involved. Whether they were manipulated or not, the point is that they got involved, and that's good. And they felt that that movement empowers them, they knew that they had made a difference, which is good. That helped a lot because they realized that if elected officials are willing to go against it then something's wrong."

The hunger strike combined spectacular media coverage and little visible support from residents, despite all indications that most shared the hunger strikers' position. At the very least, popular disconnect from the hunger strikers suggests that people did not see them as really part of the anti-plant effort. Yet the huge press turnout suggests a political savvy more likely to have come from Robles than any of the hunger strikers. But like the savvy of manipulating the arguments on Measure A in the voter information guide, it was behind the scenes.

Three additional behind-the-scenes, and particularly unwelcome, forms of anti-plant and electoral activism were thought to have Robles' signature on them. First, the No on Measure A Committee was accused of making and distributing a video that smeared political officials and candidates who were not on record as opposing the power plant. According to Luis Cabrales, the committee was threatened with a lawsuit by one of the television networks for unauthorized use of its images in a videotape that combined news clips with smear ads against pro-plant politicians. This tape, featuring clips of student demonstrations and of CBE posters, also had CBE's skull logo on its label and was distributed widely to households in South Gate. People I spoke to guessed that Albert Robles must have been behind it, but like so many anonymous negative electoral materials, the sender was never discovered. Second, Robles ran a slate of political unknowns as anti-plant candidates and spoilers against his enemies; the most conspicuous instance was a candidate with the same name as that of incumbent councilor Hector De La Torre. Robles' forces had their own slate, which included Flor Ruvalcaba running as anti-plant candidate for city clerk. The third instance had to do with an unlikely contributor to CBE. Two anti-Robles political officials told me, independent of each other, that a waste management company had made a big donation to CBE. They interpreted this contribution as buttressing the argument that CBE was being paid off by big energy, which wanted to block the adoption of SCONOx. When I asked Carlos Porras about the contribution, he confirmed that CBE had received a check from them, but that when he discovered the contribution, he returned the check.

The Pro-Plant Campaign

Sunlaw ran a well-funded public relations campaign that continued to make a case, to the South Gate electorate, for the company's civic-mindedness and in support of its power plant. Sunlaw's public relations campaign had spent some $40,000 in 2000. That amount included the Cinco de Mayo celebration, a community picnic, newspaper ads, and a float in the city's Christmas parade (Martin 2001a). Now Sunlaw turned up the heat, mobilized allies, and focused its attention on voters. Local and state anti-Robles political officials and the Los Angeles County Federation of Labor supported their own slate of candidates for the March city elections and waged a pro-plant campaign on Measure A.[6]

By the end of 2000, the grassroots anti-Robles movement was beginning to build up steam. The police, anti-Robles city councilors, and the city workers wanted him gone, and the police were beginning to do community organizing against Robles. The priority of the area's state legislators was to support the power plant, but they too were more than happy to make common cause in getting rid of Robles. In service of both, the legislators were probably instrumental in getting state officials involved in supervising the March 6, 2001, election and, subsequently, in getting the district attorney, the FBI, and the Justice Department to investigate Robles' threats and financial machinations.

The result was that this coalition ultimately built a real grassroots movement against Robles but fielded a top-down, non-face-to-face campaign in support of the plant. Like Sunlaw's publicity blitz, it delivered written and video messages to people and hired paid political canvassers but did not engage people directly on a personal level. Such muscle and passion as the pro-plant campaign had on the ground in South Gate was a corollary of the anti-Robles passion. And it wasn't much. Martha Andrade thought that "the only people who were really pushing it as being a good thing were people who worked for the pipe fitters' union, and there would always be somebody at one of these meetings saying what a great thing it is." In his analysis of the successful campaign that recalled Robles and the city counselors aligned with him, Sam Quinones (2007) argues that its success rested on organizing by existing community groups such as Community in Action and Padres Unidos. Yet in 2000 and 2001, members of those groups also opposed the power plant. For them, the issues were quite separate, even if a segment of anti-immigrant older white voters had them entangled.

RACE, RACE TALK, AND RACE SILENCE

Talk about attitudes toward recent immigrants and the avoidance of talk about them mattered to the outcome of the power plant struggle and to repertoires for building future cross-ethnic coalitions. Here we look more closely at the varieties of race talk and race avoidance: Who uses what? What message does each convey, and to whom? And what were the consequences for the outcome of the power plant struggle and the anti-Robles movement?

Race Talk

Recall that Carmen Avalos spoke (in chap. 6) to how her experience with anti-immigrant racism by whites had led her in the same direction as that taken by new citizens to support Robles. Speaking of how in 1999 she had almost voted in favor of recalling city councilor Bill DeWitt after she had read mailers accusing DeWitt (falsely) of opposition to the use of Spanish, she explained Robles-style politics with the phrase "playing the race card." That phrase is too vague. Carmen Avalos and South Gate progressives who disliked Robles' allusions to racism and xenophobia were angry that he was using Latinos' negative experiences with xenophobia in ways that benefited him but did nothing to challenge anti-immigrant practices or attitudes. Avalos said, "There are many tactics that being a Latino could be used [to] persuade our less educated voters, especially if they are newly naturalized citizens, because this to them is very new. I know that because I have only been a citizen for six years and I know what it was like to vote for the first time." In other words, selectively playing on people's knowledge about anti-immigrant sentiment against them made race talk effective—and not just among less-educated voters. When other South Gate officials explained why Robles and candidates he supported got voter support, they sounded a similar theme—that new immigrants are naive or gullible.

This discourse is a far cry from the displaced white racism encountered by the No on Measure A canvassers—that all Latina/os are bad because one Latino, Albert Robles, is a crook. Different as these strands are, the media often spin them into what in effect becomes an anti-immigrant explanation for corruption in Southeast Los Angeles' "new" Latino-majority cities. Regardless of intent, such explanations convey an impression that new immigrants are a mix of crooks and a gullible electorate. New citizens may well be gullible, but the implicit comparison is hardly true. The unspoken part of the message is that longtime citizens are somehow less crooked and less gullible than new citizens. Given the state of electoral politics in the United States, not only is this assumption implausible, but new voter naiveté is only part of the explanation for Robles' success, something many of Robles' critics know quite well. The other part of Albert Robles' rise that is often spoken about is that he has many business friends and friends in powerful places in California politics. Those friends are not new immigrants and were widely believed to have helped Robles in many of his efforts, including his squeeze on the South Gate police department in the fall of 2001.

It is hard to tell how much of the pro-plant sentiment that phone bankers encountered when calling white residents rested on anti-immigrant sentiment. Ethnicity also indexed other demographic differences, notably age, which helped produce ethnic differences in attitudes toward the power plant. Because of South Gate's history of segregation, its white and Latina/o residents were of different generations, with the former being older with grown children, and the latter younger with pre- and school-aged children. All Latina/o interviewees who mentioned school issues, regardless of their position on the power plant, agreed that education was an important priority for South Gate residents. Latina/o parents, both English- and Spanish-speaking, engaged with their children's education and participated in a variety of parent groups. Older white residents lacked comparable connections to South Gate's schools or to the intergenerational school–environmental toxics nexus because their children were long past school age.

White and Latino residents also differed in their attitudes toward industrial toxics in somewhat age-related ways, even though whites grew up under environmental conditions that were comparable to those that exist today. The white residents had grown up, raised children in Southeast Los Angeles—and survived, so for them air quality was less immediate. For Latina/os, environmental health hazards were much more immediate because they had young children.

Also, in the sixties and seventies, pollution was considered something to be borne, not least because people knew much less about its impact, but also perhaps because the industries that polluted the air were their source of good jobs and a solidly middle-class standard of living. Knowledge today about the health impacts of air pollution is much more widespread than it was forty years ago. Consequently, there is a great deal of local knowledge and concern among Latina/os about the high incidence of chronic respiratory illnesses, industrial accidents, and toxic spills; the ubiquity of industrial chemicals in the furniture, woodworking, and metalworking industries of the area; and the pollution from diesel trucks, trains, and nearby highways. The jobs available to Latino/a residents in today's South Gate also pay low or minimum wages—hardly high enough to overcome health concerns.

Race Avoidance

Both the pro-plant and anti-plant constellations included Latina/os and whites. Both groups had to deal with anti-immigrant sentiment, within their ranks or from the opposition. However, the particular challenges for each group were different. The pro-plant coalition included some vocal white residents whose interest in the power plant seemed less central than their opposition to Albert Robles. And the opposition to Robles by some of them seemed to have a strong streak of anti-immigrant sentiment.

Under these circumstances, it is understandable why a race- or ethnicity-avoidant discourse would be welcome within the coalition. Too close a look at one's allies was probably not such a good idea. Nevertheless, the vocal presence of xenophobes might well have sent a message to some Latina/o residents that confirmed their suspicions about why a power plant was planned for their city.

Anti-plant forces had their own issues around immigration and ethnicity. Race talk is at the heart of environmental justice. It made obvious sense to the high school activists who were immigrants and children of immigrants, but it did not make obvious sense to many of the white opponents of the power plant who lived with polluting industries when Southeast Los Angeles was all white; for them it was counterintuitive.[7] Even white anti-plant activists like Rhonda Nitschky weren't completely sold on environmental justice arguments in general or that the decision to put a power plant in South Gate was an instance of environmental racism.

White opponents of the power plant wanted to avoid issues of race and racism entirely and to focus on health and safety as the proximate issue joining them all together. Angelo Logan told me that some of the South Gate High teachers who were opposed to the plant didn't like the concepts of environmental racism or environmental justice. These teachers felt race was too controversial to add to the mix. He noted that these "happened to be white folks, and they didn't want to touch that with a ten-foot pole." Given the prevailing zero-sum thinking—that measures to remediate racism meant taking something from whites—it was not surprising that white anti-plant activists some-times heard environmental justice talk and talk about race as "negative" and anti-white.

Environmental justice activists certainly did talk about environ-mental racism with Latina/os, and it made immediate sense to many. But did they too avoid race talk around white allies? Nitschky was the only white anti-plant activist I met who spontaneously reflected on and talked about the workings of race and ethnicity. Early in my research, in directing me to anti-plant community activists, Huerta flagged Nitschky as a person with a valuable perspective by telling me about her exasper-ation with "these stupid white people" and his response about making

Nitschky an honorary Mexican. Both talked with me independently about the "stupid white people/honorary Mexican" exchange as a positive and reciprocal acknowledgment: Huerta signaled that Nitschky recognized racism, and Nitschky indicated that Huerta welcomed her critical acknowledgment of it. They created an empathetic bridge for cross-racial political race talk. Although it seemed to have stopped at that, this small incident underscores a larger political issue of how to explain to whites why environmental justice should matter to them, especially in ways that enlist ongoing support beyond the particulars of the Nueva Azalea campaign.

THE VOTE AND ITS INTERPRETATION

In the March 6 election, in addition to voting on Measure A, South Gate voters were also electing two city councilors, a city clerk, and a city treasurer. Most candidates for these positions were aligned with one of two slates: either the anti-plant Robles bloc or a slate that pledged to go with voters' wishes on the power plant. Although the County Federation of Labor and the Latino Caucus of state legislators supported the plant, both supported this "voters' wishes" slate, which was also perceived as an anti-Robles slate.

Because of the publicity, candidates had to speak their views on the plant. Hector De La Torre and Raul Morial were both running for reelection against a total of eight newcomers. Bill DeWitt and Pat Acosta ran on the same "voters' wishes" slate as did incumbent De La Torre. One of the other newcomer candidates (believed to be a Robles ally) was arrested for electoral fraud; another also had the name of Hector De La Torre, a coincidence no one believed was accidental. A third newcomer, Katrina Jackson, was later charged with filing election papers with a false address. Her husband, Angel Gonzalez, a printer and owner of Pyramid Press, was charged in December 2001 with printing an unsigned "hit piece" claiming that Pat Acosta had been disqualified, and illegally using the State of California's seal. Both pleaded no contest. The story notes that Gonzalez has been printing Albert Robles campaign materials for a long time. "He has also published mailers for Robles' allies, Mayor Raul Morial and Vice Mayor Xochilt Ruvalcaba" (Marosi 2001, 2002d). Among the things uncovered in the raid on the printer was the original of a 2001 anti-DeWitt hit piece (Quinones 2007, 105).

In the race for city clerk, anti-plant Flor Ruvalcaba, sister of councilwoman Xochilt Ruvalcaba, ran against biology teacher Carmen

Avalos, of the "voters' wishes" slate. The incumbent, Nina Bañuelos, in the midst of much controversy, had been disqualified for running for a third term because she failed to collect enough names on her electoral petition. There was some suspicion, however, that her ouster from the field had to do with the machinations involving the blocking of pro–Measure A arguments in the voter information booklet. Also on the "voters' wishes" slate was Albert Robles, who was running for reelection as city treasurer against businessman Joe Ruiz. Ruiz had run for city council in 1999 and been falsely accused of being a child molester in an anonymous hit piece.

On Friday, March 2, Marco Firebaugh, the state assemblyman for the district, held a press conference to make a formal request to the County of Los Angeles and the State of California to supervise transparency in the March 6 election and to have the South Gate city clerk removed from supervising it. He cited irregularities, such as absentee ballots having been issued to nonexistent people and addresses. At the press conference, Sunlaw representatives handed out documents that they said "proved certain irregularities" (Meza 2001).

On Election Day, several youth activists joined the last-minute phone bank efforts during the day and into the evening to remind the "nos" and "maybes" to vote. Channel 52 came to the CBE office to film them working the phones. People stayed at the office talking, eating still more pizza, and worrying. About nine o'clock they joined the crowd of people waiting outside city hall, where the votes were being counted.

The television stations and news reporters were there too, filming the crowds, which included students demonstrating against Measure A, and the council chambers full of people waiting for results. It was clearly a high-volume election. One older white poll worker told Fox News that she had "never seen as many people come in" as in this election. It was late when the vote count was completed. Everyone was exhausted by the time the results were announced, and the television crews filmed police carrying out the impounded ballot boxes for safekeeping.

When all the votes were finally counted, some 6,700 people had voted on the issue—4,488 no and 2,211 yes—or two to one against building the power plant (*The Press/La Ola* 2001). The result was pretty much what the anti-plant phone bank forces had predicted.

Although the vote was a clear statement on the power plant, the results of the election told a slightly more complex story. Both incumbent city councilors—one on each side of the issue—held their seats, but newcomer Pat Acosta on the "voters' wishes" slate made a strong showing (1,839 votes to De La Torre's 2,933 and Morial's 2,835). Albert Robles retained his post as treasurer, but challenger Joe Ruiz also did well (3,326 and 2,551, respectively). In a close race for city clerk, anti-plant newcomer Flor Ruvalcaba lost by four hundred votes to newcomer "voters' wishes" candidate Carmen Avalos. Voters certainly returned incumbents regardless of their position on the plant. Still, the results indicate that labor–Latino Caucus support mattered for a significant slice of South Gate voters, since many of those who voted against the plant voted for De La Torre. The vote also showed a reluctance to vote for an unknown simply because of her position on the plant—or less charitably, it showed a weakness in Robles' ability to deliver votes. The most robust first-time candidate seen as a Robles person was Flor Ruvalcaba. She got a great deal of television coverage but was otherwise unknown and unaffiliated with South Gate groups or networks. Her opponent, Carmen Avalos, was a teacher and had run a door-to-door campaign with the help of her students. Although Xochilt Ruvalcaba attributed the defeat of the power plant to the hunger strike and its coverage by television news, the strength of the grassroots anti-plant campaign by CBE and high school students, coupled with Avalos' on-the-ground campaign strategy, suggests the strength of the local for South Gate voters. As it turned out, this election marked the beginning of the end for Albert Robles as well as for the power plant.

During the victory celebration, the television news reporters predictably interviewed Alvaro Huerta and Xochilt Ruvalcaba. They also showed the anti-plant forces celebrating as well as replaying shots of the January student march and presentations to city council. All those who'd spent long hours working for this result were jubilant. And, like Jairus Ramos, they were a little surprised that it happened so fast: "I was very surprised. It was easier than I thought. Usually it takes years." Jackie Amparo spoke what others also felt. "It's stressful. I had been like doing the whole campaign: I would go to sleep at 3:00 in the morning, and I would like wake up like at 5:00. But I liked it and I did it."

Their victory confirmed what had been a leap of faith for them until that night—that people really can change things by acting collectively. They had gone through what most social movement theorists regard as the single most important experience for making lifelong activists. As Jorge Dueñas put it, "it was proof right there what people can accomplish." Although they had inklings from community canvassing and phone banking that people were opposed to the plant, Jorge was holding his breath. When the vote came in, Jorge, excited and relieved, said it felt "like it was a big breath of air." Jackie felt inspired that people her own age had accomplished it. For Jairus the experience gave new understanding to what he'd read about other social movements. And, Milton continued,

> I always knew that people together are powerful and not in a violent kind of way, but the power that is in their voice. And this proved to me that it was possible. I always knew it was possible but I never—I was never in a situation that it had happened, and so this just proved to me that we could make a difference. It was a different kind of energy than I had ever felt. It was like this warm thing—just to see all the people united and to see all these people chanting. It encouraged me to keep on—well, organizing the youth and everybody else and educating myself more to educate others.

This experience of collective action making a difference, about which these young activists speak, is the same kind of experience described by many veteran activists when they explain how and why they took the road less traveled and became full-time agitators and organizers. As we know, however, winning a grassroots campaign is not easy and doesn't happen that often. Veteran organizers and organizing schools try to give new organizers these experiences because they know that experiencing this sort of success is the best way to make lifelong activists (Brodkin 2007).

WINNING ISN'T EVERYTHING, BUT IT HELPS

After the campaign ended, CBE organizers reflected on its strengths and weaknesses, especially in relationship to their long-term goal of building an ongoing grassroots movement in Southeast Los Angeles. Some were a little disappointed that the campaign ended so suddenly— but only a little bit disappointed. They reasoned that because their win was so quick, there was little time to analyze what they were doing while they were doing it. And because it was so decisive, there wasn't the same imperative to analyze what had happened. It was a great success, and no one needed to look a gift horse in the mouth. As individuals, however, some activists reflected on the questions of what had worked and what hadn't, which goals were met and which weren't.[8]

Throughout the campaign, CBE organizers struggled to maintain a balance between stopping the power plant and doing the education and leadership development needed to build a community-based movement in Southeast Los Angeles of adults and youth. They ultimately created a campaign structure that gave people many opportunities for involvement—to leaflet as part of a group, to drop in and help at the phone bank, to take literature and talk to one's neighbors—as well as ownership and investment.

This campaign was very short as these things go. Environmental justice campaigns often go on for years. The months of October to December were mainly devoted to planning and outreach. Not until mid-December did the campaign really go public, and by early March it was all over. Yuki Kidokoro pointed out that, as wonderful as it was, a quick win also had a downside:

> I think there could be disadvantages of having a short campaign because you don't get the opportunity to really develop people, people's campaign skills, in that process because everything is so fast. At the same time, we didn't want to lose, so we didn't want to lose opportunity. I think sometimes when you are in campaign mode, you can do things that aren't necessarily developing leadership—it's kind of like ends versus means. You want to win the campaign, you want to also have a process by which people are learning and you're organizing and taking ownership over the campaign.

Kidokoro thought that some of these "ends and means" decisions needed to be evaluated, however:

> I think a lot of decisions we made were very staff driven, which I don't think is necessarily bad, but I think sometimes we could have slowed down the process so that we had meetings and really stepped through each of the decisions we made through a campaign, make sure you understood it, even understanding how stepping back and understanding strategic thinking around campaigning [is important]. Now when you talk to some people, everyone kind of thought this was our strategy. I think some of our members will understand that that was our strategy when it's shown to them, yeah, this is what we did, but I don't think they would be able to sit down with you and say, well, our strategy was we had a media strategy, we had a

city council [strategy], and we had whatever. They wouldn't be able to break it down in that way, which I think would be good [if they could]. At the same time, there is a question of if we did that, would it have allowed us to get some of these things done that made the campaign? Would we have been able to organize as many events? I don't know. I think we have differing views on that.

I personally think that we could have done more conscious development and going through the process [which is] critical when it comes to evaluation. I always have. I mean I think it's a great campaign. It's pretty amazing. I had to step back and say it's pretty amazing that we were able to fight a power plant during this kind of energy crisis.

Kidokoro, as a strong advocate of leadership development—which included evaluating what worked and what didn't—pointed to two specific areas in which she thought they could have done better. One was developing more variety in media speakers—something students also expressed. "There were people that Alvaro [Huerta] handled with the media, and he was very good from the beginning. I think that's another area that [we could have spent a] little bit more time doing some development with our members around was being spokespeople so that it wasn't one person, one staff person, being kind of the [spokesman] of the campaign, but kind of wide variety, but especially it wasn't somebody who lives here."

The other was to have involved adults who had already been working with CBE. "One thing I think in hindsight I would have liked to do better," Kidokoro noted, "is that having our existing members like our Huntington Park project advisory board and a Bell Gardens project advisory board also [more involved] to consciously make the decisions to take this on."

Staff scientist Bahram Fazeli added his belief that they had also erred in not working earlier with environmental organizations, because they too were part of an organizational community for CBE.

Although all CBE staff were committed to winning and developing community leadership and ownership of environmental justice, they varied in how much they focused on each in this campaign. Kidokoro and Logan put thinking about leadership development in the foreground, whereas Huerta focused on creating a plan of action and a media strategy. In retrospect, the combination of skill building and fostering democratic participation among active and potentially active participants, creating a campaign structure that invited participation, and getting a telegenic and clear message out to a wide public created an effective campaign.

Kidokoro also pointed out the importance of thinking about the ways campaign strategy contributed to longer-term goals of building a social movement.

> There are a lot of different pieces. I tend to feel like, because our longer goals are to build power in the community, [there are] trade-offs . . . if you lose a campaign but you have been able to get people really really on board, [you've built leadership but] people feel burned out. They don't necessarily want to go forward. If you have a win, even though you didn't do that training, that consciousness raising that gives people skills and tools of how to do a campaign, they will still be around—hopefully still be around to do that afterward and [do] some kind of evaluation process.

Building community leadership and winning battles are more than two separable goals. As Kidokoro pointed out, whether you win or lose affects participants' future involvement, and it also affects the way you evaluate your strategy of what works and what doesn't. That is, if you win, you evaluate the effectiveness of your actions in one way; if you lose, you're likely to evaluate their effectiveness differently. Kidokoro says, "It could be a lot about timing. There were a lot of different things that came together and worked well, and some of it was just really blatant mistakes on the part of the company. That was really amazing and great for us obviously. I think, had the company been a little bit smarter, we may have lost the campaign, and the evaluation would look very different." CBE organizers distinguished analytically between two tightly linked elements of movement success—winning the campaign and building a continuing community-based and community-led movement. In their retrospective analysis, organizers, having won, focused on the extent to which they could also have done more movement building.

It is also worthwhile to widen the analytic focus to examine the political context within which environmental justice activists organized. One of the more disturbing aspects of this campaign was the fact that CBE and the students faced opposition from their usual allies in labor and among progressive political officials. Another was that Sunlaw and their supporters did not always behave like the usual corporate-political suspects. Kidokoro recognized that Sunlaw's promise to leave if residents did not want the plant played a key role in defeating the plant. So too did the fact that Sunlaw honored that promise, even if it took a while.

What can we learn by comparing the campaigns for and against the power plant? The most obvious contrast is that environmental justice forces waged a grassroots campaign that emphasized direct contact with South Gate residents, whereas Sunlaw and its supporters did not. There were many indications that South Gate residents valued information that came from people they knew, whether they were neighbors or officials whom they knew by their performance in office, and information that was delivered personally, with an opportunity for dialog. These preferences give a grassroots approach an edge in credibility. So too does the central role played by high school students and their teachers. Paid canvassers and mass-circulated messages, fliers, or videocassettes do not have the same appeal. Indeed, the barrage of electoral fliers and hit pieces that circulated during the campaign created a background of confusion, which may have made personal conversation particularly welcome. All this suggests that the medium of personal contact, which is a hallmark of grassroots campaigns, is very effective in delivering its message. In contrast, as far as I could ascertain, there was not much on-the-ground activism in favor of the plant. Pro-plant forces may or may not have torn down students' signs, but they did not do much postering in support of the plant. Indeed, it seemed that both pro-plant state officials and the city workers' union were more intensely involved in their slate of "voters' wishes" candidates than they were in the power plant issue itself. In short, pro-plant forces seem to have had a divided focus and a top-down campaign, while the environmental justice campaign was about the power plant and only the power plant, and was waged in a person-to-person style.

If this was the case, we might well ask whether there was any investment on the part of South Gate residents in *favor* of the power plant that was at all comparable to the effort of those opposed to it? From what I was able to learn, such emotional investment as there was for building the plant came from pro-environmentalist state legislators at one end of the political spectrum and xenophobic anti-Robles voters at the other. Although I cannot quantify this statement, it seems from the vote count that there were many anti-Robles voters who were also anti-plant. This deduction suggests that there was not that much investment or support within South Gate for building the plant, and that the appeal of jobs and increased city funding ran far behind people's health and safety concerns.

The conclusion of this volume takes up the broader implications of this campaign. It returns to the stories people in South Gate told about what the fight was really about, and from the perspective of those stories we look at the broader lessons of this campaign for grassroots environmentalism.

Conclusion

MOST ENVIRONMENTAL JUSTICE STRUGGLES do not succeed, and of those that do, few win rapidly or decisively. So we must ask: Why were environmental justice activists in South Gate able to stop the power plant? To answer this question we need to return to the three different explanatory stories that different actors told about the power plant controversy. Each story highlights different facets of the struggle and attempts to explain different things. Each explanation of the controversy throws different elements into relief, gives us a fuller picture of what was going on, and helps explain why things turned out as they did. Because I was drawn to the controversy by the environmental justice movement and wanted to know why they won, I start with that story. Then I go on to rethink it with what I've learned from the stories told by those who supported the plant and those who wanted to get rid of Albert Robles. Following this trail should leave us in a better position to figure out what lessons this struggle can offer for building a wider grassroots environmental movement.

ENVIRONMENTAL JUSTICE: WHY DID THEY WIN?

The environmental justice story and its implicit question—What did activists do right that helped them to win?—are at the heart of this book. The answers were reasonably clear. They were able to block the power plant because their message, oriented to South Gate Latina/o voters, was clear and compelling: ethnic discrimination is bad for our health. CBE and Youth-EJ also crafted an effective grassroots campaign that had a clear message, a fine media strategy, and a plan of action that was attentive to community response, especially among newer immigrants. Most important, their message resonated deeply with many South Gate High students and a core of teachers, who became the backbone of the citywide effort to mobilize community opposition to the power plant. Their campaign politicized already existing knowledge, especially among new immigrants and their children, by connecting the dots between unhealthy air, high asthma rates, and the persistence of anti-immigrant treatment and sentiment. The mainly Latina/o working-class residents and voters in South Gate got it and voted down the plant. Their opponents not only ran a top-down and perhaps over-the-top campaign but made a crucial mistake in saying that if the community did not want the plant, they would not build it (Huerta 2001a, 2001b, 2005).

CBE and Youth-EJ members knew none of the nuances of South Gate politics or the powerful role they would come to play in the conflict, but both organizers and students had a fund of local knowledge from living and working in Southeast Los Angeles. They shared the commonsense knowledge of South Gate's Latina/o residents—the widespread awareness of ethnic discrimination and anti-immigrant sentiment, the loud public silence about racism and xenophobia, the importance of schools to the community, and the unhealthy air of the region. They may have known nothing about Albert Robles, or about Sunlaw's support from political officials when they first got involved, but they had a kind of taken-for-granted knowledge of the local landscape of everyday working-class ethnic politics. That CBE focused on schools suggests they knew or soon learned of their importance to communities.

The knowledge that animated environmental justice activists and potential constituents in South Gate is part of the wider fund of knowledge that has made environmental justice activism arguably the most dynamic strand of environmentalism. The emergence of environmental justice leaders from working-class communities of color has put working-class people of color in the forefront of the wider environmental movement. In this respect, the South Gate campaign only underscored what the larger history of environmental justice has already established—that it is a politics that comes from and speaks to the experiences of working-class people of color.

As suggested at the outset of this book, however, doing the right thing at the right time may well be a necessary condition for winning a campaign, but it is not sufficient. If it were, there would be many more decisive environmental justice victories, and most probably much greater improvements in the quality of our nation's air, soil, and water. The other two stories speak to elements of "sufficient."

THE PRO-PLANT STORY AS WORKING-CLASS ENVIRONMENTALISM: WHY DID THEY LOSE?

Environmental justice is not the only form of environmentalism that seeks to represent a working-class constituency, nationally or in South Gate. I've suggested that the pro-plant coalition has a basis for claiming itself to be a form of working-class environmentalism. Here I consider some additional evidence for that interpretation and the implications of it.

Like environmental justice activists, Sunlaw and their allies saw themselves as David battling Goliath, but not the same Goliath. Sunlaw Energy Partners was CBE's Goliath, a big power corporation wanting to try out a new emission control technology and once again using working-class communities of color as guinea pigs. Sunlaw's Goliath took the form of much bigger energy corporations that had substantial investments in the prevailing polluting technologies and a lot of political clout. Sunlaw built an alliance of underdogs, with themselves as an environmentally conscious business joined to labor and progressive officials representing a working-class constituency, a teamsters-and-turtles alliance to help workers and improve the air quality of California.

Evidence

One has to admit that agreeing to abide by the popular will is not the usual behavior of a corporate behemoth. Given the track record of the CEC in approving virtually all licensing applications and the political climate that supported building more plants, it is unclear why Sunlaw did not continue down that path despite the referendum's outcome, or why it agreed to abide by its outcome in the first place. We have seen that Sunlaw had good reason to think that its less-polluting technology was on big power's hit list.

Although I cannot speak to Sunlaw's motivations, two possible (and compatible) explanations for why the company agreed to abide by the South Gate referendum suggest themselves. The first and simplest explanation is that Sunlaw was confident that its message of cleaner power and good corporate citizenship would resonate with South Gate residents. It had active endorsements and support from the area's popular legislators and from equally popular labor unions, and it believed in its own product.

The other explanation comes from information that surfaced after the South Gate campaign ended. Although this explanation involves speculation, it links Sunlaw's fears of big power with the latter's muscle against the cleaner technology's installation on a big, demonstration-sized plant. This explanation suggests that Sunlaw might have believed—with good reason it turns out—that given big power's political connections, the CEC would be a less than friendly environment for the company. Some evidence for this line of thinking surfaced when three San Joaquin County officials and lobbyists were charged (in 2002) and convicted (in 2006) of using political influence and intimidation to pressure Calpine (a big power corporation) to withdraw from competition with Sunlaw to build a power plant at the Port of Stockton. The port decided to go with Calpine (Associated Press 2002; Scott 2006; see also Rose 2003). In 2001, Sunlaw was also assisting a community group trying to block another Calpine plant near San Jose. When it appeared that the CEC was going to override even the combined opposition of this large middle-class community group, the corporate computer giant Cisco Systems, and the city government of San Jose, to Calpine's 600-megawatt plant, this coalition offered a compromise, which was to accept the plant if Sunlaw's SCONOx emission system were installed (Hamm, Roberts, and Orma 2001). Calpine rejected the compromise, and so did the CEC; the plant has since been built.

It now looks as though Sunlaw's Nueva Azalea plant in South Gate was one of a variety of attempts by the company to have SCONOx installed on a large plant to demonstrate its effectiveness. Where community opposition alone blocked it in South Gate, in San Jose, community, corporate, and municipal government support combined were not successful in getting it installed—when the ball was in the CEC court. This last decision especially suggests, at least in hindsight, that Sunlaw may have known that it would not have smooth sailing with the CEC in South Gate. If so, the reason Sunlaw agreed to a South Gate referendum may have been because it looked like a good, or at least like the best of a bad set of alternatives, and a possible lever against anticipated CEC hostility. That Sunlaw had good reason to see itself as a David in the world of corporate and state politics would explain their fury at CBE. It also raises the possibility that the company would have been rejected by the CEC even if CBE were not on the scene.

Be that as it may, the proximate reason the plant was defeated was because the voters rejected it and the city government supported their decision. Sunlaw and its allies in labor and progressive politics lost the referendum because they did not understand that their form of teamsters-and-turtles environmentalism wasn't the only kind of working-class environmentalism there was, and because their version simply did not resonate with a majority of South Gate's residents the way that CBE's competing version of working-class environmentalism did. There are lessons to be learned by comparing these two forms of working-class environmentalism.

Differences and Implications

What did each offer in the way of priorities and moral vision to South Gate's working-class residents? How did these priorities and visions map onto larger traditions of working-class and poor people's activism, and what lessons might they offer for viable models of working-class environmentalism more generally?

For the pro-plant labor environmentalists, the story was about creating a win-win coalition between traditional adversaries, labor and business, that would support working-class concerns for good jobs and a labor-friendly green business that had invented a less toxic way of producing electric power. For labor unions and public officials, the workplace was the taken-for-granted focus of working-class interests, and jobs, specifically the good union jobs in construction and main-tenance that the plant would bring was its signature issue. Pro-plant discourse created a racially (and gender) neutral working-class actor for whom environmentalism meant good jobs with a green business.

On its face, the crux of the difference between labor environmen-talists and environmental justice was whether jobs or health was a more important working-class issue. When the pro-plant labor environmen-talists stressed the plant's relatively low emissions and its potential to improve the state's air quality, they deflected the health argument more than they addressed it. They also did not engage the environmental justice argument about racial disparities in environmental risks. Like-wise, environmental justice forces argued for health, but they too did not engage the jobs issue.

The focus on jobs did not make a clear and compelling message about why the plant was a good thing for working-class South Gate. Judging from not only the results of the South Gate referendum but also the sentiment in neighboring Downey, Bell, and Huntington Park, I believe that community and environmental health engaged far deeper and wider passions than did jobs in this working-class belt of Los Angeles County. Part of the resonance was that the site of working-class action in environmental justice is where people live, go to school—and work. Real worries about industrial toxics and environmental health resonated across ethnic lines. Jobs are fungible and finite; health as an outcome of the area's air quality is shared. Everybody in the area breathes the same air. Health also had a moral valence that the idea of "good jobs" did not. A small number of people might get jobs, but for most of the region's households, those few jobs would make no difference. Still, the mix of whites and Latina/os, old and new residents, on both sides of the issue should be a reminder that both health and good jobs remain important elements of working-class visions.

Beneath the surface, however, jobs and health were social issues that carried racial and ethnic baggage. The good union jobs that were to come with building the power plant were building trades jobs. Yet the unionized building trades have long been poster children for racially exclusionary male unionism. The labor market is as segregated as the residential housing market, and these are not the kinds of jobs that South Gate's working-class Latina/o immigrants were likely to get. Martha Andrade's comment about the pro-plant pipe fitters she saw at the South Gate city council echoes here: union pipe fitters don't live in South Gate. An overemphasis on skilled, unionized building trade jobs in this context gives the working class a white and male look, not because women and nonwhites don't want such jobs but because there are gender and ethnic barriers to getting them. "Good jobs" as an issue, then, is not as ethnic- or gender-innocent as it seems on the surface.

Health in environmental justice discourse also has ethnic baggage. Arguments that corporate polluters and their political allies target nonwhite working-class communities for toxic industry give health and working-class communities an ethnic and racial inflection (but a gender inclusiveness). As with the issue of good jobs, some of the messages are unintended and had varied receptions. Although environmental justice messages offered a welcome explanatory framework to immigrants and their children, to whites who had grown up, worked, and lived around polluting industries when the area was white, the idea that racism caused the region's toxic air was far from obvious. In earlier times, before the deadly consequences of industrial pollutants became widely known, the poor air was a concomitant of the good jobs and an upwardly mobile middle-class lifestyle. Some older residents downplayed the dangers of industrial toxics and reasoned that the power plant would also be safe to live with.

In addition, some whites believed that introducing talk of ethnicity and racism was negative, almost a form of racism in itself, because it implied that whites were part of the problem. Such talk was divisive of the unity that existed when the issue was understood as health. In general, white residents, including those allied with environmental justice activists, were more comfortable with avoiding race talk and explanations than were Latina/o residents. The way in which people heard environmental justice race talk was also shaped by a legacy of community-based activism that had elevated white racism to an acceptable form of working-class politics. During the civil rights era, as we saw, South Gate's politics were largely driven by the white working-class residents' fear of racial integration as a threat to their status and security.

The differences between pro- and anti-plant versions of working-class environmentalism are a microcosm of differences that have long distinguished two historical strands of working-class activism in general, including working-class environmentalism. One strand of labor environmentalism has roots that go back to the early environmentalism of the 1970s, to efforts to link issues of occupational safety and health in the workplace, especially the issue of toxics created during the production process, to the toxics' impacts on everyone's air, soil, and water. Gottlieb (2005, 347–388) has chronicled the history of efforts by unions, occupational health and safety groups, and mainstream environmental organizations to find common ground across class lines. He places his analysis in the context of America's long post-Vietnam economic recession, which left unions struggling for survival in the face of a sustained corporate assault. Not surprisingly they have waged a defensive war focused on preserving jobs, especially union jobs. Environmentalist attacks on polluting industries, especially nuclear and coal power, raised union fears of more blue-collar union job loss, a point made repeatedly in industry public relations campaigns. Unions have been uneasy about the consequences of environmentalism for jobs, and about environmental groups' lack of concern about blue-collar jobs. Most unions, however, have also been relatively uninterested in taking up health and safety issues around toxics, even in the workplace. As a result, Gottlieb argues, union–environmentalist alliances have been for the most part fragile and episodic. In short, labor environmentalism has historically had a longstanding political identity problem; it has focused on jobs and been uneasy about taking on anything that might jeopardize them—including environmentalism. The pro-plant coalition fits well within this tradition.

Environmental justice is part of a more civic- and community-based tradition of labor and working-class politics, which has tended to come from unions and organizations in which workers of color and new immigrants predominate (Tait 2005). Here, talk about race and racism and their impact on issues within and beyond the workplace is explicit. Although it seems natural to most Americans that unions focus solely on the workplace, in fact European unions, and some of the more radical and progressive American unions, have a heritage of working-class radicalism that includes community-based activism, support for race and gender equity, and civic political engagement with which environmental justice has more in common. These efforts are premised on seeing the job of unions as defending the whole of workers' social existence by taking on health, safety, housing, education, and quality of life as working-class issues.

Speaking about race, racism, and racial differences as lived class experience is at the heart of environmental justice politics and that of the more community-based working-class tradition. Mainstream labor and South Gate's pro-plant labor environmentalism shared an even more well-entrenched heritage of speaking (and acting) as if the working class has a single set of interests, and that racial and ethnic differences are a form of "false consciousness," more than substantively different experiences of work and neighborhood life in America's broad-based working class.

In recent decades, labor historians have called into question the effectiveness of class-transcendent perspectives. They have pointed out that, in practice, appeals to class solidarity historically have prioritized the issues and visions of white men, thus substituting interests of part of the class for the whole and erasing those of the rest (Honey 1993; Letwin 1998).

In addition, the white segregationist legacy, in South Gate and nationally, shows race and racism to be important strands of working-class "homeowner politics." That legacy persisted in South Gate as a ghostly presence that took the form of institutional and interpersonal anti-immigrant sentiment. It was underscored by periodic outbursts of xenophobia in California politics throughout the 1990s. Consequently, race and xenophobia persist in South Gate's social atmosphere, even if civic and labor leaders maintained steadfast silence on the topics. More-over, as the third story brings to the fore, these silences communicated a variety of intended and unintended messages to different groups of South Gate residents.

Before going there, it is important to keep in mind that all of the groupings—pro-plant, anti-plant, and anti-Robles, were multiethnic. There was a shared consensus that relatively new citizens were clearly opposed to the plant and that older whites were an equally clear demo-graphic base of support for the plant, whereas older U.S.-born residents whose heritage was Mexican or Central American were divided. Never-theless, the ways that racial and ethnic attitudes worked was seldom obvious. Neither side was organized on ethnic lines.

THE ANTI-ROBLES STORY

Placing the struggle over Albert Robles at the center of inquiry raises the question of how Robles managed to build and keep a strong electoral base, and why a movement arose to get rid of him. He was not the first Latina/o on South Gate's city council, and he seems not to have done much to improve the lives of the city's new immigrants. Most people I interviewed agree that Robles was an able politician and that, at least at the beginning, he did a great deal of door-to-door campaigning. I've argued that one of the things he also did was to acknowledge the xenophobia that was rampant in California in the nineties, even if only through symbolic gestures like attempting to make Cinco de Mayo the city's main celebration. Against the background of public silence about race, Robles offered an alternative. Following this thread directs us to consider the impact on South Gate residents of persistent society-wide anti-immigrant sentiment, combined with public silence about it.

The campaign to get rid of Albert Robles drew support from both whites and Latina/os. Its leadership overlapped greatly but not completely with that of the pro-plant campaign, but for most of its grassroots supporters, the power plant issue held considerably less interest and drew less support than getting rid of a corrupt politician. The stated agenda of the anti-Robles movement had nothing to do with race or ethnicity. As with the pro-plant campaign, however, race neutrality was hard to maintain in a context in which race talk had already been introduced not only by Robles but now by environmental justice activists as well. Moreover, Robles himself made already existing racism against new immigrants a magnet in the sense that opposing his corruption became a way to express resentment at changes wrought by immigration. The environmental justice campaign brought xenophobes' views of immigrants into the open and encouraged them to support the power plant, through a kind of "the enemy of my enemy is my friend" emotional logic. If Robles was against it, they were for it.

The race-avoidant discourses of the anti-Robles leadership played differently among various segments of South Gate's population. The labor and progressive public officials who led the pro-plant teamsters-and-turtles forces hoped for unity and sought to model it, verbally and otherwise, by avoiding talk about race lest it be heard as divisive. Instead, they stressed bases of agreement, especially a version of working class-ness that transcended such differences. It was a discourse of hope. To some, both Chicana/os and whites who remained in South Gate long after it became a Latina/o city, the model described their lived experience: South Gate was still a working-class city, and everyone mainly got along. Racism wasn't an issue. To others, however, especially new immigrants, this kind of talk was reminiscent of the "emperor's new clothes," a public insistence that all was well on the race and ethnicity front when they knew perfectly well it wasn't.

The class solidarity message allowed the progressive anti-Robles leadership to work with xenophobic whites without having to confront the latter's racism. One unintended consequence of the class solidarity talk was that it gave inadvertent shelter to xenophobia within the anti-Robles movement. And in turn, I suspect that the combination of white xenophobia and support for the power plant confirmed to some environmental justice supporters that anti-immigrant sentiment really did have something to do with putting still another polluting industry in their city.

Looking at the power plant controversy from three perspectives allows us to be more precise about the messages embedded in the focus of different strands of working-class environmentalism and the complex ways that race, racism, and xenophobia exert an unpredicted but significant impact on such struggles. We can view the jobs-versus-health conflict as a window on a wider conflict between a less and a more inclusive view of the working class. First, jobs are allocated to and are "properties" of individuals. Second, job opportunities are different from entitlements or guarantees. An exclusive focus on jobs emphasizes individually held resources and only a chance at access. The focus on air quality deals with a shared resource that is equally available (or not) to all who live in this working-class area.

This campaign also underscores the truism that racial and ethnic attitudes, much like their institutionalized forms of discrimination, are always present and thus part of covert as well as overt politics in America. The key challenge is to tease out the ways in which they operate. Environmental justice activists may have faced discomfort from white allies when they talked about discrimination and xenophobia, but they didn't create either the discomfort or the discrimination by speaking about them. Not to talk about things on which allies differ may well have been commonsense, polite behavior; activists on both sides of the power plant struggle did it. The pro-plant forces were very polite and didn't talk about racism at all, but that didn't make it go away.

Indeed, not talking about race in South Gate helped to support a project that would have had a racially unjust outcome, regardless of intent. The pro-plant environmentalists encouraged a racially unjust program for improving California's air quality—which was precisely what environmental justice activists called them on. Just as a class-transcendent discourse erased the ethnic variety within working-class experience and priorities, so too did the focus on statewide air quality erase its actual local variability, which is tightly linked to racial and ethnic segregation where people live and work.

Pro-plant forces and city officials were not the only ones who avoided race talk, however. White opponents of the power plant who worked alongside environmental justice activists had their own troubles with the racial dimensions of the environmental justice message. White discomfort with topics racial is an open secret in America. For the most part, white anti-plant activists did not speak about race. They treated their participation with environmental justice activists as if the fight were only about the healthfulness of the community's air quality. A few tried to discourage talking about race and racism at all because they heard talk about racial disparity as negative, as seeing whites as the enemy, or as excluding whites.

As I listened to what it was about environmental justice race talk that made their white allies uncomfortable, I realized that whites were hearing race talk as a zero-sum game. If the fight was about improving life for people of color, then sacrifices would have to be made—by whites. Rhonda Nitschky and Alvaro Huerta both told the same story to me about Nitschky's exasperated white-people-are-so-stupid response to their phone banking, and Huerta's we'll-make-you-an-honorary-Mexican reply. Both told it as a positive story, of Nitschky recognizing and challenging white xenophobia. Its importance to them was that it was an exception to the pattern.

Identifying a xenophobia that led whites to cut off their nose to spite their face is not exactly the same thing as zero-sum thinking about racial justice, however, especially among whites who worked with environmental justice activists. In zero-sum thinking, people reason that if discrimination against one group is to be remedied, another group must give up something. As we saw, the model's intellectual architecture goes back to neoconservative arguments against affirmative action in the 1970s, but the reasoning now dominates a wide spectrum of mainstream thought about affirmative action in education, jobs, and environmental health.

Most grassroots environmental movement building has centered in working-class areas, and many of these struggles are multiracial. Two cautionary analyses of interracial dynamics in working-class antitoxics struggles suggest that zero-sum thinking is not confined to whites, and that the difficulties of overcoming it are considerable.

In the first example, a community struggle in South Los Angeles looked something like another version of South Gate's jobs-versus-health struggle. Participants on both sides were concerned with working-class issues, here jobs and quality of life through urban gardens.

The South Los Angeles community group Concerned Citizens of South Central (CCSC) was a pioneering African American environmental justice organization. It had stopped the city of Los Angeles from building a solid waste incinerator in its neighborhood in the mid-1980s. The city subsequently turned the site into community gardens, and over the years largely immigrant Latina/o gardeners created an extraordinarily successful gardening community. When a private developer laid claim to that land to build a warehouse and small park, CCSC sided with the developer, arguing that the project would create much-needed construction jobs. This stance pitted them against the gardeners, who argued that their gardens were another kind of economic opportunity and that they created "a type of Urban Nature capable of renewing the otherwise bleak urban landscape" (Gottlieb 2005, 11–12).

Here too, however, jobs and quality of life had ethnic baggage. This conflict was also a black–Latina/o conflict. This area had long been a working-class African American neighborhood, but it was becoming transformed as increasing numbers of new working-class Latina/o immigrants moved into it. In this instance, the jobs-versus-gardens conflict became a proxy for intra-working-class racial friction. To some degree that friction was about neighborhood ownership, and to some degree it was about job competition. Both issues had racial subtexts. Many African Americans saw new immigrants as indirectly responsible for the loss of good jobs and strong unions, especially in the cleaning and tourism trades. With the arrival of large numbers of undocumented immigrants, non-union employers seized on their presence to lower wages and break unions that African Americans had worked hard to build. This conflict reminds us that race and the disparate experiences of working-class Americans are about more than blacks and whites. So too are the silences.

A different cautionary tale, this one about the challenges of speaking about race, comes from Buttonwillow, a small working-class town in California's San Joaquin Valley. Here, the struggle was against expansion of a large toxic waste dump run by the Canadian corporate giant Laidlaw and its devastating impact on residents' health (Cole and Foster 2001, 80–102). Slightly over half of the residents were Latina/o, and the rest were African American or white. Early on, activists struggled to have Laidlaw and agency materials translated into Spanish. Luke Cole, a participant as well as analyst of the struggle, argued that the strength of the campaign lay in the strong, self-reliant, and cohesive coalition that developed. The struggle for translation helped build that sense among Spanish speakers, but the focus on Spanish translation, especially as reported by the local press during the anti-immigrant voter initiative Proposition 187 in a conservative part of California, undermined the group's strength. Shifting the focus from the dump, where there was multiracial support, to the use of Spanish and the identification of the struggle as Latina/o, Cole argues, lost support from black and white participants, weakening grassroots power. How to maintain a multiethnic coalition in the face of systematic division? Refusal to translate information into Spanish was a form of discrimination against Spanish speakers. Not to address that form of exclusion would have worked against their participation. Yet the effort it took and its spin by the local press worked to weaken participation by black and white English speakers. Here the challenge was how to maintain the sense of ownership among English and Spanish speakers in the face of a two-pronged attempt to split them.

These campaigns reveal just how complex is the mix of elements and the tensions among them that grassroots environmentalists need to balance. The challenge from Buttonwillow was to be clear about racial justice, yet not allow it to blur the focus on the core environmental issue holding a multiracial alliance together. From South Los Angeles the message was to find ways to speak about the Latina/o–black friction that underlay and fueled competition and undermined ways of thinking about cooperation. These two cases, together with the South Gate campaign, make it clear how important and difficult it is to address race in ways that work through differences and conflicts rather than avoiding them.

The good news is that environmental justice activists in Los Angeles are now developing exciting new ways of working through such differences by on-the-ground practice. In the process they are more sharply analyzing the ways that racism abets pollution. Society-wide segregation allows corporations and their political allies to hide both the production of toxics and their connections to a wide range of diseases in low-income communities of color. Continued production of toxics is key to the survival of all too many industrial corporations. Although communities of color bear a disproportionate share of the workplace and residential burdens of industrial toxics, those hazards are hardly confined to them. On the one hand, racial and ethnic segregation have forced low-income working-class people of color onto the cutting edge of knowledge about the dangers posed by industrial production. On the other hand, even though working-class whites are also impacted, segregation has buffered them (and even more so middle-class Americans) from experiencing the corporate production of toxics up close and, as a consequence, retarded these groups' awareness and knowledge. In this respect, communities of color and environmental justice activists have had to become unwilling experts on the toxic correlates of industrial capitalism. They are much like miners' canaries for the world. This politics may connect dots across ethnic lines, but it also has a radical edge that deconstructs the conventional discourse that "America," as an aggregate of undifferentiated individuals, has to get over its materialism. It identifies corporate capitalism and its political supporters as the chief obstacles to the planet's health and safety.

In Los Angeles, CBE and other grassroots environmentalists are, on the one hand, beginning to create new kinds of campaigns and coalitions that show the links between racially concentrated, segregated production sites and their wider social impacts, and on the other develop a proactive agenda for working-class needs that offers positive alternatives to health and environment-destroying toxic industries. Toxic use reduction, or finding less toxic alternatives in production, is, as Gottlieb puts it, an "implicit call for industrial restructuring, worker empowerment, and a redefinition of the work/environment relationship [that] ... can form the basis for new kinds of social movements (2005, 385). Toxic use reduction has the additional advantage of extending the critical focus on corporate practices that have marked the environmental justice movement.

CBE is among the Los Angeles pioneers of a variant on this model. Its activists have been talking about renewable energy for a long time, but the new direction incorporates toxic reduction with broad-based alternative visions that come from the priorities of working-class communities of color. CBE is a founding organizational member of Green LA, a broad cross-class and multiethnic coalition of environmental and economic justice groups, mainstream environmental organizations, funders, city government agencies, and research institutions whose agenda offers a working-class, multiracial vision of what social justice and environmentalism can look like. The premise of Green LA is "that if the environmental quality of life is going to improve in Los Angeles, we must focus our efforts on those areas of the City where the environmental problems are the worst." Its goals for Los Angeles include the following: becoming the first city in the United States to deal with the concentration of polluters in working-class communities of color, prioritizing toxic reduction at the largest polluter, the Port of Los Angeles; making the city the leader in providing safe drinking water; expanding its urban parks, gardens, and open spaces; and improving public transportation and cutting traffic congestion. Finally, Green LA calls for the city's agencies to establish climate-neutral goals for its functioning (CBE 2007; Green LA n.d.).

Part of this program, in turn, rests on growing public awareness about global warming and the ways that industrial capitalism is contributing to it. With widespread awareness of global warming, mainstream environmental organizations have become more receptive to taking on the issues of urban air pollution and toxics that environmental justice activists pioneered. Most important is that the new coalitions and political agendas that are emerging in Los Angeles make it easier for new groups of people, especially, but not only middle-class and white ones, to see environmental justice as *not* a zero-sum game.

Perhaps the most dramatic example of the new environmentalism in Los Angeles is the multipronged ports campaign. This effort is hoping to force the adjacent ports of Los Angeles and Long Beach, the nation's largest, to cut drastically the toxic emissions that have been destroying the health of South Los Angeles' working-class communities of color. The ports campaign has been complemented by parallel efforts to clean up emissions from the rail yards that are also concentrated in South Los Angeles. In both cases, much of the pollution is caused by diesel emissions resulting from 24/7 operation of container ships and trucks at the port, and locomotives in the rail yards.

CBE and the East Yard Communities for Environmental Justice (headed by former CBE youth organizer Angelo Logan) took the lead in creating the Green Los Angeles Port Working Group. It includes a number of environmental justice organizations as well as mainstream environmental organizations like the National Resources Defense Council, the Coalition for Clean Air, the American Lung Association of California, and the Long Beach Alliance for Children with Asthma. It also has active support from labor, especially the Teamsters, as well as the Los Angeles County Federation of Labor. The latter featured the port struggle in a three-day organizing, outreach, and unity march, Hollywood to the Docks, in May 2008.

The ports campaign heated up in 2007, and in March 2008 both cities presented draft plans for cleaning up their ports. At the center of the controversy, and the plans, were the trucks that carried the cargo from the ports (and rail yards) to their final destinations. Truckers had to line up and wait many hours, often with diesel engines idling, for their turn to load. Years ago, the shipping companies and freight carriers had decided to "externalize" the drivers, that is, the truckers were no longer employees but rather independent contractors. It was a good deal for employers, who shifted the risks and costs of buying and maintaining

trucks, health and accident insurance, and retirement benefits, as well
as the cost of waiting time, onto the drivers. Drivers were not pleased.
Although technically "independent" operators, drivers are forced to
accept whatever the companies offer in order to work at the ports.
They clear very little, and less now with the skyrocketing cost of diesel
fuel. Their trucks are old, repairs are costly, and retrofitting with cleaner
alternative engines is financially out of the question for these owner
operators. To add insult to injury, truckers are among those most at risk
from diesel fumes.

Cleaning up the trucks was a classic jobs-versus-health problem
waiting to happen. Residents most affected by living near the ports
and rail yards are low-income working-class people of color. Truckers
are independent operators, but they are also low-income workers, and
many of them are men of color.

The Port Working Group collaborated with the Teamsters and the
Los Angeles County Federation of Labor, and worked directly with
truckers at both ports who wanted to be employees in law and who
were not happy with having been "externalized" by big container and
transport corporations. They succeeded in persuading the administra-
tions of both the Port of Los Angeles and the Port of Long Beach to
make the container and transport companies the employers and the
truckers their employees, and to hold employers responsible for cleaning
up diesel emissions. In June 2007 the Ports Working Group wrote to
the directors of both ports to

> congratulate you on proposing a significant first draft of a plan
> to address a major source of the port-related pollution whose
> billions of dollars in health and other costs have been shouldered
> by local communities, and indeed by all Californians, for decades.
> We strongly support your efforts to put an end to this unfair and
> unjustifiable cost-shifting by companies in the goods movement
> chain who are profiting by doing business at the Ports.
>
> We strongly agree that a trucking system which requires
> employee status for truck drivers and ensures that trucking compa-
> nies are accountable for environmental and safety maintenance of
> truck fleets is the most cost-effective and meaningful approach to
> achieving significant emissions reductions now and well into the
> future. (Logan et al. 2007)

The group also pointed out, however, that the devil was in the details of the emission standards to which transport corporations would be held. They pointed out that the ports' proposal conceded much to the corporations in stipulating an overall fleet average for emissions rather than a truck-by-truck standard, as well as not insisting on a schedule for shifting to cleaner liquid-natural-gas trucks. It pointed out the community impacts, the impacts on truckers, and the fact that the ports' steep projected growth would wipe out the minimal changes proposed (Logan et al. 2007).

By March 2008, however, when both ports announced their final plans, it turned out that the City of Los Angeles and the City of Long Beach had decided on very different solutions to the problem. The Port of Los Angeles decided to hold trucking companies responsible for cleaning up the trucks. As a delighted County Federation of Labor put it, "the Los Angeles Clean Trucks Program places the responsibility for cleanup squarely on the backs of trucking companies and their giant retailer clients, rather than misclassified 'independent contractor' truck drivers—many of whom earn little more than minimum wage" (Los Angeles County Federation of Labor 2008).

The Port of Long Beach went the other direction. It decided it would pay whoever owned the truck about 80 percent of the cost of upgrading it, but the remaining cost (about $20,000) would have to be borne by the owner. Supporters of this plan argued that it could be implemented quickly, unlike the Los Angeles plan, which, they argued, the trucking companies would keep tied up in court. Opponents of the Long Beach plan argued that the plan would not be implemented because "independent" contractors did not have $20,000, given that they cleared about $30,000 a year. At this point, the National Resources Defense Council, a member organization of the Ports Working Group, announced its intention to sue the Port of Long Beach to overturn its plan (Mittelstaedt and Gallegos 2008; Blood 2008). It is unclear what form either of these plans will finally take if and when they are implemented.

Still, it is important to note that the plans rest on differing visions of working-class environmentalism. The Long Beach plan would ultimately make "independent" truckers pay for cleaning up the air in working-class communities. The burden rests on these workers not because the plan demands it but rather because it avoids putting pressure on big employers, the trucking companies, which already hold power over truckers and benefit handsomely from the present "externalizing" arrangement. Their stated neutrality on "who owns" a truck masks a de facto support for the corporate status quo. In so doing, the Long Beach plan pits environmentalism against jobs in an all too familiar song. The Los Angeles plan is potentially much more democratic. The city would use its power to compel trucking corporations to clean up the trucks and bring environmentalism and jobs together against a status quo of corporate greed. Still at issue, however, is the big problem of which emission standards will be applied to trucks, and how they will be enforced.

CBE is also involved in another model for working class–led environmentalism. The Los Angeles Apollo Alliance is a part of a national project, the Apollo Project, whose goal is "to create good paying 'green jobs' for working-class communities throughout the U.S." Initiated in August 2006, the Los Angeles coalition includes a mix of environmental, environmental justice, social justice, and labor organizations. Its three-year goal is to create two thousand good, green, and union jobs for residents of the county's working-class communities of color and to improve the city's environment (CBE 2007).

The challenges that CBE and their allies have taken up, of working across the extraordinarily complex racial, ethnic, and class lines of Los Angeles are enormous. Not least are those associated with creating a racially informed analytic discourse for keeping the priorities of low-income and working-class Angelenos in the forefront. The goals and the potentials of these coalitions, however, are equally great for creating a grassroots environmental and social justice movement in Los Angeles that can offer new models for revitalizing environmentalism.

Epilogue

BETWEEN MARCH AND NOVEMBER 2001, when Sunlaw officially withdrew its application, California's political climate was beginning to change. The rolling blackouts continued during the summer of 2001, as did the state's efforts to stave off increasingly severe statewide energy shortages, including efforts to bail out the failing and ultimately bankrupt utilities with taxpayer money. But, with the election of President Bush, a Democratic governor and legislature were up against a conservative Republican administration. The latter refused to force suppliers to sell to California or to impose rate caps on wholesale prices.

As the situation worsened and the options continued to shrink, arguments about the true cause of the energy crisis began to become a much larger part of the political process and public discourse. In May 2001, the Bush administration's Federal Energy Regulatory Commission (FERC) began to hold hearings on price fixing against big electricity suppliers and El Paso Natural Gas, owner of Southern California's largest natural gas pipeline.

There was also a high-profile public discourse—including a June 2001 PBS *Frontline* special on California's energy crisis—that continued through and beyond 2001 (*Frontline* 2001). The discussion publicized different perspectives on the causes of California's crisis. Some argued the problem was that deregulation was only partial and did not go far enough, while others argued that big wholesale energy producers like Duke, El Paso Natural Gas, Reliant, and Dynegy were bilking California of billions.

The flawed system argument is consistent with the big-energy-bilking-the-taxpayers argument, which has come to prevail since that time. The requirement that the big three suppliers had to sell a contracted amount of energy to consumers at a fixed price created a statewide demand-at-any price for wholesale energy. Wholesale suppliers, who provided most of California's energy once the big three sold off much of their productive capacity, had a situation in which great demand existed regardless of the price they charged. These factors operated pincerlike to create conditions ripe for what we now know was "gaming the system" by the new, "independent" wholesale suppliers that had good, fast computers and programs that allowed them to spot and profit from minute (or greater) local differences in the prices of electricity in different markets. It also allowed these power producers, which, unlike the big three, had no obligation to sell power to California—or even to produce power in the plants they owned in California—to manipulate the overall supply of electricity (and hence the spot price) in California. In contrast, California's big three buyers could no longer produce all the electricity they were obligated to deliver (having sold off almost half their capacity to do so) and had to buy it from suppliers that could manipulate the price. The result was the engineered shortages, artificially high prices, and obscene profits to a few companies, of which Enron was only the most flamboyant, which have been called the California energy crisis.

As early as December 2000, in the midst of these charges, the AQMD imposed the largest fine in its history, $17 million, on AES Corporation for illegally releasing more smog-causing emissions than allowed at its Long Beach plant (Martin 2000). Then in November 2002, FERC made public a report that accused the AES Corporation and the Williams Companies of Tulsa, both of which had power plants in Southern Los Angeles County and Orange County, of conspiring to create power shortages and drive up the price of electricity. The big-power-friendly Bush administration's FERC had to be forced, by a court order sought by the *Wall Street Journal*, to release the report.

The smoking gun in that report was a tape-recorded phone conversation between employees of the two companies about deliberately prolonging a power outage at one plant because the state was paying higher prices during the outage. In another incident,

> AES shut down a power plant unit in Huntington Beach because the cost of nitrous oxide emissions credits for the plant was too high, and the company was not making enough at existing rates to

cover its costs. Like the plant in Alamitos, that plant was under a "must-run" contract with the ISO [independent system operator]. Under such a contract, the ISO was paying $63 per megawatt hour. But on the open market, it was forced to pay $750 per megawatt hour. When Morgan informed the ISO that the Huntington Beach plant was shutting down because the credits were too expensive, an unidentified ISO dispatcher, refusing to accept that as a valid reason for shutting the plant, said: "So take some of that money that you just raped us out of Alamitos (unit) 4 and buy some damn credits." After speaking with an AES lawyer, Morgan called the ISO back and presented a new reason for shutting the plant—it had to be closed for repairs. But other unidentified AES and Williams employees said in recorded conversations that the shutdown was "weird" and that "it's just some big game they're playing right now." Williams earned about $10.3 million during the 15 days that the two plants were out. Officials of the Federal Energy Regulatory Commission ordered the company to return $8 million of that in March 2001 at the conclusion of its internal investigation. (Berthelsen 2002)

As the allegations of price gouging grew, as public discourse about power companies gaming the system grew louder, and as refunds and adjustments began to be ordered by FERC and the courts, the number of new plants that were certified for construction by the CEC plummeted (California Energy Commission 2005b). Some eight projects beginning the application process in 2001 withdrew in 2002 before completing the process, suggesting that a friendly climate may have encouraged some applicants whose projects may not have been fully developed and that the change in economic weather may have discouraged other prospective applicants.

In retrospect, most analysts agree that deregulation—at least in the form it took—was largely responsible for California's energy crisis of 2001. As early as 2002, there was evidence that Enron helped to write California's deregulation legislation and, with the help of the Arthur Anderson accounting firm, profited handsomely from it (Martin 2002),

"They had a strategy, and it was to work from Washington down to the states," said Peter Navarro, a professor of business at the

University of California at Irvine who studies the energy industry. "They won the battle at the federal level, and California came next." In meetings sponsored by the state Public Utilities Commission, Enron officials passionately argued their case for deregulation. "I don't know that you can separate Enron from all the other parties who simply shared their ideological view," said former PUC board Chairman Daniel Fessler. "Their view of the world was that the government had absolutely no business designing markets. But they weren't alone in that." (Martin 2002)

Much later, the state of California filed suit against Enron, El Paso Natural Gas, and other big energy companies for market manipulation and withholding supplies to drive up the price of electricity and natural gas needed to produce power. Attorney General Bill Lockyer accused Enron of masterminding the energy crisis. "They were certainly the leader of the pack. . . . They were the company that invented a lot of the market manipulation games that allowed this to happen" (quoted in Coleman 2005, A12).

Although suits continue to wind their way through the legal system, the suit against now-bankrupt Enron has been settled, as have similar suits against the company by the states of Washington and Oregon. These settlements, reached in July 2005, award a minute fraction of their real cost to the states and their taxpayers. It is bitter justice. Enron agreed to pay $47.5 million in cash to California, Washington, and Oregon combined and to accept a $1.5 billion claim in their bankruptcy case. None of these states will be able to collect on this claim, however (Coleman 2005).

Although Sunlaw claimed that it was the victim of a fraudulent election, it asked the CEC to suspend hearings on its application a few hours after the election results were announced. The city of Downey continued to worry. Its mayor warned that Sunlaw only asked for a suspension of hearings and did not pull its application for a permit, and that the fight would not be over until Sunlaw's application was denied (Adams 2001). Sunlaw extended its request for suspension until the end of 2001 (California Energy Commission 2001). At the same time, CBE was following the state of Sunlaw's application, which by October appeared once again to be active. CBE and the students returned to the city council in October to ask the council to change city zoning regulations so that Sunlaw would be unable to build on its selected site, but on November 5, Sunlaw quietly withdrew its application to the CEC, thereby resolving the issue.

Sunlaw had no success in getting its SCONOx emission control system installed in a large plant. In 2006, they closed their Vernon plants and sold off the assets.

Having defeated Sunlaw's proposed power plant, CBE now finds itself in the midst of a community-organizing battle against another power plant. This one comes from the neighboring industrial city of Vernon, which is attempting to build a power plant nearly double the size of Sunlaw's.

CBE is continuing to create new forms of working-class environmentalism in Southeast Los Angeles. In addition to participating in the leadership of Green LA and the Apollo Alliance, it is mobilizing to stop the city of Vernon from building its own 943-megawatt gas-fired power plant in close proximity to schools and working-class neighborhoods, and to clean up pollution at the huge nearby ports of Los Angeles and Long Beach. There is now a chapter of Youth-EJ at South Gate High.

The anti-Robles forces continued their efforts to recall Robles and his allies on the city council. They gained a great deal of support when the police began a full-court legal press and recall drive to oust Robles and his allies after Robles tried to create the position of deputy chief and place an ally in that position. By October 2001, the Robles issue was dominating city council meetings. In March 2003, the anti-Robles coalition succeeded in recalling Robles, Xochilt Ruvalcaba, Raul Morial, and Maria Benavides. Hector De La Torre went on to replace the late Marco Firebaugh as the California Legislative Assembly member from Southeast Los Angeles.

Notes

Introduction

1. My discussion of California's energy crisis draws on Thornberg 2002; the California Energy Commission Web site, www.energy.ca.gov/restructuring (accessed July 2005); *Frontline* 2001; and Wikipedia 2005a; as well as conversations with Mark Abramowitz and Edward Leamer.
2. Publicly owned power companies such as the Los Angeles Department of Water and Power, those owned by the cities of Glendale and Burbank, and by Imperial County, remained public; homes and businesses served by them were unaffected by deregulation.
3. New social movement theory and its challenges have been a core contributor to analyzing political subjectivities and their relationship to movement goals and visions, while resource mobilization theories have focused on questions of movement organization and strategies. See Morris 1999; Edelman 2001 for a review of both; also Brodkin 2005.
4. On the other hand, the focus of the story is that four South Gate police officers, regarded as the city treasurer's allies, won a $10.4 million lawsuit against the South Gate police department for harassment resulting from their ties to the treasurer.

Chapter 1   South Gate Transitions

1. Ira Katznelson (1981) has argued that views like those in South Gate during the postwar decades were national in scope and drove a white working-class swing to the political right. He argued that this group defined its class interests on the job very differently from those at home, with the latter interests governing its political behavior.
2. Anonymous interview, August 5, 2002.
3. Indeed, Robles was far and away the main subject about which the *Los Angeles Times* reported for all of Southeast Los Angeles. When I asked one of the reporters why corruption in a working-class city of new immigrants was all that the *Times* found newsworthy, he told me of writing a human interest story about a woman active in her community, but said his editor insisted that people don't want to read that kind of thing.
4. The city councilors choose the mayor and vice mayor from among themselves.

CHAPTER 2   ENVIRONMENTAL JUSTICE AND COMMUNITIES
FOR A BETTER ENVIRONMENT

1. The court denied the request, saying that this was the first time racial discrimination had been raised and that the decision to locate the dump was based mainly on availability of land (U.S. Government Accounting Office 1983, 20).

2. The network grew out of what was perhaps the first environmental justice national meeting, the People of Color Regional Activist Dialogue on Environmental Justice, which brought together eighty activists from thirty-two local groups engaged in environmental justice work. The Southern California affiliate groups in the network today reflect the interpenetration of environmental and economic justice. For example, Concerned Citizens of South Central Los Angeles, Mothers of East Los Angeles, Santa Isabel, and Communities for a Better Environment are best known for their environmental campaigns, while the Pilipino Workers Center and Korean Immigrant Worker Advocates focus on immigrant worker rights and AGENDA on working-class African and Latina/o communities and job access. The Bus Riders Union is best known for its suit against the Los Angeles public transportation authority for racism in underfunding and overcrowding in public buses, compared to exurban commuter trains. That these groups all saw themselves engaged in similar struggles suggests that the concepts of environment and economic justice were tightly linked, many faceted, and robust concepts by the early 1990s. Indeed, they were all part of a vibrant immigrant workers' movement in Los Angeles during the 1990s. This movement joined labor unions, independent worker organizing, and community organizing. It redefined the face of the working class in Los Angeles as heavily Latina/o and Asian as well as African American, and female as well as male. It also redefined labor and working-class issues to include a living wage, health care, education, transportation, clean air and water, and a generally clean, safe environment (Gottlieb et al. 2005; Milkman 2000; Brodkin 2007).

CHAPTER 3   CREATING AN ENVIRONMENTAL JUSTICE CAMPAIGN

1. Pat Robertson had recently bought this refinery. It had been closed down as one of the worst polluting refineries in the region. Soon after the power plant campaign ended, CBE and Youth-EJ organized an equally successful campaign to keep the CENCO refinery closed.

2. The city was the first to hear and, on April 12, 2000, reserved its right to make requests and recommendations (Pasmant 2000).

3. That battle pitted residents of affluent neighborhoods against the gardeners. The former objected mainly to the noise and also to the dust. The gardeners argued the blowers were economically necessary. Ironically, missing from the reporting on the issue was a discussion of the environmental health consequences to the gardeners, who bore the burden of the noise, dust, and gasoline fumes, and the extent to which they were independent contractors or employees.

4. Many schools in the Los Angeles Unified School District are on year-round schedules as a way to deal with overcrowding. When students in one track are off track, that is, they have vacation time, students on another track are in session.

CHAPTER 4   SUNLAW'S NEW POLLUTION CONTROL TECHNOLOGY

1. Helpful explanations can be found at Japan Steel Works (http://www.jsw.
   co.jp/) and Cogen 3 (http://www.cogen3.net).
2. See Vernon n.d. In early November 2006, the mayor and council members of
   Vernon were indicted for electoral fraud. None of them lived in Vernon—a
   requirement for running for election. It turned out that Mayor Leonis
   Malburg, grandson of founder John Leonis, lived in the affluent Hancock
   Park neighborhood of Los Angeles (Becerra 2006a, 2006b; see also Lopez
   and Connell 2005). Wikipedia (2005b) has an accessible summary of Vernon's
   colorful politics.
3. For a description of how cogeneration can be used for cooling, see Leposky
   2003.
4. In 2004, Danziger's Web site was part of an international music site (Danziger
   2004), but it incorporated the same résumé that was once found at the free-
   standing bobdanziger.com Web site.
5. Robert Danziger, email communication, January 5, 2005.
6. California Energy Commission 2000b; I'm quoting Danziger's testimony
   from the Santa Teresa Citizen Action Group Web site, www.santaterestcitizen.
   org/sunlaw.html (accessed June 7, 2004).
7. Volatile organic compounds, or VOC, are another common airborne toxin,
   but power plants are not a source of these.
8. SCONOx is an emission control system something like a catalytic converter.
   Emissions pass through a series of chambers in two stages. In the first, the
   oxidation and absorption cycle, doors open to allow the gases to enter and the
   catalyst oxidizes carbon monoxide (CO) to CO_2 and NO to NO_2. The NO_2
   reacts with the potassium carbonate coating of the catalyst to form potassium
   nitrates and nitrites. These must be transformed back to potassium carbonate
   in order for the catalyst to oxidize and absorb carbon- and nitrogen-based
   pollutants. In the second, or regeneration, cycle, the doors close to create an
   oxygenless environment. A mix of gases is passed over the catalyst, releasing
   mainly water, and nitrogen and sulfides into the air, and turning the potassium nitrates and nitrites back to potassium carbonate, the original absorber
   of toxics. SCONOx also claims to decrease emission of volatile organic
   compounds, by absorbing and oxidizing them (Czarnecki et al. 2000).
9. According to Danziger (phone conversation with the author, July 20, 2002),
   the SCONOx patents are held by Advanced Catalyst Systems, the main
   inventor of SCONOx. Also, Danziger explained, by 2002 Sunlaw Energy
   Corporation had two subsidiary entities: Sunlaw Energy Partners, which
   is the division that proposed to build the Nueva Azalea plant, and which
   also owns and operates the cogeneration plant in Vernon; and Emerichem
   (formerly called Goal Line Technologies), which sells a variety of catalysts,
   including SCONOx, for removing toxics produced by combustion.
10. Alstom Environmental Control Systems began as a Swedish "pollution
    control" and "air handling systems" company, and acquired many European
    and North American companies through mergers and acquisitions, becoming
    Alstom Power ECS. Its Web site lists three contact offices: for the Americas,
    one in Knoxville, Tennessee; another in France for Europe, the Middle East,
    and Africa; and a third in Japan for Asia.
11. The regulations governing air quality are much more complex than indi-
    cated here. There are actually three levels of certification. BACT applies to

air quality management districts in compliance with the Federal Clean Air Act. Districts whose air is not in compliance with Federal Clean Air Act standards—that is, dirtier, as is the air in Southern California—are governed by a lowest achievable emission rate (LAER) or reasonably available control technology (RACT) (Environmental Protection Agency, Information Transfer and Program Integration Division 1999).

12. For the text and history of Senate Bill 456, see http://www.leginfo.ca.gov/pub/95-96/bill/sen/sb_0451-0500/sb_456.

13. South Gate councilman Hector De La Torre, then an employee of Edison, argued that Southern California Edison had no interest in legislation about emission control because it owned no gas-fired power plants. Strictly speaking that may have been the case when I interviewed him, during deregulation, because Edison sold many of its plants as part of the deregulation process.

14. Cone 1997b; South Coast Air Quality Management District 1997; this last citation refers to a series of articles and op-eds in the *Los Angeles Times* that brought inquiries from AQMD board members about the staff's activities.

15. As Jones and Danziger argue, however, the shift appeared to be more cosmetic than real. In the case of SCONOx, AQMD's response to the EPA was to consult with the "affected industry" and the sponsors of Senate Bill 456, as well as others, and to modify that legislation so that the cumbersome process contained in that bill would apply only in cases in which California emissions ceilings would become lower than federal emissions (South Coast Air Quality Management District 1997). Although it meant that emissions from California's gas-fired power turbines would need to meet the national standard, it also put the brakes on the possibility of California doing a better job in controlling emissions from power plants. Indeed, Danziger's claim that AQMD never enforced the emissions level of NOx that it had been forced to certify seems borne out by events.

CHAPTER 5 THE PERFECT STORM

1. Many of Robles' enemies repeated, with great relish, the story about the time he distributed door hangers telling people to take their ballot stub to 7-Eleven for a free hot dog and coke—but forgot to attach the coupons to the door hangers—and was seen handing out dollar bills in the store parking lot. After a subsequent election, a story made the rounds that a local nursery, which rented city land for a token amount, put plants on everyone's doorstep, in a kind of quid pro quo, and urged the recipients to vote for Xochilt Ruvalcaba and against Henry Gonzalez in the city council election. This nursery was owned by George Garrido, a business partner of Robles—who was indicted in 2005 as part of the Robles corruption probe (Quinones 2007, 94; Yang 2005).

2. Unsigned campaign mailers are illegal in California; all mailers must be authorized by the candidate's election committee. No one connected to South Gate city politics was ever convicted of producing the hit pieces.

3. *Arcelia* is the Spanish word for "azalea." Sunlaw gave the plant a Spanglish name, Nueva Azalea.

4. Many people noted that Albert Robles had others do his political work for him. In January 2000, Martha Hernandez, who, according to Quinones was Robles' girlfriend, served the newly elected DeWitt with recall papers

charging that DeWitt had sued the city in 1997 over a violation of the Brown Act (which required open meetings and notification processes), had won an $18,000 settlement of the suit, and thereby had wasted the city's money. As we saw in chapter 1, DeWitt's suit in fact accused the city of hiring a consultant with no posting or application process. DeWitt withdrew his suit in return for his court costs and the firing of the improperly hired consultant (Douglas 2000).

5. The governor's expedited four- and six-month application processes truncated environmental impact reporting requirements and decreased the time available for public input. Governor Davis also initiated a twenty-one-day emergency certification process for peaker plants. A peaker is a single-cycle, gas-fired plant that is supposed to run only during periods of peak power demand. These plants tend to be more polluting, and they often ran full time during the crisis. Peakers also tend to be located in working-class communities of color (Bazar 2001; Latino Issues Forum 2001; California Energy Commission 2005a). Sunlaw Energy, however, was not building a peaker.

6. Most plants approved in this year began the certification process in 2000, as did Sunlaw. More than a quarter of all capacity and more than 40 percent of all projects in the California Energy Commission's seven-year tally were approved in 2001, suggesting that the energy shortages that began in the summer of 2000, together with public support for new building, encouraged the spurt of licenses granted in 2001.

   During 1999–2005, 53 power plants were approved for licensing, for a total increase in power of 22,256 megawatts (MW). The figures for the each year are as follows: 1999, 3 plants (2,219 MW); 2000, 6 plants (4,347 MW); 2001, 23 plants (6,270 MW); 2002, 4 plants (1,045 MW); 2003, 8 plants (3,610 MW), 2004, 8 plants (4,575 MW); and 2005, 1 plant (190 MW).

   It is not possible to know for sure how many of the 23 approvals in 2001 began the application process in 2001 and how many began in 2000. Twelve of them were approvals for peakers that applied in 2001 under the twenty-one-day emergency process and were approved. Another peaker applied under longer regulations in 2001 but was online by 2002. From CEC data, it seems that at least 10 of the 23 approvals for 2001 were for the relatively small peakers (those plants produced a total of 780 megawatts), which leaves 13 facility approvals in 2001 that most probably were for larger plants that had to go through the longer, more extensive review process. It is likely that many of these applications began the process sometime in 2000, as Sunlaw Energy did.

7. When Ruvalcaba's efforts went nowhere, she asked the council to hire a consultant to study the plant's environmental impact. This action did get council support, as well as support from state assemblyman Marco Firebaugh. On June 13 the South Gate Redevelopment Agency subsequently contracted with Environmental Science Associates (ESA) of Sacramento and allocated up to $36,800 for them to perform a specified amount of work, which they completed.

   De La Torre and Ruvalcaba both remembered this contract as being for evaluation of the power plant's impact on South Gate. But ESA's project manager John Forsythe told me that "the contract was not for an evaluation of Nueva Azalea's potential impact, but rather that our role was to provide strategic guidance to the city in the process—providing information about their process and where the city could intervene. I don't think we ever got to the point where we provided detailed evaluation [of the potential impact of the Nueva Azalea plant]." The contract bears out Forsythe. It was to provide "attendance at meetings and the preparation of technical memorandum addressing procedural issues and review and comment on environmental issues relevant to the City of South Gate" (John Forsythe, Project Manager, ESA, to Oliver Mujica, Economic Development Manager, City of South Gate, December 7, 2000, Attachment A, p. 3). There were no environmental impact reports. The city discussed a second contract much later—in December 2000—that would have provided such an evaluation, but the council never approved that contract (John Forsythe, telephone conversation, July 14, 2004).

8. The rebate (in fact $1 million) was never intended to be distributed to consumers, and besides, DeWitt was not on the council at the time it happened (*Long Beach Press Telegram* 2000).

9. Benavides was also the only councilor who did not return my calls requesting an interview. She was reputed to speak to no one.

10. For the police department's case against Albert Robles, see Peace Officers Research Association of California 2003.

11. These figures are from a mailer, believed to be from Sunlaw's publicity literature, listing South Gate City expenditures for 1999–2000, by department (copy of the mailer in author's possession).

12. Robles was reported to be more than angry at this coalition. He was subsequently charged with threatening to kill Assemblyman Marco Firebaugh, rape state senator Martha Escutia, and kill her husband Leo Briones, who ran Sunlaw's publicity campaign. Robles was indicted and tried for these threats, but the trial ended in a hung jury (Marosi 2002a, 2002b).

CHAPTER 6   FINDING TRACTION AT SOUTH GATE HIGH SCHOOL

1. Interview transcript by Sylvia Zamora, 2002 (courtesy of Sylvia Zamora).
2. Ibid.

CHAPTER 7   GOING PUBLIC

1. Itemized contributions and expenditures by Friends of Measure A in 2001, from the California Tax Forms 460 and 497 (copies in author's possession).

2. The $3 million figure is from October 2000 (Catania 2000a, 29). The $6 million to $8 million figure comes from multiple newspapers. The mailer is believed to be from Sunlaw's publicity literature, which details South Gate's city expenditures for 1999–2000, by department, together with an estimated $7.8 million additional revenues the Nueva Azalea plant would bring (copy in author's possession).

3. According to Martin (2001b), Downey as well as South Gate residents were included in Sunlaw's offer.

4. This footage is from CBE's videotape collage of television coverage as well as from a collection of videotaped TV news coverage, together with campaign endorsements of anti-plant candidates and smears of their opponents (copies in author's possession).

5. I do not use parents' names when students speak about them because the parents were not interviewed.

CHAPTER 8   SUDDEN DEATH

1. CBE videotape of English- and Spanish-language television news coverage (copy in author's possession).
2. Sonya Brown did not wish to be interviewed, but she played an important role in the No on Measure A campaign, and in other activists' descriptions and analyses of the campaign. I've given her a pseudonym so that I can include activists' descriptions and analyses of her contributions.
3. I spoke with three white adults—Rhonda Nitschky, Roy Abadi, and Martha Andrade, and two Latino adults, Luis and Robert Cabrales on the committee.
4. CBE videotape of English- and Spanish-language television news coverage.
5. Ibid.
6. Miguel Contreras, head of the Los Angeles County Federation of Labor, letter to "South Gate Residents," n.d.; Marco Firebaugh, assemblyman, letter to "Friends and Neighbors," n.d.; and Martha Escutia, state senator, letter to "Friends and Neighbors," n.d.
7. Two other cities in the area, El Segundo and Huntington Beach, had CEC hearings on expansion projects for power plants in those cities. Both cities are mainly white and middle class. In neither was there an anti-plant campaign.
8. These questions might also be asked of Sunlaw's campaign and, had he said what his political goals were, of Robles' efforts as well. Because I did not have enough direct access to either Sunlaw or Robles, however, and because my focus is on grassroots environmentalism, I did not pursue these paths.

References

Acuña, Rodolfo. 2000. *Occupied America: A History of Chicanos*. New York: Longman.

Adams, John. 2001. Power Plant Fight May Not Be Over, Says Downey Mayor. *Downey Eagle*, March 16, 1.

Alfonso, Mirna. 1985a. More Study Urged on Proposed Sign Ordinance. *Los Angeles Times* (Long Beach sec.), November 10, 2.

———. 1985b. Sign Law Would Require English in South Gate. *Los Angeles Times* (Long Beach sec.), October 20.

———. 1985c. South Gate Planners to Study Idea English-Only Sign Bill Sidetracked. *Los Angeles Times* (Southeast sec.), November 17, 4.

Associated Press. 2002. Sheriff Pleads Not Guilty to Fraud, Extortion Charges. *Contra Costa Times,* December 21; http://www.contracostatimes.com/find/news (accessed July 20, 2004).

Bansal, Shipra, David Bacon, and Sam Davis. 1998. *Holding Our Breath: The Struggle for Environmental Justice in Southeast Los Angeles*. Los Angeles: Communities for a Better Environment.

Barraza, Rocio, Oscar Gutierrez, and Blanca Martinez. 2003. A "Passive" Community. Undergraduate honors section paper, Department of Anthropology, UCLA.

Bazar, Emily. 2001. Plant's Denial a True Test of Fast-Tracking? *Sacramento Bee*, June 23; http://www.sacramentobee.com/static/archive/news/special/power (accessed July 22, 2005).

Becerra, Hector. 2006a. Judge to Have Key Role as Vernon Casts Votes. *Los Angeles Times,* April 11, B1.

———. 2006b. Vernon Mayor and Ex-Official Are Indicted. *Los Angeles Times,* November 16, A1.

———. 2007. White, but His Heart Is Latino. *Los Angeles Times,* January 4, A1.

Bernal, Dolores Delgado. 1998. Grassroots Leadership Reconceptualized: Chicana Oral Histories and the 1968 East Los Angeles School Blowouts. *Frontiers: A Journal of Women Studies* 19(2): 113–142.

Berthelsen, Christian. 2002. Power Firms Spoke of Exploiting Crisis Records Reveal Talk of Longer Outage to Boost Profits. *San Francisco Chronicle*, November 16, A-1.

Blood, Michael R. 2008. LA Port Approves Plan for Cleaner-Running Trucks. *San Jose Mercury News* (online ed.), March 20.

Briegel, Kaye. 1974. Chicano Student Militancy: The Los Angeles High School Strike of 1968. In *An Awakened Minority: The Mexican Americans*, 2d ed., ed. Manuel P. Servin. Beverly Hills: Glencoe Press.

Brodkin, Karen.2005. A Better World Is Possible? *Anthropology and Social Movements Identities* 12(2): 301–313.

———. 2007. *Making Democracy Matter: Identity and Activism in Los Angeles*. New Brunswick, NJ: Rutgers University Press.

Bullard, Robert D. 1990. *Dumping in Dixie*. Boulder: Westview Press.

———, ed. 1994. *Unequal Protection: Environmental Justice and Communities of Color*. San Francisco: Sierra Club Books.

———. 2005. *The Quest for Environmental Justice: Human Rights and the Politics of Pollution*. San Francisco: Sierra Club Books.

California, State of. 1996. Health and Safety Code, secs. 40440–40459. Sacramento.

California Council for Environmental and Economic Balance (CCEEB). 2004. http://www.cceeb.org.

California Energy Commission (CEC). 2000a. Nueva Azalea Power Plant Project/ Proyecto Planta de Energia Nueva. Public information sheet.

———. 2000b. Transcript of the May 16, 2000, Evidentiary Hearing. http://www.energy.ca.gov/sitingcases/elkhills/documents/#commission (accessed May 30, 2004).

———. 2001. Order Extending Suspension through December 31, 2001. Sacramento: State of California, Energy Resources Conservation and Development Commission.

———. 2005a. Map of Peakers.

———. 2005b. Media Office Power Plant Fact Sheet: Summary. Power Plant Approvals, Applications by Year. June 22. http://www.energy.ca.gov/sitingcases/index/html.

———. N.d. Siting Cases. www.energy.ca.gov/sitingcases/metcalf/notices/2000-08-04_motionsandorder.html (accessed June 24, 2005).

Carson, Rachel. 1962. *Silent Spring*. New York: Houghton Mifflin.

Catania, Sara. 2000a. Downey to Power Plant: Drop Dead. *LA Weekly*, October 27–November 2. http://www.laweekly.com.

———. 2000b. Power Play: South Gate Is Already One of the Most Polluted Cities in California. Does It Really Need a Massive New Electric Power Plant? *LA Weekly*, October 6–12, 29, 31.

———. 2001. Lights Out. *LA Weekly*, March 16–22. http://www.laweekly.com.

Checker, Melissa. 2005. *Polluted Promises: Environmental Racism and the Search for Justice in a Southern Town*. New York: New York University Press.

Clifford, Frank. 1997. AQMD Plan Will Target Pollution in Poor Areas; Air: Board Acknowledges Concerns That Minority Communities Bear the Brunt of Industrial Emissions. *Los Angeles Times*, October 11, A1.

CNN. 1999. WTO Protests Awaken 60s-Style Activism. http://archives.cnn.com/1999/US/12/02/wto.protest.perspective (accessed August 22, 2007).

Cole, Luke W., and Sheila R. Foster. 2001. *From the Ground Up: Environmental Racism and the Rise of the Environmental Justice Movement*. New York: New York University Press.

Coleman, Jennifer. 2005. Enron Settles Price-Gouging Claims with Three States. *Register Guard* (Eugene, OR), A1, 12.

Communities for a Better Environment (CBE). 1998. *Holding Our Breath: The Struggle for Environmental Justice in Southeast Los Angeles*. Huntington Park, CA: CBE.

———. 2007. Official Web site. http://www.cbecal.org (accessed December 13, 2007).

Communities for a Better Environment (CBE) Green Team. 2000. Notes of Weekly Meetings, October–November. Huntington Park, CA: CBE.

Concerned Citizens of South Central Los Angeles. N.d. Official Web site. http://www.ccscla.org/ (accessed August 10, 2007).

Cone, Marla. 1997a. Civil Rights Suit Attacks Trade in Pollution Credits. *Los Angeles Times*, July 23, A1.

———. 1997b. EPA Criticizes Air Agencies in California. *Los Angeles Times*, August 2, A1.

Cooney, Catherine M. 1999. Still Searching for Environmental Justice. *Environmental Science and Technology* 33(9): 200–209.

Czarnecki, Larry, Jim Fuhr, Rick Oegema, and Robert Hilton. 2000. SCONOx Tm: Ammonia Free No$_x$ Removal Technology for Gas Turbines. Conference paper.

Danziger, Robert Nathan. 1979. Renewable Energy Sources and Cogeneration: Community Systems and Grid Interaction as a Public Utility Enterprise. *Whittier Law Review* 2(1): 81–100.

———. 2004. Iuma. http://artists.IUMA/Bands/BobDanziger/ (accessed July 31, 2006).

Douglas, Theo. 2000. Woman Seeks Recall of Vice Mayor. *Long Beach Press-Telegram*, January 27, A5.

Dowie, Mark. 1995. *Losing Ground: American Environmentalism at the Close of the Twentieth Century*. Cambridge, MA: MIT Press.

Dueñas, Jorge. 2001. 7 Good Reasons to March against the Power Plant. Flyer.

Edelman, Marc. 2001. Social Movements: Changing Paradigms and Forms of Politics. *Annual Reviews of Anthropology* 30:285–317.

The Energy Puzzle: One Man's Solution. 2001. Video. Los Angeles: Rice/Gorton Productions.

Environmental Justice Collaborative. 2004. Building a Regional Voice for Environmental Justice. Center for Justice, Tolerance and Community, University of California at Santa Cruz.

Environmental Justice Resource Center. 2002. Environmental Justice for People of Color Summit Draws 1,200 Delegates to Washington. *Black Commentator*. http://www.blackcommentator.com/16_re_print.html (accessed August 25, 2005).

Environmental Protection Agency. Environmental Appeals Board. 2001. Metcalf Energy Center order denying review. August 10, 2001. pdf download through http://www.epa.gov/eab (accessed February 27, 2007).

―――. Information Transfer and Program Integration Division. 1999. *RACT/ BACT/LAER Clearinghouse Clean Air Technology Center Annual Report for 1999: A Compilation of Control Technology Determinations.* Ninth supp. to 1990 ed. Washington, DC: U.S. Government Printing Office.

Frontline. 2001. The California Crisis: CA Timeline. PBS Frontline/NYT investigative report. http://www.pbs.org/wgbh/pages/frontline/shows/blackout/california/timeline.html (accessed August 15, 2005).

Gibbs, Lois Marie. 1998. *Love Canal: The Story Continues.* Gabriola Island, British Columbia: New Society Publishers.

Gottlieb, Robert. 2005. *Forcing the Spring: The Transformation of the American Environmental Movement,* rev. ed. Washington, DC: Island Press.

Gottlieb, Robert, Mark Vallinatos, Regine M. Freer, and Peter Dreier. 2005. *The Next Los Angeles: The Struggle for a Livable City.* Berkeley: University of California Press.

Green LA. N.d. A Green Los Angeles: Recommendations to the City of Los Angeles. Los Angeles: Liberty Hill Foundation and Environment Now.

Hamilton, Cynthia. 1994. Concerned Citizens of South Central. In *Unequal Protection: Environmental Justice and Communities of Color,* ed. Robert D. Bullard, 207–219. San Francisco: Sierra Club Books.

Hamm, Andrew, Timothy Roberts, and Neil Orma. 2001. Cisco Talking Compromise on Metcalf. *Silicon Valley/San Jose Business Journal,* May 4. http://sanjose.bizjournals.com/sanjose/stories.

Honey, Michael. 1993. *Southern Labor and Black Civil rights: Organizing Memphis Workers.* Urbana: University of Illinois Press.

Horton, John, and Jose Calderon. 1995. *The Politics of Diversity: Immigration, Resistance, and Change in Monterey Park, California.* Philadelphia: Temple University Press.

Huerta, Alvaro. 2001a. David v. Goliath in SE Los Angeles. *Z Magazine,* July–August, 44–45.

―――. 2001b. *Modern Day David-versus-Goliath in Southeast Los Angeles: A Synopsis of How Common People United to Stop a Power Plant in South Gate.* Huntington Park, CA: CBE.

―――. 2005. South Gate, CA: Environmental Racism Defeated in a Blue-Collar Latino Suburb. *Critical Planning* 12 (summer): 93–104.

Institute for Homelessness and Poverty at the Weingart Center. N.d. Poverty in Los Angeles. Los Angeles. http://www.weingart.org/institute (accessed April 3, 2002).

Jones, Robert. 1997a. Breathing Out. *Los Angeles Times,* February 5, B2.

―――. 1997b. Dithering over Dirty Air. *Los Angeles Times,* September 14, B1.

―――. 1997c. Hearts of the City: Air War. *Los Angeles Times,* May 14, B2.

Kaplan, Temma. 1997. *Crazy for Democracy: Women in Grassroots Movements.* New York: Routledge.

Katznelson, Ira. 1981. *City Trenches: Urban Politics and the Patterning of Class in the United States.* Chicago: University of Chicago Press.

Kidokoro, Yuki. 1999. LA's Youth for Environmental Justice. *Community Environmental Review,* no. 1, p. 4.

Kidokoro, Yuki, and Alvaro Huerta. 2000. CBE Memo re Proposed Organizing Plan of Action Draft 1. Huntington Park, CA: CBE.

Latino Issues Forum. 2001. *Power against the People? Moving beyond Crisis Planning in California Energy.* Sacramento: Latino Issues Forum.

Leposky, George. 2003. A Grocery Store Tests Cogeneration Technology. *Distributed Energy: The Journal of Onsite Power Solutions,* November–December. http://www.distributedenergy.com/november-december-2003 (accessed December 2008).

Letwin, Daniel. 1998. *The Challenge of Interracial Unionism: Alabama Coal Miners, 1878–1921.* Chapel Hill: University of North Carolina Press.

Logan, Angelo, et al. 2007. Dear Dr. Knatz and Mr. Steinke, Executive Directors of the Ports of Los Angeles and Long Beach. Open letter. June 25.

Long Beach Press Telegram. 1999. Politics Embroil South Gate (editorial). May 2, A10.

———. 2000. Wrong Fight for the WRD (editorial). October 25, A10.

Lopez, Robert J., and Rich Connell. 2005. Tiny Town of Vernon Is Focus of Inquiry. *Los Angeles Times,* April 7, B1.

Los Angeles County Federation of Labor. 2008. Major Victory in the Fight for Good Jobs! E-mail from news@launionaflcio.org.

Los Angeles Times. 1997a. Cloud of Crisis for the AQMD (editorial). September 22, A4.

———. 1997b. New Hope for Clean Urban Air: Initiative Is a Welcome Sign for Low-Income Areas (editorial). October 15, A6.

Louie, Vivian. 1990. They're Speaking the Language of Cooperation at South Gate PTA. *Los Angeles Times* (Long Beach sec.), October 21, 1.

Lungren, Daniel E. [Attorney General], and Anthony DaVigo [Deputy Attorney General]. 1997. Does the Doctrine of Incompatible Public Offices Preclude a Person from Holding Simultaneously the Positions of South Gate City Treasurer and Central Basin Municipal Water District Director? Opinion Unit, California Department of Justice, Office of the Attorney General. *Official Reports,* vol. 97-206.

MacLean, Nancy. 2006. *Freedom Is Not Enough: The Opening of the American Workplace.* Cambridge, MA: Harvard University Press.

Marosi, Richard. 2001. Printers Charged in Political Corruption Case. *Los Angeles Times,* December 8, B3.

———. 2002a. South Gate Official Posts $500,000 Bond, Is Released. *Los Angeles Times,* April 12, B1.

———. 2002b. South Gate Official's Threats Described. *Los Angeles Times,* April 9, B1.

———. 2002c. South Gate Treasurer Arrested. *Los Angeles Times,* April 6, B1.

———. 2002d. Two Plead in South Gate Election Cases. *Los Angeles Times,* July 23, B3.

———. 2003a. The Freebies Pile up as South Gate Goes to Polls. *Los Angeles Times,* January 25, A1, 18.

———. 2003b. Some Cash in Before South Gate Vote. *Los Angeles Times,* January 26, B3.

Martin, Hugo. 2000. Neighbors Fume over Backing for Power Plant. *Los Angeles Times,* December 16, A1, 7.

———. 2001a. The California Energy Crisis; Proposed South Gate Power Plant Faces Fierce Opposition. *Los Angeles Times,* January 10, A16.

———. 2001b. Firm Drops Plan for South Gate Generator. *Los Angeles Times,* March 9, A1.

———. 2001c. 2 Cities Intensify Fight against Power Plant. *Los Angeles Times,* January 25, B12.

———. 2004. Some Big Water Agencies Are Awash in Perks and Benefits. *Beachwood Voice.* http://beachwoodvoice.com/WaterIssue/wateragenciesawashinperks.htm.

Martin, Mark. 2002. California System Was Easy Pickings: Enron Helped Build Market, Then Exploited Weaknesses. *San Francisco Chronicle,* February 3, 1.

Meza, Marilu. 2001. Piden Supervisor Los Comicios de S. Gate. *La Opinion,* March 3, B1, 3.

Milkman, Ruth, ed. 2000. *Organizing Immigrants: The Challenge for Unions in Contemporary California.* Ithaca, NY: ILR Press.

Mittelstaedt, Alan, and Emma Gallegos. 2008. Ports of Harm. *Los Angeles CityBeat,* March 5. http://www.lacitybeat.com/cms/story/detail/ports_of_harm/6782 (accessed April 1, 2008).

Morello-Frosch, Manuel Pastor, Jr., Carlos Porras, and James Sadd. 2002. Environmental Justice and Regional Inequality in Southern California: Implications for Future Research. *Environmental Health Perspectives* 110 (supp. 2): 149–154.

Morris, Aldon. 1999. A Retrospective of the Civil Rights Movement: Political and Intellectual Landmarks. *Annual Reviews of Sociology* 25:517–539.

Muñoz, Carlos, Jr. 1989. *Youth, Identity, Power: The Chicano Movement.* London: Verso.

Nicolaides, Becky M. 2002. *My Blue Heaven: Life and Politics in the Working-Class Suburbs of Los Angeles, 1920–1965.* Chicago: University of Chicago Press.

Pardo, Mary. 1998. *Mexican American Women Activists: Identity and Resistance in Two Los Angeles Communities.* Philadelphia: Temple University Press.

Pasmant, Andrew. 2000. Letter to the Honorable William J. Keese, CEC: City of South Gate, City Manager. April 12. South Gate Office of the City Clerk.

Pastor, Manuel, Jr. 1997. Insight: Environmental Equity Makes Business Sense. *Los Angeles Times,* November 2, A4.

Pastor, Manuel, Jr., Jim Saad, and John Hipp. 2001. Which Came First? Toxic Facilities, Minority Move-in, and Environmental Justice. *Journal of Urban Affairs* 23(1): 1–21.

Pastor, Manuel, Jr., James L. Sadd, and Rachel Morello-Frosch. 2005. Environmental Inequity in Metropolitan Los Angeles. In *The Quest for Environmental Justice,* ed. Robert D. Bullard, 108–124. San Francisco: Sierra Club Books.

Peace Officers Research Association of California. 2000. LDF Defends South Gate POA Member against Mayor's Legal Attack. http://www.porac.org/ldf/articles/april%203%202003.html (accessed June 19, 2005).

The Press/La Ola. 2001. Voters End Power Plant Project. March 8, p. 1. Wave Community Newspapers.

Quinones, Sam. 2001. The Savage Politics of South Gate. *Los Angeles Times Magazine,* July 8, 20–24.

———. 2007. *Antonio's Gun and Delfino's Dream: True Tales of Mexican Migration.* Albuquerque: University of New Mexico Press.

Rodriguez, Val. 1985. Comment on Sign Law "Ludicrous." *Los Angeles Times* (Long Beach ed.), December 1, 6.

Romero, Simon. 1994. South Gate Backers of Azalea Festival Attack Plan. *Los Angeles Times*, October 16, A6.

Rose, Tanya. 2003. Alleged Power Plant Deal Could Have Made Politicians Wealthy, Authorities Say. *Lodi News Sentinel*, July 23. pdf accessed at http://www.valleyair.org/recent_News_Clippings/2003 (accessed August 14, 2004).

Rosenberg, Harriet B. 1995. From Trash to Treasure: Housewife Activists and the Environmental Justice Movement. In *Articulating Hidden Histories: Essays in Honor of Eric R. Wolf*, ed. Jane Schneider and Rayna Rapp, 190–206. Berkeley: University of California Press.

Rosenzweig, David. 2005. Ex-South Gate Treasurer Convicted in Bribery Case. *Los Angeles Times*, July 29, B1.

Scott, McGregor W. 2006. McFall Sentenced to over Ten Years in Prison as San Joaquin County Corruption Case Concludes. Press release, U.S. Attorney's Office, Eastern District of California, Sacramento. December 12.

Second National People of Color Environmental Leadership Summit. 2002. http://www.weact.org/savethedate/2002/2002_Oct_23.html (accessed August 2005).

Silverstein, Stuart. 2007. South Gate Officers Win Suit. *Los Angeles Times*, May 18, B1, 7.

South Coast Air Quality Management District. 1995. Company Beats Year 2010 Pollution Control Goal with New Technology. Press release.

———. 1997. Board meeting agenda. October 10. http://www.aqmd.gov.

———. 2003. Board meeting minutes. January 24. http://www.aqmd.gov/hb/030221a.html (accessed August 4, 2004).

———. 2004. History of Environmental Justice at AQMD. http://www.gov/ej/history.htm (accessed August 4, 2004).

South Gate, City of. 2002. South Gate, California (CA) Economy and Business Data. http://www.city-data.com/econ_South_Gate_California.html (accessed August 2005).

———. N.d. City Facts. Official South Gate city Web site. http://www.cityof-southgate.org/cityfact.htm (accessed August 25, 2005).

Superior Court of the State of California for the County of Los Angeles. 2001. Petitioner's Reply to Respondent's and Real Parties in Interest's Opposition to Application for Writ of Mandate. *Vivian Castro v. Nina Bañuelos*. Case no. BS067299.

Szasz, Andrew. 1994. *Ecopopulism: Toxic Waste and the Movement for Environmental Justice*. Minneapolis: University of Minnesota Press.

Tait, Vanessa. 2005. *Poor Workers' Unions. Rebuilding Labor from Below*. Cambridge, MA: South End Press.

Thornberg, Christopher F. 2002. Of Megawatts and Men: Understanding the Causes of the California Power Crisis. In *California Policy Options, UCLA Anderson Forecast*. Los Angeles: School of Public Policy and Social Research, UCLA.

U.S. Bureau of the Census. 2000. Profile of General Demographic Characteristics, 2000, for South Gate. Census tracts 5361.02, 5356.07.

U.S. Government Accounting Office. 1983. *Siting of Hazardous Waste Landfills and Their Correlation with Racial and Economic Status of Surrounding Communities*. Washington, DC: U.S. Government Printing Office.

Vernon, City of. N.d. History. Official Web site. http://www.cityofvernon.org/
   about_cov/history.htm (accessed September 9, 2005).

WARN. 2003. A Long Road to Win Environmental Justice: The Warren County
   PCB Landfill, 1978 to 2003. http://www.ncwarn.org/Campaigns/Warren
   County/12–05–03WarrenCo (accessed August 2005).

Wikipedia. 2005a. California Electricity Crisis. http://en.wikipedia.org/wiki/
   California_electricity_crisis (accessed August 14, 2005).

———. 2005b. Vernon, California. http://en.wikipedia.org/wiki/Vernon_
   California (accessed July 8, 2005).

Wilson, Janet. 2007. California Has Largest Number of Minorities near Hazardous
   Waste. *Los Angeles Times*, April 12, B1, 8.

Yang, Debra W. 2005. Federal Grand Jury Issues New Indictment in South Gate
   Corruption Case That Names Associate of Former Treasurer Albert Robles.
   Press release by the U.S. Department of Justice, Central District of California.
   March 24.

Index

Abadi, Roy: on anti-plant flyers, 100–101; initial contact with anti-plant movement, 74, 75; on irregular council meetings, 136; on recall of DeWitt, 106; on referendum, 105, 131–132, 138–140, 159–160, 165, 167

Abramowitz, Mark, 81–82, 84–85, 89, 90–91, 92

Acosta, Pat, 179, 181

activism: parents', shared with student activists, 155–156; youth (*see* youth activists; Youth-EJ)

adult school, South Gate, 69

AES Corporation, 88, 208, 209

affirmative action: and Proposition 209, 111; reframing of, by neo-conservatives, 24–25, 199; youth activist opposition to voter initiatives against, 7–8

AFL-CIO Labor Council for Latin American Advancement, 36

African Americans: appointed to chair of AQMD, 86; and Latinas/os, 45, 199–200, 200–201; shut down Warren County (NC) waste dump, 49–50; South Gate exclusion of, 36

age, and attitudes toward plant, 176–177

AGENDA, 214n.2

airborne pollutants, 203; and good jobs, 194; from Powerine refinery, 47–48; and respiratory diseases, 1, 80; South Gate a hot spot for, 8

Alameda Corridor project, 32, 53–54

Alcoa, 26–27

Alstom Power Environmental Systems (ABBES), 82, 89, 215n. 10

"alternative kids," South Gate High, 116, 129

American Lung Association of California, 203

ammonia, 72, 79

amnesty law of 1986, 34

Amparo, Jackie, 1; attends Youth in Action camp, 59, 60; on city council meeting of Jan. 23, 2001, and the march on city hall, 144, 145–146, 149, 150, 153; on early student apathy, 70; on election victory, 181

Andrade, Martha, 2; on absence of pro-plant argument from ballot, 135–136; on pipe-fitter plant supporters, 175, 193, 219n.3; and city council meeting of Jan. 23, 2001, and the march on city hall, 148–149, 151, 152–153; learns about power plant plans, 72–73, 75

ABOUT THE AUTHOR

KAREN BRODKIN writes about race, gender, and activism. She is the author of *Making Democracy Matter: Identity and Activism in Los Angeles* and *How Jews Became White Folks and What That Says about Race in America*. She is professor emerita of anthropology and women's studies at UCLA.